MANAGING QUALITY

The Addison-Wesley Middle Manager Series
Consulting editor: W. Warner Burke

Change Riders: How to Successfully Manage the Power of Change,
Gary D. Kissler

Managing Quality: The Primer for Middle Managers,
Randall S. Schuler and Drew L. Harris

RANDALL S. SCHULER and DREW L. HARRIS

MANAGING QUALITY

THE PRIMER FOR MIDDLE MANAGERS

ADDISON-WESLEY PUBLISHING COMPANY, INC.

Reading, Massachusetts • Menlo Park, California • New York • Don Mills, Ontario
Wokingham, England • Amsterdam • Bonn • Paris • Milan • Madrid
Sydney • Singapore • Tokyo • Seoul • Taipei • Mexico City • San Juan

The publisher offers discounts on this book when ordered in quantity for special sales. For more information, please contact:

Corporate & Professional Publishing Group
Addison-Wesley Publishing Company
One Jacob Way
Reading, Massachusetts 01867

Library of Congress Cataloging-in-Publication Data
Schuler, Randall S.
    Managing quality: the primer for middle managers/Randall S. Schuler and Drew L. Harris.
        p. cm. — (The Addison-Wesley middle manager series)
    Includes bibliographical references and index.
    ISBN 0-201-56326-6
    1. Total quality management. I. Harris, Drew L. II. Title.
III. Series.
    HD62.15.S38   1992
    658.5′62—dc20   91-33166

Cover design by Hannus Design Associates
Text design by Wilson Graphics & Design (Kenneth J. Wilson)
Set in 10 point Palatino by Technologies 'N Typography

ISBN 0-201-56326-6

Printed on recycled and acid-free paper.
1 2 3 4 5 6 7 8 9-MA-95949392
First Printing,   June 1992

The authors would like to dedicate this book to their fathers, Wilson Schuler and Milton V. Harris.

CONTENTS

Foreword xi

Preface xiii

Acknowledgments xv

Introduction xvii

Chapter 1 **WHY LOOK AT QUALITY AND THE MIDDLE MANAGER?** 1

Why Be Concerned about Quality? 2

Quality Is Important 2

Quality Saves Money 4

Making a Commitment to Quality Is Difficult 5

Quality Has a Role as a Proprietary Competitive Strategy 6

What Can Middle Managers Do about Quality? 8

Managers in Organizations with Executive Support for Quality Improvement 9

Managers in Organizations with Quality-Improvement Programs but No Support 11

Managers in Organizations without Quality-Improvement Programs 12

A Plan for Quality Improvement 14

The Sphere of Influence 15

Summary 17

References 18

Chapter 2 **WHAT IS QUALITY?** 20

Management Philosophers: Quality as a Phenomenon 20

Joseph Juran 21

W. Edwards Deming 23

Decomposing Quality: Getting Chunks Small Enough to Work on 26

Information as a Dimension of Quality 30

A Composite Definition 32
A Process View of Quality, Productivity, and Costs 36
  Business Systems 36
    Inputs 38
    Process 39
    Outputs 39
  Quality and the System 41
  What Is Quality from a Systems Viewpoint? 43
Summary 47
References 48

Chapter 3 **TOOLS FOR IMPROVING QUALITY** 49
General Process and Strategy 50
A Quality-Improvement Project 52
  1. Identifying the System 53
  2. Selecting the Project 55
  3. Selecting and Developing the Team 65
  4. Assessing the Current Process 66
    System Stability and Capability 66
    Measuring Stability and Capability 67
    Attribute-Control Charts 67
    Additional Notes on Control Charts 72
  5. Diagnosing the Problem 74
    Flowcharts 74
    Cause-and-Effect Diagrams (Fishbone, Ishikawa) 75
    Other Diagnostic Tools 78
  6. Testing Theories in the Workplace 81
  7. Quantifying and Maintaining Results 83
  8. Publicizing and Expanding Quality Improvement 84
Summary 86
References 87

Chapter 4 **QUALITY ENHANCEMENT, THE MANAGER, AND THE HR FUNCTION** 89
New Roles for the Manager 90
Transformation of the Human Resource Function 92
  The Line Manager as HR Manager 93
  The Vice President of Quality 95

Systematic Human Resource Management 96
   To Be or Not to Be Systematic 96
   Being Systematic 97
   Human Resource Management Philosophies 98
      Accumulation 98
      Utilization 99
      Facilitation 100
   Choosing a Human Resource Management Philosophy
   101
      Alternative Mind-Sets 101
      Alternative Behaviors 102
   Competitive Strategies: Beating the Competition 103
   Matching Philosophy with Competitive Strategy 105
Summary 106
References 106

Chapter 5 **CHOICES IN HUMAN RESOURCE MANAGEMENT** 107
Linking Human Resource Practices with Competitive
Strategy 107
Quality Enhancement and Required Role Behaviors 108
Typology of HRM Practices 109
   Planning Menu 110
   Staffing Menu 112
   Appraising Menu 113
   Compensation Menu 114
   Training and Development Menu 115
   Labor-Management Menu 116
Human Resource Practice Choices for Quality
Enhancement 116
   Planning Practice Choices 116
   Staffing Practice Choices 118
   Performance-Appraisal Practice Choices 120
   Compensation Practice Choices 128
   Training Practice Choices 131
   Labor-Management Practice Choices 134
   Putting It All Together 136
Summary 139
References 139

Chapter 6 **QUALITY FROM EXTERNAL RELATIONSHIPS** 141
Expanding the Definitions of Customer and Supplier 141
Relationships 143
  Suppliers 143
  Customers 148
Differences between Internal and External Relationships 150
Summary 151
References 153

Appendix A **The Case of Ensoniq Corp.: Applying Deming Quality Improvement in a Small Business** 154

Appendix B **Case Study of the HR Department at Swiss Bank Corporation: Customerization for High-Quality Customer Service** 168

Appendix C **Beginning Reading List in Quality** 182
  Glossary 185
  Index 197

Foreword

A decade ago, it was excellence; today, it is quality. As you consider that opening statement, do you detect a note of cynicism? If so, the implication of cynicism is quite deliberate. After all, quality—or TQM (total quality management), to use the popular acronym—is yet another fad in corporate America and, like all fads, will soon pass from the scene, right?

TQM may indeed be a fad in corporate America, but so was corporate culture a number of years ago, and that concept seems to have stuck. Executives and managers today, a decade after corporate culture first became popular, clearly recognize the importance of understanding an organization's culture. Will TQM still be around when we enter the twenty-first century? Apparently—even industrial-organizational psychologists, some of the most confirmed skeptics I know, think so. A recent issue of the Society for Industrial-Organizational Psychology's membership quarterly contained a brief article entitled "TQM Is More Prevalent Than You Think," which admonished us industrial-organizational psychologists to "get with it." The article's primary points were that: (1) TQM is here to stay, (2) we industrial-organizational psychologists have something to contribute, and (3) we are late. My point is this: If some of the world's greatest skeptics, psychologists in general (not to mention my brand of colleagues in particular), are true believers in TQM, then the concept must be real and here to stay.

Although I remain a skeptic and cynic about a number of things, I am a true believer when it comes to the critical importance of TQM for America's work organizations. The proof thereof is my support for the publication of Schuler and Harris's *Managing Quality*. The book is a superb primer on the subject and should prove helpful to all levels of managers, but particularly those in the middle—those managers who are held accountable every working day for quality products and services but who may not be sufficiently clear as to what this accountability means.

As stated in my Foreword to *The Change Riders*, the first book in this Addison-Wesley series for managers, our objective for this series is *not* to present fluff, the latest rage in management, or books that are either overly academic or overly "practical." Instead, our intent, also as noted in that Foreword, is to build bridges between what we know to be sound and what can therefore be depended on in practice. *Managing Quality*, the second title in the series, clearly meets these standards.

W. Warner Burke
Pelham, New York

Preface

Increasingly, battles for competitive superiority are being won by achieving outstanding quality. Whether from manufacturing or service businesses, customers demand high-quality goods and services. Although to a certain extent quality may be in the eye of the beholder, one senses a growing consensus about what constitutes high and low quality. When customers perceive high quality, they willingly pay a premium for it. Consequently, many organizations aggressively pursue quality.

Successful organizations pursue quality according to the new paradigm—building quality in rather than inspecting postproduction while committing to continuous innovation and improvement. When they deliver goods and services in this new way, these organizations discover unexpected results: Costs do not rise; more often, they diminish. Employees find new interest, challenges, and rewards in their work. For these organizations (and their competitors), improving quality is no longer a choice but an imperative.

All this is easier said than done. The new approach requires extensive analysis of work systems; those leading the quality transformation must know that if the work force does not possess the right skills and cannot exhibit the right behaviors, success will be impossible. This directs attention toward the need to reevaluate and possibly change all the traditional human resource management practices—selecting, training, developing, and compensating. These practices must be consistent with the new thinking.

Commitment to continuous quality improvement is a new way of doing business. Although support from senior management can be vital in making the transformation, for the middle manager, both the challenges and the rewards are great. The challenges come from delivering the right analytic tools (with training), leading projects, reducing resistance to change, and creating an environment conducive to continuous improvement. The rewards come from achieving clear-cut gains: Quality is up, a mind-set of continuous improvement is in place, customers are happy and market share has risen, and jobs and opportunities are expanding.

The purpose of this book is to help the middle manager meet these challenges and reap these rewards. From explaining the meaning and measurement of quality to reviewing analytic tools and their appropriate use to rethinking human resource practices, this book provides a guide to initiating and sustaining quality-improvement programs, whether in manufacturing organizations or in service companies. Because the chapters tend to dissect a process that is necessarily very integrative, two extensive case studies are provided in Appendixes A and B to bring all the parts together.

If this book is judged valuable, it will be because readers take the ideas and suggestions presented herein and apply and extend them in their own work. Those who find value will see this book as a starting point, for our presentation cannot be considered complete—quality improvement is an ongoing process.

Acknowledgments

We wish to thank several individuals for generously helping in the writing of this book. They include Michael Mitchell at the Swiss Bank Corporation, Bruce Crockett at Ensoniq Corporation, and David Schweiger and Steve Noble of the Human Resources Planning Society for allowing us to use the case study materials from Swiss Bank and Ensoniq. Matthew Harris of Provost Consulting helped enormously with encouragement, feedback, and editing. Lloyd Provost, also of Provost Consulting, provided comments that proved helpful in improving Chapter 3. Katharine C. Weldon of Ernst & Young, along with two anonymous reviewers, offered quite valuable suggestions for improving the early drafts.

The administration at New York University's Stern School of Business, especially the Management Department, provided support for this project. For that we are grateful.

Finally, we would like to thank W. Edwards Deming. Although he had little direct input into this project, his influence in creating a world-wide concern for quality, in shaping our views on how to achieve quality, and in inspiring our efforts can be seen throughout our work and in this book.

Randall S. Schuler
Drew L. Harris
New York, New York
May 1992

Introduction

This book approaches the topic of quality from a new perspective—that of the middle manager. To date, most books and articles about quality have been addressed to the executive. The executive group controls the resources and power required to direct organizationwide quality-improvement efforts; however, in the kind of efforts that result in or reflect a shift in operating philosophy, the middle manager is far from impotent in the change process. Indeed, if executives want to implement a quality-improvement program, that effort must be carried out by middle management.

Here is the first challenge for middle managers: what to do, how to respond, when confronted with the command "Improve quality!" All too often that command is accompanied by little or no guidance. This book is designed to help middle managers take the first steps toward an ongoing quality-improvement process.

In addition, managers who feel driven to initiate a quality-improvement effort for their own reasons should find this book useful in beginning the process. Although this latter route may be more difficult than initiating a program at the behest of executives, it may also prove more rewarding. Careers and companies have been turned around by managers willing to take a chance on making a difference. *Managing Quality*, in short, provides a rationale, a road map, and a set of tools, both for self-starters and for those directed from above.

Chapter 1 begins establishing the rationale by providing an overview of the importance of quality in today's competitive environment. Quality is identified as the basis of comparison in the global marketplace. Testimony reveals that as new thinking about quality takes hold and new approaches to quality are successfully implemented, costs go down and productivity goes up. American organizations are therefore becoming increasingly concerned about quality. Chapter 1 also expands on the difficult and varied roles that middle managers play in the quality-improvement process.

Chapter 2 analyzes and defines quality. First, an examination of the teachings of leading quality "gurus" provides a broad view of quality, which gives an overall direction to quality improvement, an understanding of the big mission. Then, quality is decomposed into attributes of products and services so that attention can be focused on specific areas needing improvement. Finally, a systematic view of quality shows how to think about and diagnose quality and how to direct corrective actions in order to reduce the defect rates (variance) or focus more effectively on desired outcomes (targets).

Once the framework for analyzing quality has been established, Chapter 3 reviews a prototypical quality-improvement process. This process takes into account the potentially tenuous position of a middle manager yet applies equally well to a fully supported, companywide quality-improvement program. The prototype project includes a description of various tools and techniques commonly used in quality-improvement efforts. For some readers, these descriptions will suffice for immediate application. For other readers, these descriptions may serve to direct their attention to tools of interest but will not fully prepare them to act. The chapter therefore provides references to more complete texts or sources that detail the use of each tool.

Chapter 4 builds a case for harmonizing human resource practices with a quality-improvement strategy. Following a general discussion of human resource philosophies and competitive strategies, philosophies are matched to strategies. The quality-improvement and cost-reduction strategy is determined to be consistent with a human resource philosophy called "accumulation." In addition to arguing for a good match between strategy and human resource philosophy, Chapter 4 argues for the systematic development of human resource practices. It also presents evidence suggesting that middle managers are becoming increasingly important in determining those practices.

In Chapter 5, the accumulation philosophy is systematically applied to a "menu" of human resource activities. A discussion of options shows how an internally consistent set of human resource practices can reflect and support a commitment to quality improvement.

Chapter 6 takes a look outside the company at relations with vendors and customers. Vendors are seen as partners and as important sources of both quality (good and bad) and innovation. Customers are also seen as partners in defining quality targets (a process that sometimes leads to innovation) and as important sources of information on how the organization is performing with regard to quality.

Managing Quality as a whole aims to introduce the manager (or executive) to a practical view of quality. If even one reader, upon completing this book, says, "I now have a clear idea of how to think about quality and where to begin improving quality in my organization," then our efforts will have been worthwhile. With that thought in mind, we begin by asking . . .

Chapter 1

WHY LOOK AT QUALITY AND THE MIDDLE MANAGER?

In this chapter, we answer three important questions. First, why consider quality? Is quality just another management fad, or is it a fundamental issue that will shape the business world and every life it touches? We believe the latter case is more likely. The idea of simultaneously improving both quality and productivity now holds the attention of companies throughout the world. One can hardly imagine turning back once organizations have recognized the benefits.

Second, what role does quality play in competitive strategies? Quality touches every dimension of strategy and also plays a unique and proprietary role in establishing an organization's competitive position. When sources of competitive advantage are examined, it can be seen that quality influences or defines every generally accepted source of advantage (e.g., cost leadership, technology, distribution channels). Quality in products and services functions as a unique source of competitive advantage since quality cannot be duplicated; each organization takes a unique approach to quality. Because quality is comparative, or relative to the competition, a company must continue improving quality or risk being overtaken by competitors that are committed to continuous quality improvement.

And finally, what role do middle managers play in delivering quality products and services? Why should middle managers be concerned about quality? Although the answer ultimately rests with each manager, some commonly encountered reasons include survival, career advancement, responsibility, and pride. Some middle managers enjoy the luxury of company support for ongoing quality-improvement programs. More often, however, middle managers find themselves being charged with quality improvement but given no direction or support from above. Other managers will not wait for corporate programs; they feel compelled to act on quality now.

1

In order to enable middle managers to develop a concrete plan directed toward the ultimate goal of quality, we will focus on *why* quality is so important, *what* quality means, *how* middle managers can affect quality, *how* they can manage human resources to achieve quality, and *who* are the other participants in quality improvement—external suppliers and customers who influence the definition of quality and affect the organization's chances of delivering high-quality products and services.

WHY BE CONCERNED ABOUT QUALITY?

The widespread application of Baldrige standards [the quality-improvement standards used to measure applicants for the Baldrige Quality Award] could add 7 percent to the gross national product.

> —Armand V. Feigenbaum, head of General Systems Company, based on a model of the economy that includes measures of gains from quality improvement among Baldrige Award applicants (Holusha 1990: F12)

We've entered the second phase of quality. Now, it's the personality of the product that dictates quality.

> —Richard D. Recchia, executive vice president of Mitsubishi Motor Sales of America, Inc. (Woodruff et al. 1990: 84)

I'm not sure the Big Three [U.S. automakers] even recognize that there is a stage two [in quality].

> —Christopher W. Cedergreen, a J. D. Power senior analyst (ibid.: 86)

Quality is a matter of survival. We have divested over 70 businesses in the past several years, and it's questionable whether we would have divested all 70 if they had embraced quality years ago. If you are really the best in your business, you are going to survive.

> —John Marous, chairman of Westinghouse Corporation (Main 1990: 106)

QUALITY IS IMPORTANT

The preceding quotes tell a story about quality in America. Even as America awakens to the international clamor for quality, defined as meeting specifications, a new level of competition is being defined by other nations. The costs to our economy and standard of living are enormous: entire industries lost (e.g., consumer electronics and dynamic random-access computer memory); plants shuttered and jobs lost in the automotive, steel, and textile industries; businesses being sold to foreign investors that know how to turn them around and create quality products. Yet the message is now being heard, and the American business community is waking up to the cold reality that quality—defined first as freedom from defects and then as properties that delight and fascinate—is the playing field of the future.

Quality has become one of the hottest topics in business today. The popular business press rarely prints an article on any company without mentioning the quality of its products or services. The topic of quality most clearly and uniquely captures the struggle of products and services competing in the global market. As a symbol of national importance, and following the model of the Japanese "Deming Award," the U.S. government now sponsors a national quality competition, whose winners receive the Baldrige Award. Since 1988, this competition has become a rallying point for many quality-improvement efforts. According to Jerry Junkins, CEO of Texas Instruments, "If you measure yourself against the criteria laid out by the Baldrige award, you have a blueprint for a better company" (Main 1990: 101).

But quality and a blueprint for a better company have not always been pressing concerns. After World War II, America was the only industrial nation whose production capacity remained intact. In fact, America had developed volume production methods to such an extent that it could produce enough to satisfy its own needs and still supply goods to hungry markets throughout the world. If American industry could make something at a reasonable price, irrespective of quality, America could sell it. Our industry grew—and in many cases, it grew fat and complacent.

Perhaps more dangerous for the United States was the distorted learning that took place during this period. Because virtually anything made could be sold, management practices were not tested as they are now. Since cause and effect were not linked, managers (and business schools that shaped future generations of managers) came to believe that the current practices represented the best possible approach. Most of today's managers were brought up believing that the "American way" of the 1950s and 1960s was the best (and maybe the only) way to manage a business. Competitors from other nations and fast learners here are now showing the United States that there *are* alternative approaches.

As nations rebuilt after World War II (most with U.S. aid), they were forced to consider ways to compete with the phenomenal capability of American industry. Some chose to compete on price (the South American metal and cattle industries, Hong Kong manufacturing); some chose complete isolation (the Soviet Union, China); and others closed parts of their markets while pursuing exports in other areas (most of Europe and Asia). But within some of those rebuilding nations, there were a few companies and industries that rebuilt to gain a competitive advantage that transcended national boundaries and provided opportunities for premium returns. That competitive advantage was quality.

Products from Japan, Germany, Sweden, and (in selected industries such as watchmaking, leather goods, and fashion design) other countries have come to be synonymous with quality. Because of globalization, benchmarks for quality are no longer local; products from one country are now routinely compared with the highest-quality products in the world. In automobiles, consumer electronics, machine tools, steel, and a variety of other products, the Japanese establish the benchmarks for quality. German engineering and craftsmanship are renowned. In furnishing, clothing, and appliances, Italian designers set the pace. As the tigers of Asia (Korea, Taiwan, Singapore, and Thailand) advance, their products are also measuring up to quality expectations. As the economies of Eastern Europe open themselves to the rest of the world, they face the daunting task of playing catch-up to other nations, which are far advanced in quality production. It has now become rare for any nation's industries to initiate global competition on the basis of quantity and price alone; quality must always be considered.

QUALITY SAVES MONEY

However, quality, quantity, and price have improved in unison for most of the successful global competitors. (Although the dramatic increase in the price of Japanese automobiles over the last few years might seem to contradict this assertion, economic analysis reveals that the majority of the increase can be attributed to limitations on supply created by trade restrictions. In fact, prices might have dropped had the United States not imposed quotas and tariffs as it did during the 1980s.) Contrary to the traditional view, the world-class companies of all nations are finding that improved quality results in improved costs and productivity.

Said David T. Kearns, former chairman of Xerox, when speaking of the company's early discoveries as Xerox began systematically focusing on quality: "Pretty early in the process we realized the cost of non-conformance [to quality specifications in manufacturing] was costing us 20% of revenues. The opportunity was enormous" (Holusha 1989: D1, D11). Similarly at Motorola, improvements in quality yielded a 25–30 percent improvement in costs. Chief executive George M. Fisher said, "Americans used to fall into the trap that high quality costs more. But high quality and low cost go hand in hand" (Therrien 1989: 114).

Notable leaders in the worldwide quality-improvement process offer similar estimates. According to Joseph M. Juran, about a third of the U.S. economy is expended on rework due to low quality (Juran 1989: 199). A. V. Feigenbaum, a leading authority on quality, estimated that 15–40 percent of the cost of manufacturing almost any American product is consumed by waste (Feigenbaum 1977). Some obvious costs take the form of rework, detection (inspection and monitoring), scrap, warranties, and repairs. However, manufacturing may not be the largest source of quality problems. Richard Beutow, director of quality at Motorola, guesses that 90 percent of the errors made by Motorola employees have nothing to do with manufacturing; instead, they involve filling out forms correctly, acting quickly, and providing service ("Corporate Performance," 1990: 168). Even within manufacturing, the costs of quality are not concentrated in production. Juran and other experts estimate that no more than 20 percent of defects can be traced to production; the other 80 percent result from design or purchasing policies that value low prices over higher quality.

Increasingly, product and service liability, both direct and in the form of insurance costs, consume a huge portion of organizations' budgets. In businesses as diverse as maternity medical services, alpine skiing, private aircraft, and waste hauling, liability costs can account for over half the price paid by the consumer. Furthermore, W. Edwards Deming contends that these direct costs constitute only a small share of the real costs to most companies; their biggest costs come from customer dissatisfaction and defection to competitors. For many companies, this leads to a lost customer base and a lost future. These costs, albeit unmeasurable, are nonetheless critical.

MAKING A COMMITMENT TO QUALITY IS DIFFICULT

So why do managers and executives express concern, frustration, and anger when quality is mentioned? One simple answer is that the rules of the game are changing, and no one likes to have the rules changed in midgame. U.S. companies developed a number of habits that worked during the heyday of American business superiority following World War II but are proving ineffective in the competitive, global markets of the 1990s. Other members of the world community now define the rules of the new game, and organizations have little time to respond or hesitate. Today's competitive rules do not include grandfather clauses; no one has a permanent hiding place.

A common industrial response is to demand trade protection: Keep the rules the same! When trade protection is used as a temporary shield to give an entrenched industry some response time, the effects can be quite positive: Harley-Davidson's recovery and reemergence as a solid, high-quality international competitor illustrates how effective such limited-duration protection can be:

On March 17, 1987 Harley-Davidson announced it no longer needed the special tariffs that had been imposed on Japanese motorcycle manufacturers since 1983: 'We're taking this action now because we believe we're sending a strong message out to the international industrial community: U.S. workers, given a respite from predatory import practices, can become competitive in world markets. But U.S. industry must also be aggressive and take the initiative to regain competitiveness.' (Reid 1990: 130)

The last part of the preceding quote contains the key to protection: U.S. businesses must aggressively remake themselves if they are to become competitive. If a protected industry's practices are sufficiently backward, if the industry does little to reform itself, and if protection is granted indefinitely, domestic competitors (or indeed, whole new competing industries) will emerge. For example, big American steel companies such as USX and Bethlehem found themselves competing with and losing market share to minimills like Nucor and Chaparrel even though they received significant protection from foreign competitors (Schroeder and Konrad 1990: 76).

Furthermore, there is a limit to how long consumers will put up with the harmful side effects that typically accompany trade restriction (i.e., higher prices, less variety, and lower quality). In the United States, automobile manufacturers are encountering resistance among consumers and legislators to the manufacturers' efforts to block tougher mileage and clean-air standards—a form of competitive protection since importing companies, both European and Japanese, hold advantages in these two areas (Woodruff et al. 1989: 83A). Even in Japan, which has a long tradition of protecting internal markets and a culture that emphasizes conformity and acceptance of authority, early signs of consumer revolt and social unrest reveal resentment over the highest cost of living in the world—a phenomenon closely tied to restrictive trade practices (Buell 1990: 52). Japanese consumers cannot get the high-quality, low-cost food and consumer items that America and other countries would gladly supply.

QUALITY HAS A ROLE AS A PROPRIETARY COMPETITIVE STRATEGY

According to Michael E. Spiess, a vice president of the Wallace Company, "We decided to use quality to differentiate our business from others in the same field." Since 1987, when the company—a supplier of industrial pipes, valves, and fittings—began pursuing this strategy, sales have grown 69 percent, and profits have grown sevenfold. In 1990, the Wallace Company won the Baldrige Award (Holusha 1990: F12).

Growing competition in the manufacturing and service arenas leads companies to look for competitive advantages. Quality fills this requirement in ways that other competitive advantages do not. Quality in an organization's products and services cannot be copied by another organization in exactly the same way. Quality is not the result of technology that can be bought off the shelf and used. It may be unique in that regard.

When they describe situations in which one organization has a competitive advantage over other organizations in the same industry, management theorists tend to focus on a number of characteristics—specialization, brand identification, channel selection, technological leadership, vertical integration, cost position, service, and price policy, among others. Sometimes (though not always) product or service quality is mentioned. However, the descriptions of each of the aforementioned characteristics do include the implications for quality in products, services, and relationships. A closer examination of several of these characteristics will serve to illustrate how quality influences each.

Specialization. When an organization specializes, it focuses on a particular product, service, and/or market. However, in most instances, competing companies can focus on the same or similarly targeted segments; specialization can be copied. Although being the first on the market with a specialty often yields certain short-term advantages, it is quality that creates the long-term advantage for the specialist. Osborn and Kaypro computers led the market for portable computers as specialists; when Compaq began shipping higher-quality products, those two competitors (along with many others) disappeared.

Technological Leadership. Technological leadership has been America's primary competitive strategy during the last two decades. However, as the Japanese have shown, new-product innovation can be bought. American innovators frequently sell or lease their technology quickly in order to maximize short-term gains. As the widespread dispersion of personal computer technology illustrates, this strategy can rapidly create vigorous and sometimes overwhelming competition. Often, after acquiring rights to a technological innovation, international competitors improve the technology or its application so that the end products are of higher quality. For example, the Japanese, unlike the Americans, did not develop innovations in automotive technology during the 1960s, 1970s, and early 1980s, but they did improve their manufacturing processes so that their automobiles dominated world standards for reliability, cost-effectiveness, durability, and overall consumer satisfaction. By contrast, General Motors has spent billions of dollars on technology in the form of robots and computing power without understanding the nature of quality in manufacturing; during the same decades, GM's reputation for relative reliability, cost-effectiveness, and customer satisfaction consistently dropped.

Cost Leadership. As already mentioned, the new view of quality almost always has a favorable impact on costs. Rarely does a company have exclusive access to cheap resources, and even in global competition, lower input costs do not always translate into lower total costs. Manufacturing offshore may yield lower labor costs, but higher transportation costs often offset those gains. As the case of Japan and Korea illustrates, cost advantages from lower input costs, such as wages, can disappear in short order; Japanese autoworkers now cost more per work-hour than American autoworkers, although the overall cost of manufacturing an automobile remains lower for Japanese manufacturers than for American manufacturers.

As these examples suggest, quality impacts every aspect of an organization's competitive position. It cannot be duplicated, for what any particular company does to create quality will differ from what any other company does to create quality. Quality is proprietary in that sense: It belongs to its creator. Quality cannot be transferred, given up, or stolen. Quality is unique among the broad range of factors that affect competitive position. Any other competitive action that a company might take can be duplicated, at least in form. Because it affects all other competitive strategies, is unique, and requires constant attention due to its comparative nature, quality is the dominant issue in today's global markets.

WHAT CAN MIDDLE MANAGERS DO ABOUT QUALITY?

Its focus on the middle manager makes this book a little unusual. Most books on quality are addressed to executives—and with good reason. As studies from the 1950s and 1960s show, the ratio of management-controllable quality factors to line-controllable factors is roughly 4:1 (Juran 1989: 149). Executives control the resources, set the priorities, and determine the rewards (or punishments) for their organizations. They alone have the leverage to enact sweeping, organizationwide changes, such as a total revamping of thinking on quality.

So why address middle managers? Because middle managers, from first-level supervisors up to the levels below division heads (and henceforth referred to simply as managers), actually implement the changes that are required to improve quality. Managers need to know why, when, and by what means they can effect change. Furthermore, managers concerned with quality typically find themselves in one of three difficult positions with regard to this issue:

1. In the best of situations, the organization's executives may launch a quality-improvement process that includes plans for improving quality.

2. In more typical situations, the executives will launch what is to them a quality-improvement program with slogans and exhortations but with neither a clear idea of how to accomplish the desired improvement nor a concrete plan for doing so.

3. In some cases, managers may feel compelled to pursue quality improvement for their own reasons (some good reasons commonly cited include integrity, sanity, career improvement, loyalty/responsibility to their company and coworkers, quality of work life, and pride).

MANAGERS IN ORGANIZATIONS WITH EXECUTIVE SUPPORT FOR QUALITY IMPROVEMENT

Innumerable books share the primary focus of persuading organizational leaders to adopt a philosophy of continual quality improvement for increased productivity and improved competitive position (e.g., Deming 1986; Crosby 1979; Peters and Waterman 1982; Juran 1988; Scherkenbach 1987). Many consultants likewise advocate such a change in thinking. When executives have made a real commitment to quality (as evidenced by plans for *how* to improve quality, not just how much), they will begin by training people in the new roles expected of them and the new tools and techniques required in the quality environment. A real commitment will probably include changes in policies and reallocation of resources. In this new environment, the manager's first task is to understand the new role, to learn as quickly as possible how to become a change agent.

Even in this best possible scenario, managers still feel tremendous pressure. Executives will expect a change in both the managers' role and the hourly employees' role, as well as a change in the relationship between executives, managers, and employees. Many say that a real commitment to quality puts more pressure on managers than on anyone else in the organization.

Studies (e.g., Steers and Porter 1987) show that managers often suffer from a change in role identity due to a lack of preparation for their new role. In organizations where quality is being emphasized from above and taught to employees below, managers find that their job differs markedly from the traditional managerial role. Instead of being controllers and counters, managers become consultants and motivators. Instead of being the ones who push, the ones who take numbers and kick ass, managers must now be leaders, people who motivate without using fear and coercion, who help workers generate their own numbers and derive meaning from them. The new managers must coach and counsel when problems arise. The managers' role shifts from control to empowerment. Chapter 5 expands on these issues of managerial responsibility in the new quality-enhancement environment.

For managers, the transition can be painful, as Pehr G. Gyllenhammer, president of Volvo during its transition to high-quality work methods, explains:

> At every level, management of group working is a different phenomenon. . . . Instead of giving orders the management has to listen, argue, motivate, and often compromise. This process takes longer. Decisions are slower. But it works out better in the long run because, once they are made, the decisions are accepted and implemented.
>
> We have learned something else from the group working at Torslanda [one of Volvo's largest plants] and other factories. The success and failure of an idea is often attributable to whose idea it was, rather than the intrinsic goodness or badness of the idea. If it is the union's idea, or if it comes from a work group, an innovation has a good chance of working. If it is a management idea, its chances are slimmer. (Gyllenhammer 1977: 501)

J. K. Bakken, former vice president of corporate quality and engineering services at Ford Motor Company, expressed the difficulty similarly:

> We expect the transition to full and complete quality thinking to take a generation. Some managers and staff simply will not make the change. They are too stuck in their ways. They have been so thoroughly indoctrinated in their old habits [through former compensation programs] that they cannot or will not change. No amount of training or cajoling seems to move them. . . . For those who won't adopt the philosophy and practices, when we can find them, we try to put them where they will do the least damage. We can't fire them if we are going to truly practice what we preach. (Interview with one of the authors, July 1988.)

Not every company is as dedicated to improving quality as Ford. Often, managers who do not join the program are left out, as at Ford, or fired. Many companies regard downsizing managerial ranks and flattening organizations as fundamental steps toward quality improvement. By acting on the ideas introduced in this book, the reader should be better prepared to compete in organizations that are starting programs to enhance the quality of their products and services.

MANAGERS IN ORGANIZATIONS WITH QUALITY-IMPROVEMENT PROGRAMS BUT NO SUPPORT

After winning the Baldrige Award in 1988, Motorola told thirty-six hundred of its large suppliers that they, too, must be prepared to compete—or else (Main 1990: 101). Motorola, IBM, Ford, GM, and other large companies are telling their divisions and suppliers that they must institute quality-improvement programs and prepare to compete for the Baldrige Award. Although some of these companies provide direction and consulting (e.g., Ford's Q-1 vendor-certification program), many simply demand improvement. So executives in the organizations whose improvement is sought then demand improvement in turn, but too often, these executives do not specify how to improve, nor do they provide adequate resources or increased rewards, either tangibly or through demonstrated appreciation.

In these environments created by fiat or coercion, executives may rely on symbolic gestures to support their call for quality improvement. They may blanket the workplace with slogans (e.g., "Do it right the first time," "Zero defects," "Never make a mistake," "We must tighten our specifications," "Let no product through that does not meet the highest standards"); they may hold a big annual quality-review meeting; they may dictate the creation of quality circles and councils. Increasingly, they say, "Make sure we meet the standards of the Baldrige Award; we want to win that prize." In such situations, the manager's job is doubly difficult. Although these slogans sound impressive, they provide no concrete guidance for converting the current process into one that produces quality. Despite management's hope that the flurry of activity will somehow prove motivating, these quotes, committees, and threats offer nothing more than a vague idea of the desired outcome.

The executive who truly understands the commitment to a quality-improvement process will start with an education program. If the reader's organization is calling for improved quality but has no educational program and is taking no steps to show *how* to improve quality, then it may be assumed that the organization has made no real commitment to quality. Instead, it has merely applied yet another pressure. Its executives expect change but have not made the required commitment in resources, nor have they committed to changing the organization's philosophy in all the areas that must be changed in order to impact quality. In all probability, these executives are not truly concerned about quality; rather, they want to be perceived as being concerned about quality.

The following chapters should provide managers in this situation with enough guidance to get started on quality improvement. With additional reading and training (suggestions are offered in Appendix C), a manager could become a leader in quality improvement. In all probability, there will not be enough cooperation across organizational boundaries to enable dramatic changes to be made, but managers can still make meaningful changes within their own sphere of influence (discussed in the final section of this chapter). Once some measure of success is achieved, resources and cooperation should become more available, leading to greater opportunities and exposure. When executives call for quality improvement but do not commit resources to the effort, the prepared manager has an opportunity to become a star by being one of the few who can deliver the requested improvements.

MANAGERS IN ORGANIZATIONS WITHOUT QUALITY-IMPROVEMENT PROGRAMS

When an organization's managers are concerned about quality but its executives have made either no commitment to quality or only a symbolic commitment, the situation is different. These managers will experience less pressure but can expect fewer resources and less cooperation. Independent managers may even need to operate in a guerrilla fashion, hiding or masking quality-improvement efforts until positive results can be shown. In these situations, guerrilla managers, if discovered, might be perceived as sabotaging formally stated goals (e.g., cutting costs) or questioned by peers as to ulterior motives (e.g., trying to get an edge in the competition for the next promotion). Guerrilla managers must scavenge resources and be willing to take risks, both in changing policies and procedures and in doing things differently from the way they have traditionally been done. Without such changes, no improvement in quality will be achieved.

This is a potentially dangerous course. By changing not only rules but perhaps policies and standard operating procedures as well, these managers run the risk of offending executives. Even though the managers' intentions are good, they could be labeled as troublemakers. Some career opportunities may be lost (if the effort is unsuccessful). It is not an undertaking for the fainthearted.

So why would managers try to improve quality when their organization does not support such efforts? There are some practical reasons. Managers who succeed in creating better quality within their sphere of influence will be recognized. In most instances, executives look for managers who can get things done, and those managers who achieve improvements in quality, together with the commensurate improvements in costs and productivity, will be perceived as getting things done. Furthermore, managers who understand the quality-improvement process will be in a position to make greater changes with greater authority. Not only will these managers be regarded as better and more effective by executives and subordinates; they will in fact be better managers.

If a particular employer does not recognize the benefits of a quality-improvement effort, other avenues are readily available to the trained manager. As more and more organizations become concerned about quality, the demand for knowledgeable managers with a proven track record in quality improvement increases. Moreover, organizations following a true path to quality are good places to work; they will grow and prosper while providing opportunities for employees to work in a participative environment.

Increasingly, managers with a background in quality are choosing another alternative: They are becoming entrepreneurs, using their knowledge of quality improvement to create competitive advantages immediately. For example, an engineer at Exxon Corporation studied part-time with Dr. Deming. After learning how to apply quality thinking and techniques, she became frustrated with her management's lack of interest and began applying quality principles to a part-time endeavor—running a kennel. As she said:

> Within weeks, I began to see a difference in the business. We began saving money, and customers noticed an improvement in service. I think the dogs even began noticing a difference. If things get much worse at Exxon, I may just run the kennel full-time. I now know I can make a success of it. (Overheard by author from participant in Dr. Deming's class, "Managing for Quality, Productivity, and Competitive Position," New York University, November 1987.)

Perhaps the main reasons for pursuing quality improvement as a way of work life are personal. Humans have a fundamental desire to influence or control their environment. Most want to do good things, to be perceived as good people. What better way to exercise control over one's environment and accomplish something worthwhile than to improve the quality of both one's work product and, quite probably, one's work environment? Studies repeatedly show that people want to take pride in their work; they want to feel they have made a difference. Improving the quality of the work product makes a difference. Not only will the manager make a difference, but because continuous improvement in quality requires involvement by subordinates at all levels, their working conditions will improve as well. According to John Grettenberger, general manager of the Cadillac division of General Motors, a 1990 winner of the Baldrige Award, "The great benefit is to the corporation itself. When you go around the offices and plants you see people smiling again" (Holusha 1990: F12).

Loyalty to the organization, peers, and subordinates can be a powerful motivator as well; if poor quality threatens the organization's existence, then everybody will suffer. There are also those who consider quality improvement a moral responsibility: If one knows how to make things better, isn't there some responsibility (to the organization, friends, self) to improve the process? And finally, pride in one's work still exists, even at the managerial level.

A PLAN FOR QUALITY IMPROVEMENT

So managers have multiple reasons for pursuing quality. Managers who are reading this book probably already have a reason that is better than any of the aforementioned, simply because it is *their* reason. But reasons for pursuing a quality approach are not enough. Managers must also have a plan, especially if they are operating without executive support. The plan must fit their particular circumstances, and only the managers who are directly involved can decide whether those circumstances warrant proceeding. With that in mind, the following steps outline a generic plan for quality improvement, which can be adapted to many environments:

1. Understand what quality means. Know the various aspects of quality and how change may be effected in each of these areas. (This is the topic of the next chapter.)

2. Recognize the sphere of influence (discussed later in this section) and accept the limitations imposed by it.

3. Choose a target project for improvement from a large list of potential projects. Suggestions for list generation and project selection are given in Chapter 3, "Tools for Improving Quality."

4. Decide on the staff, tools, techniques, and learning that will be required to complete the project successfully. Again, suggestions can be found in Chapter 3.

5. Conduct the project and document the process and the resulting progress. Chapter 3 offers suggestions for this as well.

6. Stabilize the gains made by instituting new processes. Again, this is discussed in Chapter 3.

7. Cycle through steps 3–6 with new projects, gradually including more areas in the sphere of influence and expanding the sphere of influence while publicizing successes.

8. With each new project and each of the preceding steps, build a reference library of books, articles, project descriptions, success-story documentation, references for training and consultants, and other support material. The change agent must be prepared to defend actions, show progress and success, and help guide the followers. A lending library of these materials will become invaluable as recognition grows.

9. As appropriate within projects and within the manager's sphere of influence, alter the human resource practices to create an environment conducive to quality. This is so important that both Chapters 4 and 5 are devoted to the change in human resource management.

The foregoing are general steps. In the following chapters, these steps are reviewed and illustrated through examples and minicases. Fundamental to this approach is the understanding that in the case of the middle manager, quality improvement must necessarily be an incremental process. Incremental change (although the increments are sometimes large) and gain holding are the way to achieve lasting quality improvement. A manager attains each increment through a project—a deliberate, contained effort to improve a specific aspect of quality. Eventually, quality improvement should occur as a matter of course; quality-improvement projects should be a part of the standard business process. Only by proceeding one project at a time, showing gains, educating subordinates, peers, and executives, and maintaining constant vigilance can the manager make a lasting change in the habits and attitudes that govern the process.

THE SPHERE OF INFLUENCE

Managers just beginning the quality-improvement process will find that some projects are simply not feasible. Key participants may refuse to cooperate; resources may be unavailable. This points to the concept of the sphere of influence (SOI). Recognition of the SOI will give managers a better perspective and greater understanding of the possible impacts of their actions. Without this perspective, managers will quickly become discouraged and abandon the quest for quality.

What do we mean by the SOI? It is the facilities, people, tools, and processes over which a manager can exert some control or influence. A manager has a certain number of direct-report employees, who are responsible for a variety of tasks involving equipment, materials, and procedures. All these are within the manager's direct SOI. Often, below the manager, subordinates may manage subunits. Since the manager has considerable influence and responsibility when it comes to setting goals, allocating resources, monitoring outcomes, and reporting on the performance of the subunits, those areas can also be regarded as within the manager's direct SOI.

But everyone has influence beyond direct reports. In a sequence of processes (such as the handoff between ticket counter and baggage handling at an airport), there is some influence on the processes immediately preceding and following the process under a manager's direct control. These could be considered part of an indirect SOI (that is, unless the manager has an adversarial relationship with the managers of adjacent activities). Often, a manager has personal influence through peer relationships, collegiate contacts, or affiliations outside the workplace. All these sources of influence expand the manager's SOI.

Since one would be hard-pressed to find an ethical dilemma in using relationships to improve quality, the manager should not hesitate to use and apply influence wherever it may improve quality. However, the strength of the influence may determine the practicality of using a particular relationship. The following examples illustrate this point:

1. If a manager in an advertising group has influence with the manager of a typing pool, this may give the advertising manager some leverage to discuss the quality of the work being produced by the typing pool. By using influence to bring up the subject in a nonthreatening and non-accusatory way, the advertising manager might be able to start a dialogue, which could lead to a change in the nature of the interactions between the typing pool and the advertising staff. Such a change might involve improving the feedback loops—typists could explain things that are difficult for them to understand, and users of the typing pool could offer feedback regarding their problems in a nonthreatening way.

2. An assembly manager might be unable to persuade the purchasing manager to buy a particularly sensitive component from a single supplier. Although the assembly manager may know that her preferred vendor produces very high-quality parts that result in less rework and therefore lower overall costs, the purchasing agent has been taught to

buy each batch from a different vendor to maintain multiple sources of supply. If the assembly manager has influence with the design engineer, she might work with the engineer to redefine a specification so that only the preferred vendor's parts qualify for purchasing. In this case, the assembly manager uses a source of indirect influence to overcome a lack of direct influence.

These are examples of the guerrilla tactics that must be employed by managers whose organizations provide little or no support for the quality-improvement program. Other examples might include changing policies regarding attendance, job structure, process flow, work-area layout, and so on.

One must question how rational it is to buck the system in a quest for higher quality. Many people contend that the only way to get ahead is to play the game as it is defined by the existing organizational rules. And many people do in fact lead their lives this way. But for managers who want to make a difference, improve, shape their careers, and be recognized as special, there is no more effective way than to improve the quality and productivity of their work unit's output. The world is clamoring for managers who know how to improve quality, who have embraced the role of the quality manager, and who understand the required techniques.

SUMMARY

This chapter has introduced the concern for quality and explained why middle managers, in particular, must play an active role in the quality-improvement effort. Faced with rapidly increasing competition, American industry simply has no choice but to improve quality. Organizations that do not adopt a policy of continuous quality improvement run the risk of falling behind and eventually being driven from the marketplace.

Quality plays a role in every major source of competitive advantage. Attention to quality can in itself be a source of significant competitive advantage. Since each organization pursues quality along its own unique path, quality constitutes a proprietary source of competitive advantage. However, because quality is relative (to the quality of other organizations' products and services), organizations must continue to improve quality lest others leapfrog them.

Middle managers face unique problems in the quest for quality. Even if they have support and direction from above, many changes must still be made, and these managers can use all available help in effecting the transition. If the managers have no support from above, then they must develop a plan for changing quality, discover the tools and techniques required, and chart a course of action. Managers will shoulder this burden, for both practical and personal reasons.

However, to remain sane and effective, managers must recognize the opportunities and limitations arising from their sphere of influence. Although managers have limited control and influence over the entire organization, they have more than just direct reports in their SOI. These multiple areas of influence become resources in the struggle to improve quality. As managers engage in a sometimes clandestine pursuit of quality, careful handling of politically sensitive issues will improve their chances for success.

Now that the concern for quality has been established, we are prepared to address the meaning of quality.

References

Buell, B. 1990. "Japan's Silent Majority Starts to Rumble." *Business Week* (Apr. 23): 52–54.

"Corporate Performance." 1990. *Fortune* (Oct. 24): 168.

Crosby, P. B. 1979. *Quality Is Free.* New York: McGraw-Hill.

Deming, W. E. 1986. *Out of the Crisis.* Cambridge, Mass.: MIT Center for Advanced Engineering Studies.

Feigenbaum, A. V. 1977. "Quality and Productivity." Quality Progress (Nov.).

Gyllenhammer, P. G. 1977. "How Volvo Adapts Work to People." From *Harvard Business Review* (July-Aug. 1977): 102–111, as reprinted in Richard M. Steers and Lyman W. Porter, *Motivation and Work Behavior* (New York: McGraw-Hill, 1987).

Holusha, J. 1989. "Stress On Quality Lifts Xerox's Market Share." *New York Times* (Nov. 9): D1, D11.

———. 1990. "The Baldrige Badge of Courage—and Quality." *New York Times* (Oct. 21): F12.

Juran, J. M. 1988. *Juran on Planning for Quality.* New York: Free Press.

———. 1989. *Juran on Leadership for Quality.* New York: Free Press.

Main, J. 1990. "How to Win the Baldrige Award." *Fortune* (Apr. 23): 101–116.

Peters, T. J., and Waterman, R. H. 1982. *In Search of Excellence.* New York: Harper & Row.

Reid, P. C. 1990. *Well Made in America: Lessons Learned from Harley-Davidson on Being the Best.* New York: McGraw-Hill.

Scherkenbach, W. W. 1987. *The Deming Route to Quality and Productivity: Road Maps and Road-blocks.* Rockville, Md.: Mercury Press/Fairchild Publications.

Schroeder, M., and Konrad, W. 1990. "Nucor: Rolling Right into Steel's Big Time." *Business Week* (Nov. 19): 76–81.

Steers, R. M., and Porter, L. W. 1987. *Motivation and Work Behavior.* New York: McGraw-Hill. In particular, see Chapter 10.

Therrien, L. 1989. "The Rival Japan Respects." *Business Week* (Nov. 13): 108–118.

Woodruff, D., Miller, K., Armstrong, L., and Peterson, T. 1990. "A New Era for Auto Quality." *Business Week* (Oct. 22): 84–96.

Woodruff, D., Zellner, W., and Cahan, V. 1989. "Does Detroit Have the Oomph for the Hills Ahead?" *Business Week* (Nov. 20): 83A–83C.

Chapter 2

WHAT IS QUALITY?

Quality is recognized as critical to modern competition. It has placed harsh burdens on middle managers, executives, companies, and industries. They need to know how to improve quality if they are to survive. Yet before anyone can improve quality, he or she must know what it means.

All too often, a manager comes face to face with an attitude like "I can't define quality, but I know it when I see it." Unfortunately, such an attitude tells nothing about how to achieve quality. Defining quality at three levels may help everyone understand the concept of quality so that something can be done about it. These three levels build on each other and should aid managers in talking about quality, identifying opportunities for improving quality, measuring quality, and acting to improve quality.

Quality at an abstract level has been defined through the words and guidance of two masters in the field, Joseph Juran and W. Edwards Deming. They have created a mind-set, provided a language for communicating about quality, and built the foundation of quality thinking. Their thoughts also help with the next level of detail: decomposing quality into components (attributes or aspects). This helps isolate areas needing improvement and suggests boundaries for improvement projects. Finally, an operational view defines quality as a product of the business process. This view helps pinpoint sources of quality problems and suggests further boundaries for possible improvement projects.

MANAGEMENT PHILOSOPHERS: QUALITY AS A PHENOMENON

Although many consultants, executives, and educators could be considered leaders and are quoted elsewhere in this book, two men have had a world-wide impact on quality (Garvin 1987). Joseph Juran and W. Edwards Deming easily qualify as the grand old men, or masters, of quality. More important, they are the ones who really created a popular awareness of quality and spearheaded the drive toward quality improvement. In the following sub-sections, their views are presented in increasing complexity and depth.

JOSEPH JURAN

Joseph Juran consulted with the Japanese in the 1950s and 1960s and is considered second only to W. Edwards Deming in having influenced Japanese thinking on quality. In the United States, Juran may be more widely known in the business community than Deming—in part because of the Juran Institute, which he founded in 1979. The institute now serves as a base for consulting, seminars, conferences, publications, and videotapes associated with Juran. The institute and its activities and products provide an ongoing forum for the dissemination of Juran's message.

Although Juran's definition of quality has changed over the years, it can best be summed up as "fitness for use" (Juran and Gryna 1980). This means that a product or service should do what the user needs or wants and has a right to expect. Juran defined five dimensions of quality:

1. *Design* specifies what a product or service is and what it should do; it distinguishes a truck from a car.

2. *Conformance* reflects the match between design intent and actual product delivery. Conformance is directly impacted by process choice, input materials, work-force training and supervision, transitory environmental influences, and adherence to testing programs.

3. *Availability* encompasses aspects of reliability, maintainability, and durability; it reflects a product's freedom from disruptive problems (i.e., the product is available to the customer for use).

4. *Safety* examines risks to the user from product hazards that may be associated with one of the other dimensions.

5. *Field use* encompasses the other four dimensions, but with emphasis on use in the customer's hands. Field use is affected by packaging, transportation, storage, and field-service competence and promptness.

Managers probably have more control over conformance and field use than over the other dimensions. Design, when performed according to Juran, involves multidisciplinary cooperation. Safety is dependent on design and conformance. Availability relies on all the other dimensions. Typically, conformance means producing something according to design and with minimum variance. Although each manager may be responsible for only a part of the end product, within that part, conformance is most often within the manger's control (although some other area, such as purchasing, may prevent conformance). Similarly, packaging, transportation, storage, and field service often fall within a single manager's sphere of influence (SOI). The greater the SOI, the greater the likelihood that the manager can influence the outcome.

Juran offered a number of techniques, tools, and methods for improving quality along his five dimensions. His general approach is to examine each dimension from initial product concept through design, vendor relations, process development, manufacturing, inspection and testing, distribution, customer relations, and field service. Each step of the process is dissected and analyzed for opportunities to address appropriate dimensions of quality. The analytic tools range from statistical techniques to various group problem-solving techniques, some of which are addressed in more detail in Chapter 3.

Juran also advocates a cost of poor quality (COPQ) accounting system, which would account for the costs "that would disappear if there were no quality problems"; these include the cost of making, finding, repairing, or avoiding defects (Juran 1989: 50). There are four types of costs: internal failure (defects discovered before shipment), external failure (defects discovered after shipment), appraisal (assessing incoming materials), and preventive. Using the COPQ approach, the goal is to provide the highest quality with the lowest COPQ. This is accomplished by expending efforts (and dollars) on assessment and prevention activities until the costs of such activities equal the costs of defects (Juran estimates that 50 percent to 80 percent of the COPQ comes from the cost of internal and external failure rather than from the cost of prevention). Juran points out that zero defects may not be a practical goal; appraisal and prevention costs could rise so substantially that the COPQ might not be at a minimum with zero defects.

To focus the attention and efforts of managers, Juran suggests a three-pronged approach. In the early stages of a quality-improvement effort, a company's failure costs usually greatly exceed its prevention and appraisal costs; during this period, "breakthrough projects" are feasible. A breakthrough project addresses a chronic problem, such as the need to revise tolerances, change vendors, change work flows, or revise forms. After success has been achieved with breakthrough projects, a "control" sequence (mainly a big feedback loop) is required to consolidate and maintain gains. The third prong attempts to capture and hold the attention of top management through annual quality programs centered around COPQ reporting and planning quality objectives.

W. EDWARDS DEMING

W. Edwards Deming is the father of modern thinking on quality. He is widely credited with leading the Japanese quality revolution. Although Deming was advocating his philosophy and techniques in the United States as early as the 1930s, it is only during the last ten years that organizations in this country have finally started listening to him. Deming has authored books, teaches at New York and Columbia universities, gives seminars throughout the world, and is a consultant on quality to major U.S. and Japanese companies. Although Deming has created no institutional structure to carry on his philosophy, the numerous companies successfully practicing his techniques (such as Ford and many of its suppliers, Nashua Corporation, and Florida Light and Electric) as well as organizations created by others to promote and spread his philosophy assure continuing support for and development of Deming's teachings.

Deming suggests that although quality includes matching product attributes to customer demands, it must go beyond that. Despite his training as an engineer and a statistician, Deming's definition of quality seems very unquantitative: A product or service is of high quality if customers perceive good value for their purchases, remain loyal in their purchases, urge others to buy the product or service, and transfer those sentiments to other products or services from the same vendor. According to Deming, quality is global and competition-based; consumers ultimately define true quality based on their tastes, expectations, responsiveness to new stimuli, and subjective comparison to other products. (The foregoing overview of Deming's views on quality was gleaned from lecture notes, discussions, and personal correspondence.)

Deming's approach challenges managers, for he asserts that managers are responsible for 85 percent of all quality problems, in that they define and control processes, policies, personnel practices, equipment, facilities, and supplies. Therefore, management must take the lead in improving quality (Deming 1986). Deming prescribes fourteen points that can help managers achieve this improvement. The wording of these points has changed over the years, and the following version is taken from Serlen (1987: 18):

The World According to Deming: His Fourteen Essential Points for Managers

1. Create constancy of purpose toward improvement of product and service, with the aim to become competitive and to stay in business, and to provide jobs.

2. Adopt the new philosophy. We are in a new economic age. Western management must awaken to the challenge, must learn their responsibilities, and take on leadership for change.

3. Cease dependence on inspection to achieve quality. Eliminate the need for inspection on a mass basis by building quality into the product in the first place.

4. End the practice of awarding business on the basis of price tag. Instead, minimize total cost. Move toward a single supplier for any one item, on a long-term relationship of loyalty and trust.

5. Improve constantly and forever the system of production and service, to improve quality and productivity, and thus constantly decrease costs.

6. Institute training on the job.

7. Institute leadership. The aim of supervision should be to help people and machines and gadgets to do a better job. Supervision of management is in need of overhaul, as well as supervision of production workers.

8. Drive out fear, so that everyone may work effectively for the company.

9. Break down barriers between departments. People in research, design, sales, and production must work as a team to foresee problems of production and in use that may be encountered with the product or service.

10. Eliminate slogans, exhortations, and targets for the work force asking for zero defects and new levels of productivity. Such exhortations only create adversarial relationships, as the bulk of the causes of low quality and low productivity belongs to the system and thus lies beyond the power of the work force.

11a. Eliminate work standards (quotas) on the factory floor. Substitute leadership.

11b. Eliminate management by objective. Eliminate management by the numbers, numerical goals. Substitute leadership.

12a. Remove barriers that rob the hourly worker of his right to pride of workmanship. The responsibility of supervisors must be changed from sheer numbers to quality.

12b. Remove barriers that rob people in management and in engineering of their right to pride of workmanship. This means, inter alia, abolishment of the annual or merit rating and of management by objective.

13. Institute a vigorous program of education and self-improvement.

14. Top management will accomplish the transformation.

Embedded in these points are several key ideas that form the foundation of Deming's philosophy and touch on every aspect of organizational endeavor. The first and primary idea is that variation is present in everything. Although this may seem obvious, Deming provides insight that transcends the obvious.

There are two sources of variance: common-cause, or systematic, variance and special-cause variance. Common-cause variance shows up as random variance generated by the entire system's working together; it cannot be attributed to a single, isolated source. Common causes of variance in a production system might include product design, equipment not holding tolerance, misplaced priorities due to ineffectively designed compensation systems, or a breakdown in communications due to personnel practices that create communication barriers.

Special causes of variance are nonrandom and can be attributed to a specific cause. Special causes include such factors as operator inattention, lack of knowledge or skill, an unusually poor shipment of raw materials, natural disaster, or an operator's personal problem, such as drug abuse. When they can be controlled, common causes are the responsibility of management, and special causes are the responsibility of operators. Much of management's current practices and problems stem from treating common causes as special causes.

Deming popularized another fundamental idea: Productivity increases as quality increases. Prior to Deming, the common wisdom was that higher quality meant lower productivity and higher costs. Deming pointed out that quality (high or low) is manufactured into all products. (The quotations in Chapter 1 bear witness to this fact.) Conventional final inspection and rework approaches to quality control mean that low-quality products require more processing and increased costs to become high-quality products, and any attempts to improve quality in this way would surely raise overall costs by increasing both detection costs and subsequent rework costs. Deming points the way out of this conundrum: Processes must be designed to produce high quality to begin with, before costs are tied up in a defective product.

Executives and managers may find a third key idea more difficult to accept. Deming claims that the most important costs of quality cannot be measured. The cost of a defective product or service reaching a consumer is an example of a critical cost that cannot be measured. The true cost, which goes way beyond simple replacement or repair, determines the consumer's future relationship with the organization—i.e., whether the consumer will repurchase this or other products and services and whether he or she will rave about a good product or rant about a poor-quality one. Although such costs cannot be measured, they determine an organization's success in the long term.

Deming does not imply that organizations should refrain from assessing countable costs and taking other measurements; they are critical to understanding the capability of a process. Rather, Deming insists that executives and managers look beyond tangible measures when trying to assess the value and true costs of their quality efforts. Juran agrees on this point, suggesting that the costs of poor quality on major projects are so great that even very rough estimates work fine (e.g., although $2 million differs quite a bit from $4 million either amount will justify a project!).

A variety of tools are used to implement Deming's recommendations. Statistical tools differentiate between common causes of variation and special causes. Among these, the control chart, developed by Walter Shewhart at Bell Labs in the 1920s, is of greatest use and is discussed in more detail in Chapter 3. Problem-solving tools and techniques as well as experimental design, control, and evaluation are also used. These, too, are discussed in Chapter 3.

In summary, each of these two masters offers some important views on quality. Deming supplies the broadest view, encompassing and combining the dictates of global competition, enthusiastic customers (beyond merely satisfied or happy), and a philosophy dedicated to continual improvement. (At the age of ninety-one, Deming still listens attentively when someone with knowledge and experience speaks.) He suggests that quality can be found only through the application of profound knowledge, which he defines as including an appreciation for a system, a theory of variation, human psychology, and a theory of learning and knowledge (Deming 1990). Juran's general views on quality are quite similar to Deming's; in addition, his views on COPQ and his specific implementation recommendations can be extremely useful. A manager picking up the quality banner will do well to read from both these masters. (See Appendix C for a suggested reading list.)

DECOMPOSING QUALITY: GETTING CHUNKS SMALL ENOUGH TO WORK ON

Although Juran discusses five dimensions of quality, several of these include a variety of different processes and responsibilities. A more detailed breakdown of the dimensions of quality might allow managers to focus more clearly on what can be accomplished within their sphere of influence. Decomposing quality into categories may provide a descriptive framework that will lead to a better understanding of the concept. Decomposition also establishes a structure for researching, testing, and discussing quality. Surprisingly little categorization has been done in the case of quality (perhaps because America's concern for quality is a fairly recent phenomenon). Fortunately, at least one good description is available.

David A. Garvin (1987) proposes eight critical dimensions or categories of quality:

1. Performance

2. Features

3. Reliability

4. Conformance

5. Durability

6. Serviceability

7. Aesthetics

8. Perceived quality

These dimensions provide a framework for examining a product or service. The recognition that a product or service merits a high rating on one measure and a low rating on another can be used to direct quality-improvement efforts. Managers may have to make trade-offs between dimensions (depending on the product or service) and may therefore have to make a choice to compete on one dimension or another. Furthermore, managers may have limited influence over some of the dimensions—in which case they must again remain focused on the things they can change.

Performance.   Performance refers to a product's primary operating characteristics. In the case of a computer, this may mean its processing speed, memory and storage capability, and the like; in the case of a bank, it may mean yields on investment products, response time at tellers (human or automated), accessibility of tellers, and availability of funds after deposit. Regardless of whether tangible objects or services are involved, performance can normally be measured and compared over time and against competitors. Usually, performance is measured as a rate, the most common measure being units per time (e.g., calls handled per hour, meals served per day, projects delivered on time per year).

Features.   Although sometimes considered a secondary aspect of performance, features are the "bells and whistles" whose characteristics supplement the basic function. This dimension is more volatile than other dimensions; features quickly become subsumed into performance. For example, remote tuners on television sets might have been considered a feature a few years ago; now, all but the lowest-cost televisions have them. A feature today might be multiple screen displays. The choice of features may also be regarded as a reflection of quality; if a company offering mutual funds does not provide a range of funds and permit free and easy transfers, many investors would consider the company's offerings to be of low quality. Features are usually measured in terms of variety (how many) and strength of appeal (preference rankings).

Reliability. The reliability dimension reflects the probability of a product's malfunctioning or failing within a specified time or of a service's not being delivered consistently over time. Typical measures for products include mean time to first failure, mean time between failures, and failure rates per unit of time. For services, the measures are not so clear-cut but might include on-time deliveries as a percentage of all deliveries, percentages of fees at or below estimates, and the number or percentage of correct answers provided by an information service (such as the IRS hot line). Reliability increases in importance as downtime, maintenance, predictability, or timeliness become more critical (expensive) to the customer. Financial services and computers, farmers and harvesting equipment, and soldiers and weapons are obvious examples of customers in critical need of reliable products. Today, even the casual consumer has come to expect reliability in most products and services. Once some company has demonstrated product or service reliability (especially if such reliability is offered without charging a premium price), consumers will expect all companies to meet similar reliability standards or be thought of as lower-quality producers.

Conformance. Conformance involves matching competitors' offerings and meeting consumers' expectations in terms of established standards for design and operating characteristics. Standards are often expressed as specifications that indicate a center or target and some acceptable degree of deviation or variance; this is the essential issue in conformance, traditional quality control, and statistical quality control, although each examines the issue differently. Conformance effectiveness often drives reliability, durability, performance, and perceived quality. Because of its central importance and because this area can often be influenced by managers, much of Chapters 3, 4, and 5 addresses conformance issues through the use of tools (Chapter 3) and through human resource approaches (Chapters 4 and 5).

Durability. Durability measures product life in both technical and economic dimensions. With products that cannot be repaired, such as light bulbs, the technical life and economic life are the same. With other products, consumers weigh the expected costs (in both dollars and inconvenience) of future repairs against the investment in and operating expenses of a newer, more reliable model. In this case, durability may be defined as how long a product can be used before it breaks down and/or replacement is preferred over the expense and inconvenience of making expected repairs. Deciding to replace a used car with a new model is an example of durability evaluation. Durability and reliability are closely linked; a product that often fails is more likely to be scrapped earlier than one that is more reliable. However, apparent increases in durability may actually reflect some other change. For instance, the fact that the life expectancy of automobiles rose to an average of fourteen years between 1975 and 1985 may not have reflected a real increase in durability; during those years Americans drove fewer miles per year due to higher gasoline prices and a weak economy.

Serviceability. Speed, courtesy, competence, and ease of repair or replacement define serviceability. Customers are concerned about several aspects of serviceability: Once a product breaks down, how quickly can service be restored? How timely are service appointments? What is the nature of the dealings with the service personnel? How effective is the repair effort? And what remedies are available when a repair effort has not been successful? Although each customer has a different standard of acceptable service, the truism "No one likes surprises" suggests that gathering data and making information about performance capability available to customers will help manage their expectations and hence their perceptions of quality in serviceability. Typical measures include mean time until a service representative arrives, mean time to repair, average number of service calls required to correct problems, and mean waiting time to speak to a customer-service representative when calling about problems. Although personal behavior, such as courtesy, is difficult to measure, this is often the most critical aspect of perceived serviceability. Serviceability can constitute a powerful competitive advantage; surveys indicate that over 40 percent of households initiating complaints were dissatisfied with the results. Complaint resolution correlated closely with consumer willingness to repurchase the offending brands. The moral may be that *how* a complaint is handled is more important than *whether* a complaint arises in the first place.

Aesthetics. How a product (or service) feels, looks, sounds, tastes, or smells is very subjective, reflecting personal preferences. Even though aesthetics are difficult to measure, a great deal of marketing research has revealed certain general patterns. For example, people tend to like quiet automobiles (although sports car enthusiasts might not agree). This suggests opportunities for niche marketing; it is impossible to please everyone with one aesthetic interpretation.

Perceived Quality. Consumers do not have complete information about a product or service; they rely on indirect sources of information as well as signals sent by the company that produces the product or service. Among these sources of information are company or brand reputation, image, advertising, warranties, and guarantees. Reputation may be the most significant source of perceived quality; consumers refer to reputation unconsciously, using it as an anchor or starting point from which to evaluate specific products or competitors. Reputation has an interesting property: It is claimed that up to ten years may be required to build a good, widely recognized reputation, whereas that good reputation can be lost in a matter of months. For these reasons, successful companies manage their reputation carefully. To cite but one example, Volkswagen has an automobile plant in Tennessee that has a reputation for building lower-quality cars than its German factories; Nissan has a truck factory in Tennessee that has a reputation for building better trucks than its Japanese plants. Both companies resist identifying the source of their vehicles because they believe that their overall quality is high and that to compete internally (i.e., domestic production versus imported production) would diminish their general reputation for quality.

INFORMATION AS A DIMENSION OF QUALITY

Although each of these eight dimensions can be applied to services as well as physical products, an additional dimension—information—is critical in representing service quality. For consumers, information has two primary aspects: availability and accuracy.

Information availability affects quality in a number of ways. Withholding directly requested information is the obvious example: How many times has a clerk, teller, or salesperson simply failed to respond to a question? If a salesperson does not respond (perhaps because he or she wants to "control" the discussion), the customer immediately becomes suspicious, and the dimension of perceived quality is negatively affected. If a clerk or teller is not paying attention, the customer becomes angered by the poor performance. If a service representative wants to withhold information as a way of exercising power, the customer becomes irritated. Such abuses, whose cost to companies cannot be measured, quickly become the basis for the horror stories that people love to tell their friends.

Greater losses may come from partial withholding of information; a couple booking a weekend at a resort were told all sorts of wonderful things about the view, the facilities, the recreational opportunities, and the great food (all of which came true). However, they were not informed that the only available room, the one they were given, was next to the game room. All weekend long, the couple were kept awake by the noisy comings and goings of patrons using the game room. By Sunday afternoon, they were cranky and irritable; they felt cheated. Not only would they never return to that resort, but they would discourage their friends from going there as well. Had the couple been allowed to make an informed choice, their expectations, and therefore their perceptions of the weekend, would have been different. Withholding information allowed the resort to book that room for one weekend but lost an untold number of future bookings. Had the resort provided the couple with full information, it might have booked the weekend anyway without incurring the negative results because the couple would have known what to expect. (The resort could also have changed its room-assignment policy; a family with children would probably have preferred that room to one three floors away from the game room.)

A variation of information withholding is answering a direct question by rote while ignoring the real, indirect question. When the scheduled train was canceled, the traveler inquired, "When is the next train to Verona?" The response: "In ten minutes." The traveler boarded that train, which turned out to be a local train that took three hours to reach Verona. Within fifteen minutes after the traveler's departure, an express train to Verona passed the local train; it reached Verona in an hour. Had the information clerk answered the *real* question—"Which train will get me to Verona the quickest?"—the traveler would have saved two hours and a great deal of annoyance. How many times has goodwill been irretrievably lost over similar failures to respond to a consumer's real concerns? "Buyer beware" may be an appropriate stance to take in court, but it does not win loyal customers!

A related issue is useless offerings (of information, products, or services). A software company may publicize a toll-free information and troubleshooting telephone number. In one such company, no one answering the phones actually knows how the software functions; by contrast, at the WordPerfect Corporation, the phones are answered by well-trained representatives because customer service is a critical part of the organization's strategy.

A small electronics device costing $8.00 has a lifetime warranty; the fine print explains that to obtain warranty service, all one has to do is mail in the device along with a $6.00 check for return postage and handling. A store offers an unconditional exchange policy: Just bring the item back in its original packaging. However, opening the package to test the item requires tearing the package; the store then refuses to make an exchange because the packaging has been damaged. These examples involve a form of deception. A company cannot practice deception without risking serious damage to its reputation. Again, these are the tales of woe that people love to tell their friends.

Understanding these eight dimensions and the impact of information provides a framework that can help managers identify the quality-improvement opportunities that lie within their SOI. Table 2.1 suggests a cross-reference between functional areas (such as accounting, production, and customer service) and quality dimensions. It focuses on matches that have the greatest probability of making an impact on quality (although these are certainly not the only matches that can make an impact).

A COMPOSITE DEFINITION

These various approaches may suggest a complex definition of quality, and rightly so. Quality means delivering products and services that will generate intense customer loyalty and premium returns for the producer and service provider. To do this, quality must be delivered along all eight of Garvin's dimensions (and subsequently along all five of Juran's dimensions). This can only be accomplished by delivering quality with a single effort (no remakes, returns, or rejects, especially in service, where the product is consumed at the point of creation). That kind of effort requires an expectation that top quality can be produced. It also requires an understanding of variation and common and special cause, as well as knowledge of how and where to look for opportunities to reduce that variation.

This complex definition—*high quality means delivering loyalty-producing products and services along all dimensions of quality with a single effort*—will be most effective if applied to all functional areas in an organization. However, managers and their business units may contribute to overall quality without the cooperation of other units. The following subsections illustrate some contributions that can be made by business functions.

Operations. Operations can have a direct impact on conformance, reliability, durability, and perceived quality. If allowed to contribute early enough in a product-development cycle, operations can also affect performance,

Table 2.1 Cross-Reference between Aspects of Quality and Some Traditional Departments

Aspect	Department								
	Mktg.	Sales	Design	Eng.	Mfg.	Pack.	Dist.	Svc.	Acct.
Performance	1,2,4	3,4,5	1,2,7	7,8,9	9	10	9,11	1,2,3,4,5,6,9	12
Features	1,2,4	3,4,5	1,2,7	7,8,9	9	9,10	9,11	1,2,4,5,6,9	12
Reliability	3,4	3,4,5	2,7	7,8,9,12	9,13	9	9,11	1,4,5,6,9	12
Conformance	—	5	2,7,8	7,8,9,12	7,9,13	9,10	9	9	12,13
Durability	3	3,4,5	2,7,8	7,8,9,12	9	7,9	9,11	4,6,9	12
Serviceability	1,2,3	4,5	2,7,8	7,8,9,12	9	7,9,11	7,9,11	1,3,4,5,6,7,9,12	12
Aesthetics	1,2,4	4	1,2,7	7,8,9	9	1,2,7,9	7,9,11	9	—
Perceived Quality	1,2,4	3,4,5	1,7	7	13	1,2,7,9,10	3,5,6,7,9,11	1,3,4,5,6,7,9	9
Information	3	3,5,6	—	9	13	7,9,10	3,6,7,9,10,11	4,6,7,9,12	6,9,12

1. Analyze customer needs.
2. Analyze competitors.
3. Promote accurately.
4. Create customer expectations.
5. Sell to capability.
6. Respond completely and accurately to inquiries.
7. Explicitly include.
8. Choose function with form.
9. Look upstream to get/give information.
10. Include appropriate documentation.
11. Place in appropriate channels.
12. Provide relevant measures.
13. Provide timely vendor support.

features, and serviceability. Contributions come from identifying and correcting sources of variance, delivering good products with a single effort, and providing feedback to those who support and define their functions (research and development, engineering, suppliers, etc.).

Sales and Marketing. Sales and marketing can impact all dimensions through their direct involvement in the customer-feedback loop. Even without the cooperation of other functions, marketing can have the greatest impact on perceived quality. Its efforts can be directed at positioning products in consumers' minds so that they perform within or above expectations. Marketing also plays a critical role in disseminating information.

Accounting and Finance. Accounting and finance can not only improve their own functions but also influence everything except aesthetics and perceived quality. These departments contribute through policies and budgets that factor in both the full cost of programs and the full returns from them. (As Deming points out, this task is impossible using current cost-accounting methods; Juran's admonition to estimate could help cost accounting.) In performing their calculations, these departments must attempt to take into account the value of customer loyalty and spontaneous support.

Customer Service. Customer service directly affects serviceability, durability, and reliability as well as perceived quality. By participating in the customer-feedback loop, customer service can also affect all the other dimensions of quality. Its primary tools for improvement include identifying sources of variance (in such areas as average response time and efficacy of response) and acting as disseminators of information.

Research, Design, and Engineering. Research, design, and engineering impact every dimension of quality through the design of products. Here, a manager can apply techniques to search for ways of reducing variance, especially systematic variance, in every subsequent process.

Although combining the efforts of all these functional areas can assure the generation of the highest-quality products, each functional area acting alone can have an influence on quality. That is to say, quality improvements at a functional level help even if the big picture is not being addressed. In addition to improving the quality of output from a particular activity, an almost inevitable consequence of improved quality in one area will be improved quality in other areas. The following subsections present three examples from various business segments. (Appendixes A and B provide two more complete cases, those of Ensoniq Corporation and Swiss Banking Corporation, which illustrate the ripple-out effect of improving quality.)

Operations in a Book-Distribution Center. Customers want their books delivered quickly, correctly (i.e., they want to receive the books they ordered), in good condition, and with an invoice for the right amount. If operations can deliver these attributes effectively, customers will gain confidence in ordering and in the predictability of correct order fulfillment and billing. Even if the items delivered are not of the highest quality, customers may well continue to buy and encourage others to buy if the service on delivery is of high quality (e.g., Reader's Digest Association has built its business on quality service in distributing its magazine).

But the benefit does not stop at immediate customer satisfaction. If books are always (or very nearly always) received without delay or error, a whole category of customer complaints is removed from the customer-service backlog (one could view operations as a supplier to customer service— i.e., it can supply customers with causes for complaints, which are then brought to the attention of customer service). If billing is correct, accounting should have fewer disputes over collections and simpler assets to track (cash is easier to track and protect than are accounts receivable). Accounting should also find itself with a shorter accounts-receivable cycle, giving the company a lower cost of funds and greater freedom to expand. If marketing and sales know that operations can deliver more reliably than competitors, then they can direct customers' attention to that attribute with the expectation of matching (and shaping) their perception of value.

Accounting in Any Company. Many organizations adopt the approach of paying vendors only after a protracted period of time and perhaps only after receiving multiple requests for payment. Usually, some relatively complex form of buyer/manager sign-off procedure is required as well (often as an excuse to lose documentation and further delay payment). If instead, vendors were paid promptly, with minimal or simple sign-off procedures, then vendors and line managers (both customers of accounting) would be happier. Higher quality for the accounting department would come from handling invoices fewer times (ideally, only once); responding to fewer complaints; spending less time investigating requests; solving billing problems while they are still fresh (rather than at some later date when considerable investigation may be required); and in many instances, receiving discounts for prompt payment. Reducing the accounts-payable cycle time necessarily reduces one source of systematic variation.

For other departments, the quality payoff comes from better vendor service, simpler processing steps for handing the payment of invoices, greater confidence when placing orders, and greater confidence in the health of the organization.

Sales. Often, a salesperson feels pressured to promise (or allude to the possibility of) higher levels of performance than the company can deliver. For example, a custom-software sales representative may promise delivery in two months. Although the customer might otherwise have been happy with delivery in four months, once the two-month time frame has been suggested, this becomes the customer's standard. If the company cannot deliver, the quality of its offering will be judged as poor due to a low level of performance, conformance, reliability, and perceived quality. Had the customer not been led to expect a quicker delivery, he or she might have perceived every dimension as being of higher quality for exactly the same transaction.

By positioning a company's products so that they will perform in accordance with user expectations, fewer complaints and disputes will arise. The customer will perceive higher quality because products behave as well as, or better than, the customer had been led to expect. If products meet high standards, then the customer is likely to perceive high levels of performance, conformance, and serviceability.

A PROCESS VIEW OF QUALITY, PRODUCTIVITY, AND COSTS

The foregoing examples and the various definitions of quality have established a conceptual framework for discussing the tools and techniques that a manager might use to improve quality. However, before we address that topic (in Chapter 3), there is another key aspect of quality that must be examined. Namely, in order to measure quality and its improvement, managers require a more operational view of the issue. That is, they must be able to identify what and how to measure across each of these attributes. Then, they can identify objectives—either changing the goal across the attribute or more consistently delivering the attribute. Such an operational definition of quality arises from viewing a business process as a system.

BUSINESS SYSTEMS

Business systems or *systems* means the entire process of doing business as well as subprocesses within the larger organization. A business system consists of inputs to a process, a function or conversion process, and all outputs. This general description includes both planned and unplanned inputs as well as planned and unplanned outputs.

All sources of input are referred to as "suppliers," and all consumers of output are referred to as "customers." Unplanned customers, such as the recipients of air pollution (an unplanned, or at least undesirable, product), are included. Unplanned suppliers, such as an elevator bank that supplies radio frequencies that might interfere with an office computer, must also be taken into account. A few quick examples should serve to clear up any ambiguity in terminology.

On a companywide basis, a bank could view its business system as follows:

- *Inputs:* Supply of deposits, regulations, rates from competitors, demand for loans, employees from many sources, a host of paper and electronic products, utilities, land and buildings, public-relations companies, advertising, etc.

- *Process:* Make judgments regarding the use of funds, deploy personnel, create and maintain facilities for safekeeping assets, create vehicles for delivering security and financial opportunities, etc.

- *Outputs:* Security, investment opportunities, sources of funds, economic activity, demand for land and buildings, convenience for customers, etc.

Within a bank, an office has a business system as well. The department that clears and sorts checks, for example, may have a system that looks like this:

- *Inputs:* Documents from branches and offices, employees from personnel (or from outside sources of recruitment), equipment such as sorting machines, offices and utilities, specification of procedures, etc.

- *Process:* Sort documents and route to appropriate destinations.

- *Outputs:* Correctly sorted documents, some incorrectly sorted documents, employment, some scrap paper, etc.

The decomposition could continue down to the level of individual transactions. In some instances, such detailed decomposition is required in order to detect the causes of poor quality. At each level, business systems will be decomposed into six classes of inputs, the process, and two classes of outputs, as explained in the following subsections.

Inputs

1. *People:* This almost always means employees or those acting at the direction of the business unit.

2. *Materials:* These are the physical raw goods used to produce outputs. For a manufacturer, this class of inputs includes the material in the final product, packaging, office supplies, and other material employed in the process. In a service environment—say, an accounting firm—this would include work papers, binders, and other office supplies but might also be viewed as including data, client documents, and regulations.

3. *Tools or equipment:* These are the implements of technology used to convert materials into finished products (i.e., products that are finished vis-à-vis the particular business system). In a plastics factory, this might include extrusion equipment, bins and loading devices, cleaning equipment, forklifts, etc. In a law firm, it might include data-processing and word-processing equipment, dictating machines, typewriters, a legal library, etc.

4. *Procedures:* These are the internally defined "rules" for how to produce the products. An engine-assembly facility might specify in minute detail the components that are combined to form a finished product, including sequences, tools, and torques. As part of an operator's procedures, the outbound-calling department of a telemarketing organization might specify a script, time of day, whom to call, and notes to be taken.

5. *Environment:* This encompasses the location and surroundings in which the work takes place—the factory floor or the accounting department's offices. Although so-called externalities could almost always be included under one of the other headings, the language of economics suggests that they be treated separately. Externalities are factors such as laws governing strict liability, emission-control standards, acts of nature (e.g., an earthquake), and other externally imposed events or conditions. Traditional economics treats these as external to, or not governed by, the marketplace. One could argue that all legislation and publicly imposed restraints on production reflect a market for quality of life—a view endorsed by many of today's environmental economists. Because such factors are rarely under the influence of the middle manager, they are usually omitted from discussions of systems.

6. *Measurement:* This class of inputs specifies how and when measures are taken. Relevant considerations range from the obvious (e.g., using the same uniformly calibrated tools for measuring pipe-wall thickness) to

the not-so-obvious (e.g., using consistent and reliable survey methods to assess customer attitudes). The critical aspects of measurement include using reliable devices and standardized or calibrated measures, establishing procedural consistency, and ensuring the reproducibility of results.

Process

Once the aforementioned inputs are brought together, specified procedures are performed to convert them into products. This conversion system is called the process. In most instances, the manager is responsible for bringing the inputs together and initiating the operation of the system.

Some consider the separation of inputs from process as too complicated; the environment, people, procedures, and measurements drive the conversion process. We separate these ideas to point out potential sources of variation that feed the process and contribute to variation in output.

Outputs

Products of the conversion process are classified as planned, or intended, outcomes and unplanned, or unintended, outcomes. For the manufacturer, examples of planned outcomes include the products to be sold, employment, dividends for shareholders, and even some scrap materials; some unplanned outcomes include pollution, liability suits charging faulty design or manufacturing, and strikes by employees. For the internal accountant, planned outcomes might include reliable statistics on business performance, procedures for protecting assets, and forms and procedures for creating an orderly flow of information and funds throughout a company. Unplanned outcomes might include restrictions on the flow of funds that hamper business processes, spending more to protect assets than the assets are worth, and creating incentives for individuals to avoid participating in the orderly flow of information. This system is illustrated in Figure 2.1.

Suppliers and customers could be identified in this process as well, but for the sake of simplicity, they are defined as being included within the terms *input* and *output*.

In the case of many business activities, especially service activities, the customer and the supplier may often be the same entity. For example, the public accountant provides the client (customer) with tools for sending signals to the client's various information customers (e.g., audited financial reports for banks); a primary input to those reports is information furnished by the client (here acting as a supplier).

Figure 2.1   A SYSTEM VIEW OF BUSINESS PROCESSES

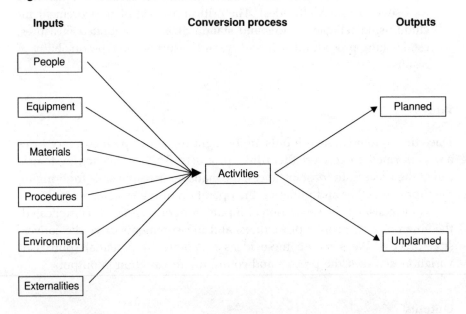

Clearly, the business system may not be purely linear, as Figure 2.1 might appear to indicate. Although a linear view is useful when analyzing processes, and linear systems lend themselves to being understood intuitively, the circular or cyclical view is often more productive for improving quality. If systems are represented in a linear fashion, the manager should also consider the cyclic possibilities (Figure 2.2) by taking into account all conceivable suppliers and customers of intended and unintended outputs.

Graphically, supply and suppliers are represented as entering the process from the left and will henceforth be referred to as being "upstream" in the system. Outputs and customers are represented as being on the right, or "downstream." This terminology establishes a framework for analyzing relationships and sources of quality.

Figure 2.2   CYCLIC WORK FLOW: EFFECTS OF UNPLANNED OUTCOMES

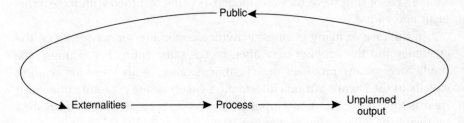

QUALITY AND THE SYSTEM

From a product point of view (regardless of whether the product is a physical entity or a service), two major parameters affect how a customer views quality: the target product and the variation from that target.

The *target product* means the idealized product—what it should be or is intended to be. Every organization intends to deliver functionality (transportation, convenience, sustenance, glamour) through specific products (cars, pop-top cans, fresh vegetables, perfume). In developing a product, the organization has a concept of the product—e.g., a sporty car with styling, handling, and accessories that will appeal to young drivers and must therefore be manufactured at a low cost so it will be affordable. This concept gets translated into specifications—a specific power-to-weight ratio, manufacturing costs of less than X, fewer than Y mechanical defects over the first five years of use, etc. Together, the concept and specification represent the ideal or target.

From the customer's point of view, an important element of quality is how well the ideal or target product matches the need (or expectation of need) experienced by the customer. If the vendor's target product has certain specifications—say, a car weighing between five thousand and fifty-five hundred pounds with a seventy-horsepower engine that consumes gasoline at a rate of twenty miles per gallon and has an expected defect rate of two defects per year over its first five years of use—but the customer's expectations or needs call for a car weighing under four thousand pounds with a seventy-horsepower engine delivering gas mileage of thirty-five miles per gallon with no defects over the first five years of use, then the customer will not view the target product as being of very good quality.

If a vendor's target product matches a target desire among customers, the next issue in perception of quality is product variation. Although the ideal, target product may exactly match the customers' need, the actual, delivered product may not meet that need if it varies from the target. Even if much of a system's output hits the target, if enough does not, thereby creating uncertainty, customers will view the product as being of low quality.

The normal bell curve can be used to represent this concept of variation and target value (see Figure 2.3). The mathematical properties of this approach are not discussed in great detail herein, but Figure 2.4 and the following description may help readers who do not intuitively understand the meaning of the curve. Generally, the center line represents the target product for the producer as well as the "center" or dominant (average) target for customers. The notion of a center or dominant target reflects the truism that no two customers want exactly the same things. This variability of taste (or in the producer curve, the variability of output) is represented by the

Figure 2.3   FREQUENCY OF OUTCOMES FROM NORMAL PROCESS

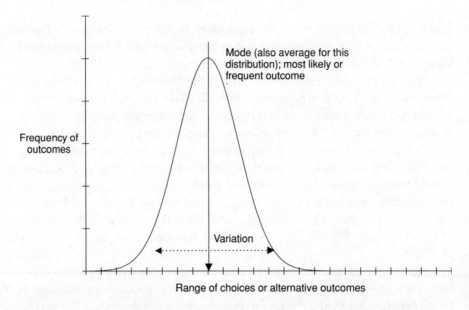

Figure 2.4   DISTRIBUTION OF NORMAL OUTCOMES, LIKLIHOOD OF OCCURRENCE

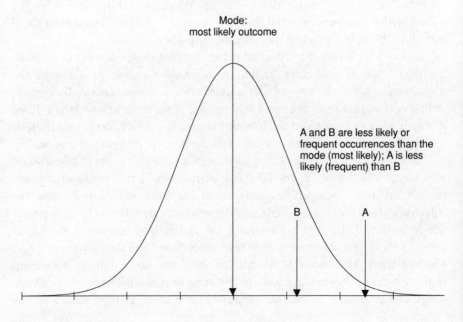

spread of the curve. The height of the curve or the area under a section of the curve represents the frequency or the probability of occurrence of the event directly under that section of the curve. The higher the curve, the greater the likelihood that the event under the curve will occur or the greater the frequency of its occurrence. Readers who wish to know more about the mathematical properties of this representation will find several good sources in the "References" list at the end of the chapter.

Two curves can be used to represent the influences of target product and variation. One curve represents the process output and is called "the voice of the process"; the other represents customer needs and is called "the voice of the customer." (One of the authors first encountered this terminology in a presentation given by William W. Scherkenbach at a March 1988 conference on Statistics for Educators at New York University.) The area where the curves overlap represents opportunities for sales; it identifies instances in which some customers may perceive good quality. Figures 2.5–2.10 illustrate the primary conditions experienced in matching these needs:

- *Good quality:* Close match on target and similar variation (Figure 2.5).

- *Poor quality:* Bad match on target; similar variation allows some sales (Figure 2.6).

- *Poor quality:* Acceptable match on target but too much variation in process (Figure 2.7).

- *Unclear:* The voice of the process target matches the voice of the customer target, but there is much greater variation in customer needs (Figure 2.8). Because the voice of the customer has several "humps," the customer market should probably be segmented into multiple markets (Figures 2.9 and 2.10).

The next chapter provides some guidelines for developing these types of diagrams. However, the reader is encouraged to create conceptual diagrams (i.e., diagrams that are not mathematically precise) when faced with the need to analyze discrepancies between the voice of the process and the voice of the customer.

WHAT IS QUALITY FROM A SYSTEMS VIEWPOINT?

The process view suggests an operational supplement to our definition of quality. High quality means delivering loyalty-producing products and services along all dimensions of quality with a single effort *by creating products whose target attributes match the target attributes desired and needed by customers*

Figure 2.5   GOOD QUALITY: CLOSE MATCH ON TARGET AND SIMILAR VARIATION

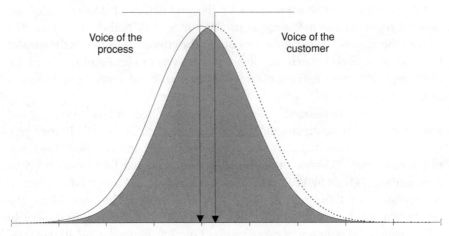

The area of overlap represents the opportunity for quality sales

Figure 2.6   POOR QUALITY: BAD MATCH ON TARGET BUT SIMILAR VARIATION

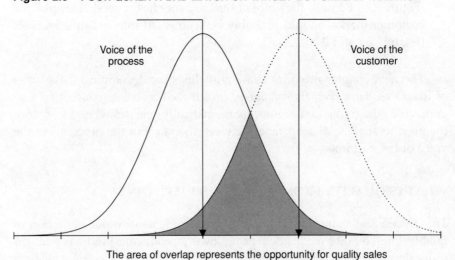

The area of overlap represents the opportunity for quality sales

Figure 2.7   POOR QUALITY: GOOD MATCH ON TARGET BUT BIG DIFFERENCE IN VARIATION

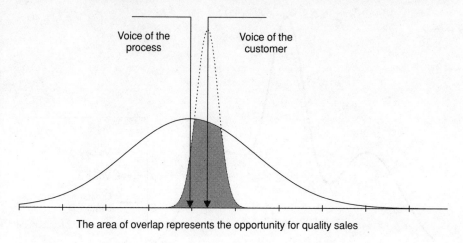

The area of overlap represents the opportunity for quality sales

Figure 2.8   MIXED QUALITY: CLOSE MATCH ON TARGET BUT MIXED VOICE OF THE CUSTOMER

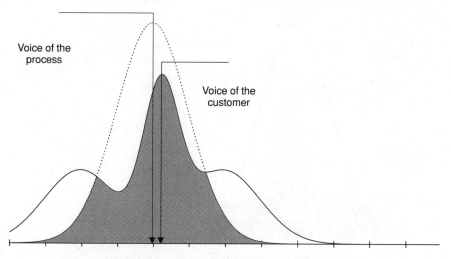

The area of overlap represents the opportunity for quality sales

Figure 2.9   MIXED VOICE OF THE CUSTOMER SEEN AS THE SUM OF SEGMENTED CUSTOMERS

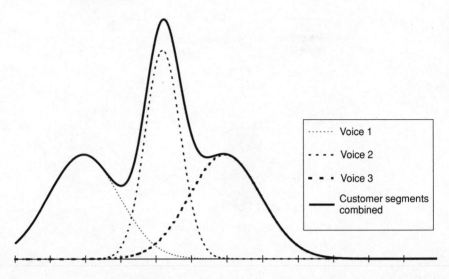

Figure 2.10   MATCHING THE VOICE OF THE PROCESS TO THE VOICES OF CUSTOMER SEGMENTS

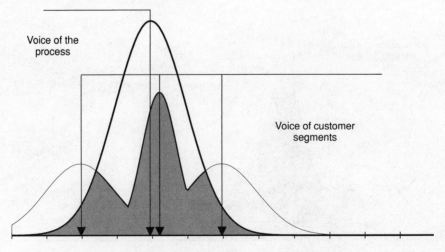

The shaded area represents opportunity for quality sales

and whose variation is within the variation bounds expected and needed by custom-ers. Given enough attention to detail and careful segmentation of customers, this will probably work as a near-operational definition of quality.

Although this definition is fairly complete, it does require applying the dimensions of quality, understanding the system, and examining the match between the voice of the customer and the voice of the process. Consider the possibility of conflicting matches on various attributes (some attributes match some customers' desires; other attributes don't). Decomposing the voice of the customer and carefully examining the eight dimensions of quality should better enable managers to correct the dimensions that are out of alignment. This definition also allows managers to consider the impact of marketing on shaping customer attitudes (target and variation in the voice of the customer) and on the introduction of innovative products for which there are no customer expectations (e.g., what did the first customer of electric lighting expect?). In some ways, this definition leads to an under-standing of the role of strategic marketing—creating or shaping the voice of the customer so that delivered products and services will match that voice.

SUMMARY

This chapter has explored three views of quality. First, the philosophies and approaches of the two grand old men of quality—Juran and Deming—pro-vided the consumer-driven view of quality. Juran and Deming blend specific recommendations with general guidelines through an overriding philoso-phy regarding human relations, variance, and business.

Following the categorization proposed by Garvin, we decomposed qual-ity into eight aspects or dimensions: performance, features, reliability, con-formance, durability, serviceability, aesthetics, and perceived quality. For services, we added two concerns involving information: availability and accuracy. This approach points to the possibility that a product may rate high along some dimensions of quality while rating low along others. After a weak dimension has been identified, corrective action can be taken to improve quality along that dimension.

Finally, a process view of quality highlighted the critical role played by variation. Every organization is seen as a process involving the transforma-tion of inputs into outputs. Large organizations can be broken down into suborganizations, which are also processes involving the transformation of inputs into outputs. By controlling the process in terms of both its target or goal and its variation, the organization can control the quality of the process. Generally, managers must look "upstream" at the suppliers and at early steps in a process in order to control variation, and they must look "down-stream" at customers in order to control the target.

Now that quality has been defined in operational terms, we can examine specific steps that may help improve quality.

References

Deming, W. E. 1986. *Out of the Crisis.* Cambridge, Mass.: MIT Center for Advanced Engineering Studies.

————. 1990. "Foundations for Management of Quality in the Western World." Revision of a paper presented at a meeting of the Institute of Management Sciences in Osaka, Japan, July 24, 1989.

Garvin, D. A. 1987. "A Note on Quality: Views of Deming, Juran, and Crosby." Harvard Business School publication 9–687–001, rev. June 1987.

Juran, J. M. 1989. *Juran on Leadership for Quality.* New York: Free Press.

Juran, J. M., and Gryna, F. M., Jr. 1980. *Quality Planning and Analysis.* New York: McGraw-Hill.

Serlen, B. 1987. "W. Edwards Deming: The Man Who Made Japan Famous—for Quality." *NYU Business* (Fall/Winter 1988): 16–20.

Chapter 3

TOOLS FOR IMPROVING QUALITY

When companies pursue quality, middle managers are the ones who must implement the program. Too often, executives merely issue mandates instead of providing the guidance, direction, and specialized support that managers need. When the impetus for quality improvement comes from managers, they must discover how to be effective in this new area. In today's quality environment, managers can enhance their career prospects considerably by learning how to improve the quality of their organization's output.

Quality, when defined as "fitness for use," focuses on a combination of customer expectations and competitor offerings. Innovation in products and features surprises current customers and captures new ones. Innovation in processes improves output and reduces variation and costs. A systems view of innovation calls for focusing on the target value (product) and the variance (process). In general, efforts to change the target value require looking "downstream" in the system, and efforts to reduce variance require looking "upstream."

Once they have become concerned about quality and have armed themselves with definitions that allow them to examine and evaluate quality, middle managers still need tools for working on production systems. Beyond knowing what tools to use, managers must have a plan for coordinating the use of those tools in a quality-improvement program. The generic quality-improvement project presented in this chapter illustrates where and how such tools can be used.

The following are the major steps in a typical quality-improvement project:

1. Identify and document the current systems.

2. Isolate potential projects for improvement and choose a project from among them based on situation-specific criteria.

3. Select and develop the team.

4. Assess the capability of the current process.

5. Diagnose the problem by pinpointing potential sources of trouble.

6. Experiment in the workplace to verify the causes and solutions that have been identified.

7. Solidify the project's gains and document its results.

8. Publicize the project's successes and expand the quality-improvement effort.

A variety of tools are available to help the manager move the quality-improvement project along, employing techniques that range from the technically simple to the statistically complex. This chapter uses a fictitious case study to present some tools appropriate to each of these steps. The explanation of each tool is necessarily elementary, since this discussion is designed to point toward the appropriate use of tools rather than to provide a detailed "how-to" textbook.

GENERAL PROCESS AND STRATEGY

Quality does not improve spontaneously just because someone wants better quality. Nor does quality improve as a result of "being more careful," "doing it right the first time," "working smarter, not harder," or any other well-meaning slogan. The entire production system, of which employees are only a part, produces quality. The system is what determines the outcome; if employees are to work smarter, harder, more carefully, and right the first time, it will be because the system supports this result.

A manager trying to improve quality must adopt the attitude that employees want to do a good job, are working to the best of their ability (within the limitations of the system), and will help improve the process (if they believe it to be in their best interests to do so). Without this attitude, (1) the manager would have little reason to believe in the possibility of achieving improvements, and (2) any attempt at improvement becomes counterproductive, seemingly resulting in *less* effort on the part of employees, because if workers are already trying their best, telling them to work smarter, harder, and more carefully is not only useless, it is insulting. Many quality-improvement programs die at birth because they kick off with slogans that alienate the work force.

So how can quality be improved? By changing the work system—which is more easily said than done. On a large scale, making a companywide commitment to quality improvement probably requires a change in company culture. Such changes are difficult and seem to require the active support of top executives. (A number of authors—among them, Tushman and Romanelli 1985; Tushman et al. 1985; Nadler and Tushman 1990; Miller and Friesen 1980; and Miller 1990—have documented how hard it is to change an organization's overall direction and culture. In general terms, their findings are that the organization and its top management must undergo a crisis that leads to a conscious effort to redirect the organization. Success comes through breaking down the currently held views of the organization and then recreating the organization in a new image. Often, incumbent executives must step aside in order for the transformation effort to be successful.)

In contrast, middle managers must settle for more incremental changes, at least to begin with. Through step-by-step improvements, managers not only build skills and a track record, but each successful project creates a level of cognitive dissonance that may contribute to the emergence of a new culture.

Quality-improvement projects alter inputs: tools, methods, people, facilities, the environment, measurements, and usually combinations of these. Quality is upgraded in a step-by-step manner through projects that improve one or two aspects of the work product at a time. As Dr. Deming has said, "There is no instant pudding" (Deming 1986: 126). Each improvement is the result of a series of deliberate efforts, first to change the system and then to retain the benefits of the change.

In most situations, managers will find almost unlimited opportunities for improvement. The challenge lies in developing an improvement strategy that will achieve the greatest benefits and has the highest probability of success. A well-developed strategy then builds on earlier successes to improve both the quality and chances for success of current and future projects.

As noted earlier, the case presented in the following section, which provides a structure for introducing the use of quality-improvement tools, is largely fictitious and offers a somewhat prescriptive view of quality improvement. However, it is consistent with success stories documented by experts in the field (e.g., Schuler and Walker 1990; Schaffer 1989; Scholtes and Hacquebord 1987; Juran 1989).

A QUALITY-IMPROVEMENT PROJECT

Entertainment Distribution, Inc. (EDI), had been growing rapidly for the last ten years. The company distributed a variety of entertainment products through several specialized channels. Its gross sales last year exceeded $400 million. New opportunities led the company to expect sales of $600 million in the coming year.

Toni Adams, EDI's controller, was concerned about the quality and quantity of work expected from her staff. In particular, she was charged with maintaining her current staff through the projected period of growth. However, complaints from vendors and internal staff had increased over the last six months. Payments to vendors had been late and occasionally inaccurate. Budgets had received incorrect charges. Even with increased inspection, the problems seemed to multiply. Completing the quarterly financial statements had become a chore because the general ledger (GL) required too many correcting entries. Each day, the staff seemed to fall a little further behind.

Toni's assistant controller, Susan Carey, and Don Harmon, a systems consultant used frequently by the department, had been pushing for a program to improve quality and productivity in the accounts payable (AP) department. Most of accounting's problems seemed to originate in AP, due either to delays or to miscoding. Since AP was the entry point for the majority of accounting transactions at EDI, it was the most upstream activity with respect to Toni's area.

After much pushing from Susan and Don, Toni visited an organization that had implemented a quality-improvement program. She came away with a new perspective that led her to read a number of books on the topic. Finally, she decided to commit to conducting several projects in AP to see whether such an approach would work at EDI.

When Toni raised the subject with her boss, Steve Aron, his response was, at best, disinterested: "Don't do it if it costs money or slows down processing; we can't afford delays or fancy projects." Something about that attitude made Toni more determined to try to improve her situation on her own.

She knew she would have to be subtle about conducting change projects. If she publicized her efforts and anything went wrong, both she and the projects would be blamed. Also, since her first attempt might not work perfectly, why attract unnecessary attention from the inevitable naysayers? Finally, although Toni would ideally have wanted her staff to be directly involved in the selection of improvement projects (so that they would own and commit to the projects), at this early stage, neither they nor she had the team skills required to steer the selection process toward potentially successful projects. Toni regarded this last point as critical; the chosen project should have a high likelihood of success. To increase that likelihood, she mapped out a program consisting of the steps presented at the start of this chapter.

1. IDENTIFYING THE SYSTEM

Although Toni and Susan had decided that the AP department needed attention first, they had very little documentation on the AP system. The department had grown large enough that the staff were no longer sure of every step in the process. Since EDI's auditors had been after Toni for some time to produce a flowchart of the process, this seemed like the logical place to start.

Not only can flowcharts be used to describe systems, but they can also be invaluable tools for locating possible sources of problems. Flowcharting symbols (Figure 3.1 shows the basic ones) are connected with arrows to illustrate the sequence of processing steps and decisions.

Although widely used, flowcharting has several weaknesses: Considerable expertise and patience are required to illustrate complex systems effectively with this technique, and it can be difficult to depict processing that occurs either simultaneously or in nonspecific sequences. Organizational boundaries and documents are not always clear, nor do flowcharts indicate the time required to complete the various stages of the process being depicted. Furthermore, it is often difficult to choose the level of detail. Despite these problems, Toni felt that flowcharting was the most useful tool for describing the AP system.

However, before deciding on the flowcharting approach, Toni also considered other useful tools, including bubble charts, CPM (critical path method), and PERT (program evaluation and review technique) charts. (Appendix C lists sources that explain these techniques in detail.) Bubble charts help in depicting organizational interaction and document flow and can also be used to present layers of detail, but they do not show either decisions or time. CPM and PERT charts depict time and activity dependency. If events are well sequenced and timing is critical, these techniques can be used to present systems effectively. However, they do not depict choices and ambiguity well.

To supplement the flowchart, Toni also decided to develop a narrative description of the system. Although they cannot be grasped as quickly as one of the graphic presentations, narratives can completely describe all system issues. By developing both, Toni hoped to cross-reference them and thereby strengthen each.

Figure 3.1   FLOWCHART SYMBOLS AND USAGE

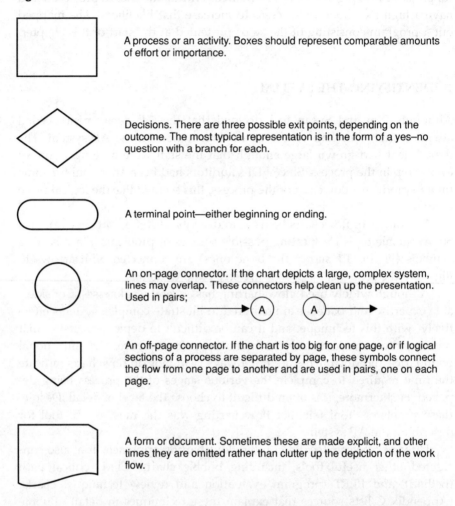

A process or an activity. Boxes should represent comparable amounts of effort or importance.

Decisions. There are three possible exit points, depending on the outcome. The most typical representation is in the form of a yes–no question with a branch for each.

A terminal point—either beginning or ending.

An on-page connector. If the chart depicts a large, complex system, lines may overlap. These connectors help clean up the presentation. Used in pairs;

An off-page connector. If the chart is too big for one page, or if logical sections of a process are separated by page, these symbols connect the flow from one page to another and are used in pairs, one on each page.

A form or document. Sometimes these are made explicit, and other times they are omitted rather than clutter up the depiction of the work flow.

A wide variety of other symbols are used for special-purpose flowcharting. In particular, flowcharting for computer programming includes many symbols for forms, terminal processing, file storage and retrieval, and other special activities. The symbols presented above will usually suffice for describing a business process.

Plastic templates with these symbols are available at most bookstores. In addition, many PC graphics packages include a flowchart symbol set. A number of special PC programs will generate flowcharts, either from descriptions or through the use of commands in the programs.

To develop this documentation, Toni decided to use a team approach. First, each person in the department wrote a narrative describing his or her job. Susan then compiled and edited them. To develop the flowchart, Toni called on Jim Kyle, one of the clerks who showed an interest in computer systems. Toni also used Don, the consultant, to help Jim get started. They produced two levels of flowcharts. A summary-level flowchart depicted major exchanges between departments and functions. For each block on the summary chart, a detail-level flowchart was prepared depicting decisions and activities within that block. Figures 3.2 and 3.3 show the summary-level flowchart and one of the detail-level flowcharts.

After completing the flowcharts, Jim and Don reviewed them and the narrative with the staff to obtain feedback that would be used for corrections and clarification. Later, Toni asked each staff member to explain his or her part of the flowchart to her, thus providing her with an opportunity to learn how the system had evolved, demonstrate an interest in her subordinates' work, and informally solicit ideas for problem areas and potential solutions. This team approach and review process gave each person a chance to provide his or her unique perspective on how the system worked. A number of misunderstandings about process flow were corrected simply by developing and sharing the flowcharts and narrative.

2. SELECTING THE PROJECT

Toni's next step was to develop a list of likely improvement projects. She reviewed complaints from vendors, staff, and internal clients (other departments) as well as correction efforts and compared those with the comments she had solicited during the system description review. Susan, Don, and Jim offered further ideas regarding improvement projects. Table 3.1 provides a brief list of the projects they considered.

For reasons mentioned at the start of this section, Toni felt it advisable to develop her initial project list without a formal group. In planning future projects, however, she hoped to include more staff in the project identification and selection process, using brainstorming to generate a list of likely projects. Brainstorming is one of the most popular group techniques, not just for generating ideas but for building teams by encouraging full group participation in a nonjudgmental setting. The procedure for using this technique is simple:

1. A group of four to ten participants assemble along with a facilitator, who reviews the ground rules and acts as a moderator for the process. The

Figure 3.2   SUMMARY-LEVEL FLOWCHART OF THE AP PROCESS

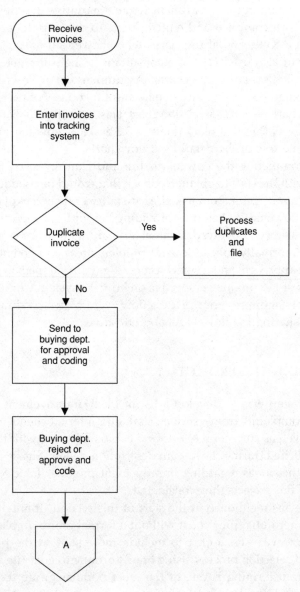

Figure 3.2 (*Cont.*)

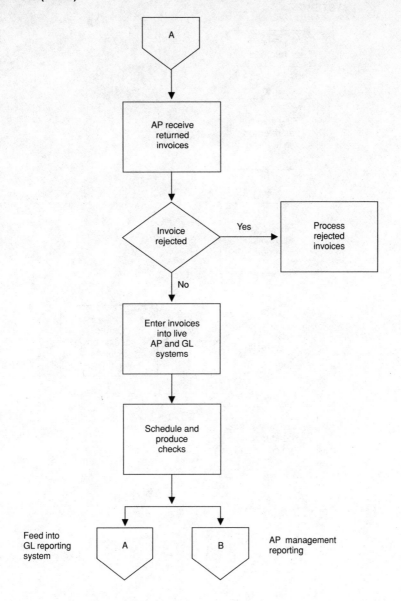

Figure 3.3   DETAIL-LEVEL FLOWCHART OF INVOICE ENTRY INTO LIVE AP AND GL SYSTEMS

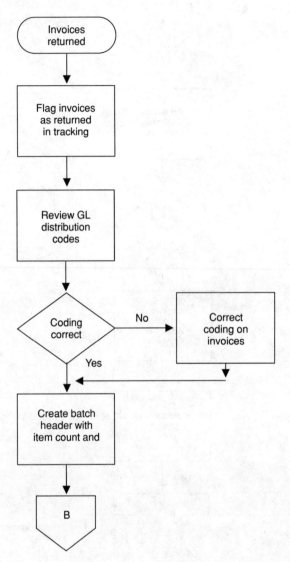

Figure 3.3 (*Cont.*)

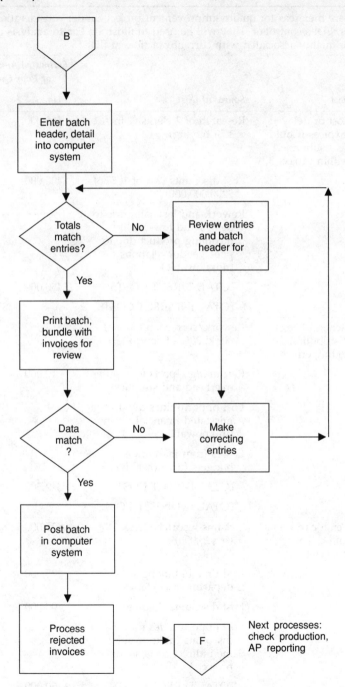

Table 3.1 Estimates of the Costs of Poor Quality

There are the areas for quality-improvement projects under consideration by Toni Adams, EDI's controller. They will be used to illustrate Pareto analysis of the cost of poor quality associated with current practices at EDI.

Project	Source of Costs	Estimated Annual Cost of Poor Quality	
		Direct	*Indirect*
1. Lost or delayed invoices (Could be a subproject within project 3.)	Research of 2 clerks (1 in AP, 1 in buying)	$50,000	
	Lost discounts (2% of 10% of $200,000,000)	400,000	
	Rework and lost sales due to delays and low-quality incoming product due to poor vendor relations (unknowable)		$3,000,000
	TOTAL DIRECT COSTS	$450,000	
	TOTAL INDIRECT COSTS		$3,000,000
2. General Ledger distribution coding errors	Rework/correction (50% of clerk, 20% of controller)	$32,500	
	Rerunning reports (computer overhead and supplies)	10,000	
	Lost opportunities due to misstated financial position (unknowable)		$1,000,000
	Losses from inaccurate budgets (unknowable)		1,000,000
	TOTAL DIRECT COSTS	$42,500	
	TOTAL INDIRECT COSTS		$2,000,000
3. Vendor relations (other than project 1)	1 claims-research clerk (@ $25,000)	$25,000	
	Lost time in buying department (1 clerk)	25,000	
	Lost discounts (known)	100,000	
	Lost opportunities for discounts (unknowable)		$ 500,000
	Same indirect costs as for project 1		3,000,000
	TOTAL DIRECT COSTS	$150,000	
	TOTAL INDIRECT COSTS		$3,500,000

Table 3.1 (*Cont.*)

Project	Source of Costs	Estimated Annual Cost of Poor Quality	
		Direct	*Indirect*
4. Reruns on computer system	Cost of reruns	$10,000	
	Cost of detecting the need for reruns (5% of clerk)	1,250	
	Delays due to lost cooperation (unknowable)		$500,000
	TOTAL DIRECT COSTS	$11,250	
	TOTAL INDIRECT COSTS		$500,000
5. Inaccuracies in check production (overpayment, underpayment)	Cost of reruns (if errors are caught)	$10,000	
	Cost of detecting the need for reruns (50% of clerk)	12,500	
	Loss due to overpayment (unknown)		$50,000
	Loss due to underpayment (unknowable)		500,000
	TOTAL DIRECT COSTS	$22,500	
	TOTAL INDIRECT COSTS		$550,000
6. Responsiveness to information requests from external vendors	Cost of research (2 staff)	$50,000	
	Cost of current information filing/retrieval	250,000	
	Cost of buying time (1 staff)	25,000	
	Loss of goodwill/cooperation (unknowable)		$2,000,000
	TOTAL DIRECT COSTS	$325,000	
	TOTAL INDIRECT COSTS		$2,000,000

group directs its attention to the problem at hand and begins developing ideas about causes and/or possible cures.

2. The facilitator records the ideas so that they can be seen by the entire group. The notes should probably be written on large sheets of paper, so that they can be saved for future reference and additions and deletions can be made.

3. All ideas offered by participants are welcomed and recorded. At this stage, no judgment is made. Studies have repeatedly shown that passing judgment reduces the number and quality of ideas offered. Part of the facilitator's job is to record all ideas and stop any judgmental comments.

4. Piggybacking is encouraged. Adding to or extending ideas allows everyone a chance to express his or her perspective.

5. If the group runs out of ideas, five or ten minutes are allowed to pass in silence. Although prolonged silence commonly makes participants uncomfortable, it can stimulate deeper thought and will often result in the emergence of excellent ideas.

6. A time limit should be set and adhered to (unless ideas are still emerging rapidly, in which case, the time limit was probably too short). Effective time limits usually range from a minimum of twenty minutes to a maximum of one hour.

7. The ideas should be rearranged, grouped, and evaluated only after the idea-generation phase has been completed.

From her list of potential projects, Toni had to choose one to start with. Juran (1989) recommends selecting quality-improvement projects on the basis of the current cost of low quality and using estimates when accurate costs are not available. Deming (1986) adds the notion that the most important costs cannot be measured (e.g., the cost of lost goodwill when a product fails). Both Deming and Juran suggest that the importance and costs of low quality may reasonably (and liberally) be estimated, with that estimate being used as a starting point for selecting projects.

Juran coined the phrase *Pareto principle* to describe a condition that is typical in most organizations—namely, 80 percent of the problems (trouble, costs) come from 20 percent of the sources (activities). Others have called this the 80–20 rule. With this in mind, managers should compare the costs of competing projects to identify those that fall into the 80-percent category. A handy way to evaluate projects is with graphic displays. Table 3.1 (shown earlier in this subsection) presents rough estimates of the cost of poor quality associated with six potential accounts-payable projects. Figures 3.4 and 3.5 show a graphic approach that can be used to analyze these alternatives.

The table and figures show the six quality-improvement projects that Toni was considering. The bar charts in Figures 3.4 and 3.5 helped Toni focus on the potentially high-payoff projects. Reducing the cost of information requests, improving vendor relations, and reducing the number of lost or delayed invoices have the highest direct costs. These also have the highest total costs, but in a different order. Toni also realized that projects designed to improve vendor relations and the organization's response to information requests had substantial overlap. This helped narrow her choices. But in making a final decision on a first project, Toni felt that other criteria besides costs were important. Her additional concerns included:

1. The probability of successfully completing the project (especially, did the means for succeeding fall within her SOI?)

2. The meaningfulness of the project to the staff (staff members are the first ones who must be convinced if future projects are to have a chance)

3. The likelihood of building a team that would support the project

4. The chances of being able to measure the results and then attribute those results to the improvement efforts

5. The extent to which other departments would benefit from the results

Figure 3.4   COST OF POOR QUALITY, SORTED BY DIRECT COSTS

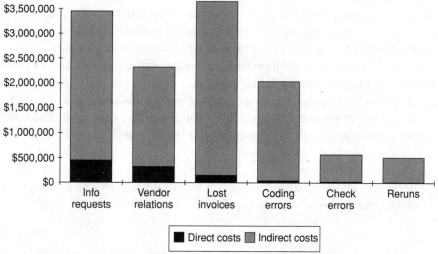

Figure 3.5   COST OF POOR QUALITY, SORTED BY TOTAL COSTS

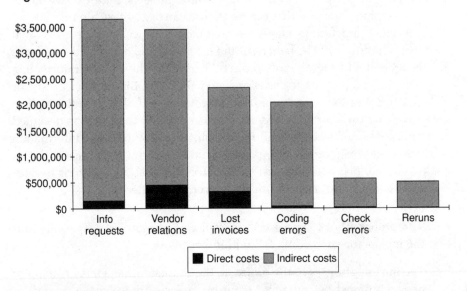

Applying these criteria, Toni noted that for several projects, considerable cooperation would be required from the purchasing department and possibly from outside vendors, neither of which fell within her SOI. Each of the three most costly problems required more cooperation than Toni felt she could get for the first project. Of the three remaining problem areas, errors in coding invoices had the highest direct and total costs. Toni believed that with a small project, her staff could successfully reduce the number of errors in GL coding. If they reduced those errors, the results would be obvious to many: Budgets would be more accurate; financial statements would be delivered more quickly; and project analyses would be both more timely and more accurate. In short, reducing coding problems seemed to offer a high potential for success and a high payoff throughout the organization. It seemed to be the kind of improvement project that could be used to build credibility and support for future projects.

Let's take a minute to review Toni's efforts to this point: She started by making a list of potential projects and estimating the costs, both direct and indirect, associated with current quality levels. By using Pareto analysis, she eliminated two low-payoff projects. Based on an awareness of her SOI and its impact on probable success, she eliminated three other projects. Pareto analysis of total costs, consideration for team building and technical development, and awareness of her political environment led to Toni's final choice.

3. SELECTING AND DEVELOPING THE TEAM

Having chosen a project, Toni faced the next challenge—selecting and developing a team to implement it. (For an excellent primer on building teams, see *The Team Handbook* [Scholtes 1989].) At this stage, support from above would have been particularly useful since team development often requires training and possibly the use of an external facilitator. However, not only did Toni lack support from above, but she knew that in order to be able to conduct the project as she wished, she would actually have to conceal her efforts. Fortunately, Don, the systems consultant, had some experience in running groups; Toni decided to use Don as a group facilitator and, if asked, portray their efforts as a system-design project.

Don and Toni agreed that the team should include members from each level of the department. They chose Susan, the assistant controller, both because she seemed the most enthusiastic and prepared person on the staff and because she had the most complete hands-on knowledge of the system. Jim Kyle, who represented the lowest-level processing clerk, was also chosen since he had some diagnostic skills. Joan Caruso, the clerk responsible for entering the GL coding into the computer system, was asked to join the group as well. Joan presented an interesting challenge and opportunity. She seemed chronically unhappy, rarely thought that things were done correctly, and was skeptical about any change in the system. Mostly, she seemed to want to be left alone. Toni felt that if Joan could develop some enthusiasm about quality improvement, she could become one of the most successful promoters of the process, especially since everyone was aware of Joan's skepticism.

Finally, because user and buyer departments were responsible for the initial coding of invoices, Toni wanted to include someone from one of those areas. She chose Bob Coburn, a media buyer who had regularly complained about the current process and offered many suggestions for change in the past. Despite Bob's frustration with the process, though, his relationship with the AP department had remained cordial.

Toni thought that this could be an effective team. It contained a mix of participants who had different viewpoints on the problem. She would act as team leader, pushing and pulling the team along while providing resources. Don would act as the facilitator to help ensure that the team functioned effectively.

Toni's decision to include Don, Susan, and Jim was based partly on their knowledge and skills. She hoped that their experience would, by example, help train the less experienced team members. She also hoped at some point to be able to provide formal training to prepare team members for their roles in future projects.

Furthermore, as the quality-improvement effort achieved success and gained credibility, Toni planned to follow the example of many others by having future teams visit successful, "model" companies and examine their processes. Many successful companies are opening their doors to visitors, and visiting model companies has become a standard activity among organizations pursuing quality. In fact, one of the conditions of applying for the Baldrige Award is agreeing to allow outsiders to visit the company and learn how quality can be achieved (Main 1990: 112). On visits such as these, Toni knew that the members of her team would interact with peers at each model company and learn what processes must be followed to improve quality. She also knew from her own experience that they would receive specific suggestions and hints for action as well.

4. ASSESSING THE CURRENT PROCESS

A business process contains three main points of concern for quality-minded managers. First, they must know how the process operates. Second, they must know whether the process is stable; does it produce consistent, predictable results? Put another way, managers need to be able to identify the sources of common-cause variance (stable) and special-cause variance (unstable). Finally, they must know the current capability and capacity of the process.

Using the flowcharts and system narrative that were prepared in the system-identification stage, Toni could determine how the process operated. She still did not know the capability of the current system or whether the system was stable. Documenting capability would show Toni what changes she could expect. A similar analysis after the quality-improvement effort would show the gain attributable to the project. Toni planned to use the contrasting results to publicize the present project and attract support for future projects.

System Stability and Capability

Before measuring capability or, in most instances, while measuring capability, one should also examine system stability. All mixes of inputs result in variable outcomes. Each day, new supplies arrive, equipment is subjected to wear and tear and is serviced or adjusted, people's moods and attention vary, the environment changes, and sometimes procedures are modified. So each day, even each hour, the system will function slightly differently than the day or hour before. When looking for stability, a manager checks to see whether the variation is random.

If a system exhibits random variation only, then the system is stable. In stable systems, outcomes vary both up and down from the average, but within predictable bounds. Here, the quality-improvement challenge is to remix the inputs to generate a new, stable system that yields greater quality (i.e., a system with less variation up and down and a new target, if such is required). When a system exhibits instability, either a special cause of variation has been introduced or the system is inherently poorly designed. Special causes of variation could include a new input (a new supplier, worker, or machine) or a change in input (such as additions to the general ledger or the introduction of new divisions). In these situations, the first step toward improving quality is to root out the special causes of variation and stabilize the system. This can be done with a project such as those described herein. However, unless the system design is to blame, special causes of variation can often be discovered and corrected through direct actions on the part of the manager.

Measuring Stability and Capability

Perhaps the most widely and effectively used tool for assessing process stability and capability is the Shewhart control chart, named for its inventor, Walter Shewhart of Bell Labs. (Hereafter, Shewhart charts will just be called control charts.) The control chart simplifies statistics into a graphic display that yields its meaning to even the casual observer. Control charts come in many varieties and can become quite complex, although simple control charts are often the most useful. Entire books have been written about control charts and their use (Appendix C provides a list of sources). Obviously, the subject of control charts cannot be covered in detail here, but a basic introduction will serve to show their power.

Attribute-Control Charts

Attribute-control charts are useful when some important attribute of a process is identified and counted as a normal course of activity. One typical situation involves errors (defects) that occur infrequently but are detected with a high degree of probability. Although attribute-control charts are not the simplest type of control chart, they have features that make them appropriate for this project. (The terminology and formulas used to produce the control charts in the balance of this subsection are taken from *Process Control, Capability, and Improvement,* published in Southbury, Connecticut, by The Quality Institute, one of IBM's Corporate Technical Institutes. Similar formulas and terminology can be found in Duncan [1986] and Ishikawa [1990], among others.)

A "U chart" measures the number of attributes (in this case, errors) that occur in a sample. For the AP department, the entire set of coded invoices constitutes the sample. Due to the uneven flow of invoices, this sample size varies from day to day. The U chart accommodates unequal sample sizes by reporting the errors as a rate (e.g., errors per 100 invoices). It also has variable control limits, reflecting the greater or lesser probability of getting an average rate of errors in especially large or small samples.

With this in mind, Toni and Susan devised a simple recording method for measuring both error count and total transactions coming into the AP computer system. First, Joan reviewed and corrected the coding on each invoice before entering it into the computer system. She could easily count the number of corrections she made to the invoices and recorded these counts in a PC spreadsheet. The computer system routinely provided counts of the numbers of transactions entered, which were also recorded in the spreadsheet in the sequence in which they occurred. Table 3.2 shows the data that Joan collected.

With Don's help, Joan constructed a chart for the first month. She began by converting the raw data into errors per 100 invoices (because an invoice could have more than one error, this is more appropriate than analyzing the proportion of defective invoices). For each day, she divided the number of errors by the number of transactions and multiplied by 100 (shown in Table 3.2). In plotting the data, the horizontal axis represents time or sequence of events; the vertical axis is the scale for errors per 100 invoices. Figure 3.6 shows the incoming invoice coding errors by day (based on the information in Table 3.2).

After Joan had recorded about twenty days, Don helped her calculate important lines on the chart and examine the system for stability. First, they calculated the average rate of errors (approximately 2.2 per 100 invoices) and drew a line parallel to the horizontal axis through 2.2 on the vertical axis. This is called the center line (CL). Next, they calculated two more sets of values for each point: the upper control limit (UCL) and the lower control limit (LCL). Formulas for the control limits are as follows:

$$UCL = P + 3 \times \sqrt{(P/n_i)}$$

$$LCL = P - 3 \times \sqrt{(P/n_i)}$$

Table 3.2 Incoming GL Transactions and Errors before Changes

Day	Type of Error Account	Project	Total Errors	Transactions per day	Errors per 100 Transactions
1	2	2	4	200	2.00
2	1	1	2	178	1.12
3	2	1	3	350	0.86
4	2	0	2	224	0.89
5	0	0	0	112	0.00
6	0	0	0	157	0.00
7	1	0	1	15	6.67
8	1	1	2	212	0.94
9	1	0	1	31	3.23
10	0	2	2	152	1.32
11	5	20	25	254	9.84
12	0	15	15	198	7.58
13	0	14	14	155	9.03
14	2	6	8	257	3.11
15	3	6	9	233	3.86
16	2	1	3	27	11.11
17	1	0	1	231	0.43
18	1	0	1	48	2.08
19	0	0	0	62	0.00
20	0	1	1	189	0.53
21	1	3	4	291	1.37
22	2	1	3	375	0.80

Figure 3.6   PLOT OF THE INCOMING CODING ERRORS

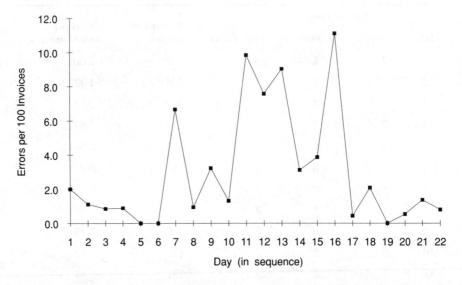

Day (in sequence)

In other words, the average proportion, P, plus (in the case of the UCL) and minus (in the case of the LCL) three times the square root of the average proportion divided by the square root of the sample size for the data point. Don and Joan did not calculate the control limits for each of these data points separately; instead, they used a spreadsheet to calculate and print the results presented here. (Note: For control charts in which data come from fixed sample sizes, the control limits are calculated for all the data at once, not for each data point. U charts require more calculation than most control charts.) In the case of Joan's data, the LCL is negative for each point, so she had no lower control limit. (In this case the LCL line is drawn through 0.) When Joan plotted the CL and UCL on top of the proportion data, she got a chart like the one shown in Figure 3.7.

In one of the first team meetings, Don and Susan interpreted the control charts for the group. The center line showed average performance—what the organization could expect in terms of incoming errors, on average, day in and day out. The UCL and LCL define the range of "normal" performance. For any stable system that has a somewhat symmetrical distribution, the overwhelming portion of all occurrences will fall within these control limits. Put another way, when the process is stable there is a very small likelihood that an event (count) will fall outside the control limits by chance. Such an out-of-control event can probably be attributed to a special cause. (When the distribution of outcomes is stable and symmetric the probability

of events occurring outside the control limits by chance alone is less than
.14 percent.)

Having all points on a control chart fall within the control limits is an
indication that the process is stable. Having points fall outside the control
limits is an indication that the process is unstable. An out-of-control point
(also called an outlier) tells the observer exactly when something in the
system went wrong. This information can then be used to locate special
causes of variance.

On Figure 3.7, it can be seen that points 11, 12, and 13 fall outside the
control limits. When the issue was raised, Joan was immediately able to
explain why those points were out of control:

> That was when we killed the "Planet Movement" project, which had the project
> code "MOVE," and introduced the "Move or Die" project, which had the code
> "MOD." Everyone assumed that the code for "Move or Die" was "MOVE." It
> took a bunch of phone calls to get all the departments to quit using the
> "MOVE" code.

In short, those three points could clearly be accounted for as being
attributable to a special cause. They were removed, and the chart was
recalculated and redrawn without them, resulting in the new chart shown
in Figure 3.8. Although point 16 is out of control, it too could be accounted
for: The effects of the project-coding mistake were still lingering, and the

Figure 3.7   ATTRIBUTE (U) CONTROL CHART FOR INCOMING CODING ERRORS

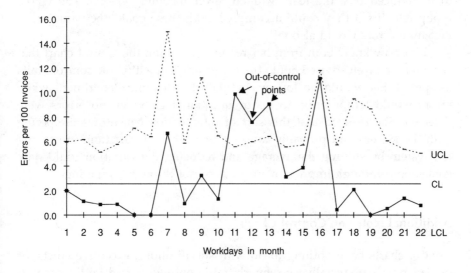

Figure 3.8   ATTRIBUTE (U) CONTROL CHART WITH ORIGINAL OUT-OF-CONTORL POINTS

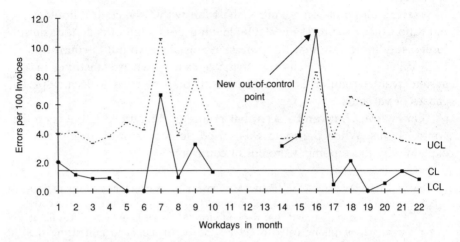

sample size that day was particularly small (which tended to narrow the width of the control limits). Otherwise, the system of incoming errors seemed stable, but with a great deal of variation. On average, almost 2 percent of incoming coding was in error, but on any given day, the error rate could range from 0 to over 10 percent.

The quality-improvement team saw two clear quality goals. First, the opportunities for special causes of variation had to be eliminated from the system. Second, the total number of each day's incoming coding errors had to be reduced (i.e., the team wanted fewer incoming errors). The whole group felt that if they could accomplish both these goals, the variation of incoming errors would also fall.

Toni now knew both from her reading and from the control chart that she would be well advised not to treat any variation within the control limits as special. She would no longer complain to a coding department when errors would temporarily go up or question Joan when no errors were detected. She realized that this sort of intervention constitutes tampering with the system and probably causes greater overall variation. Improving the system by shifting the average and reducing the variation could only come about through improvement projects, not through tampering.

Additional Notes on Control Charts

Control charts have nothing to do with specifications, executive edicts, or quotas, which are usually set semiarbitrarily without regard for the capabilities of the system. A control chart tells what the system can actually do. It can also function as an on-off switch for examining the system. If the process goes out of control (i.e., outside the control limits in the direction of poor performance), it should be examined for special cause. If the severity or cost of the unusual errors is high, the system may need to be shut down while the cause is investigated and removed. If the system goes outside the limits in the direction of good performance (such as seven consecutive error-free days), then the conditions that yielded the outstanding results should be examined to see whether the system can be changed to duplicate those conditions on a regular basis.

Other types of control charts apply to different conditions. X-bar and R charts are used in pairs to show sampling averages and variation. They are appropriate when census data are not available or when product characteristics can be measured. These conditions call for sampling and sampling statistics; the X bar is the sample average, and the R comes from the sample range. Examples of the use of X-bar and R charts include such activities as measuring the diameter of ball bearings, checking the accuracy of power bills from a municipal utility, testing satisfaction with 800-number customer service, estimating gallons of gasoline distilled in a day, estimating the size of the fish population in a river, and testing the life of light bulbs.

P charts apply to concerns about proportions or percentages of classification data in processes where the sample size is constant. Examples include measuring the proportions of various colors of clothes sold, the proportions of accounts-receivable invoices falling into various aging categories, and the proportion of direct-mail advertising that elicits a response. This type of chart tells when proportions are out of their normal range.

In the case of both X-bar/R charts and P charts, the user will probably develop a sampling plan. Most authorities on control charts suggest that with X-bar/R charts, the most practical and useful approach is to schedule sampling frequently, using a sample size of three to five units. The sampling schedule should follow practical steps. For example, samples might be taken at the beginning, middle, and end of a shift or, if activity is great enough and errors critical enough, at each hour during processing. With proven stability, samples may be taken less frequently. For attribute measures, U charts (such as those shown in Figures 3.7 and 3.8) may be used. If the attributes were simply good/defective (or some other classification), a sampling plan would lead to using P charts. (For example, Joan could have taken a random sample of ten to twenty invoices from each day. If she had classified invoices as with error(s) or without error(s) she could have used a P chart. However, she wanted to capture the possibility of having more than one error per invoice, so she used the U chart). Each of the references on control charts in Appendix C offers more detailed suggestions regarding sampling plans.

Control charts can be applied to almost any process capable of being measured. Although process capability can be measured, averages calculated, and stability assessed without the use of control charts, such charts capture all the information in an easily recognizable and interpretable form. In addition, when the charts are created and monitored by the staff members responsible for the process, they receive immediate feedback about their participation. The manager should be forewarned that once the staff begin to see graphic representations of their system, they will be less patient about shouldering the blame for system-generated problems.

Furthermore, many organizations in the United States create control charts for processes but then fail to use them. These charts look great and are taped to machines, tacked on walls, and carried to meetings, but they are not actually used to control, study, and improve the process. They become another ritual, usually because managers do not empower their staff to act on the information displayed in the charts. Occasionally, one sees situations in which control charts are used to determine rewards and punishments for the staff; in such cases, the control charts almost certainly contribute to lower quality and are probably falsified out of fear.

Used correctly, control charts tell staff and managers when to examine a process because it is out of control. They reveal the steady capability of a process and indicate its stability. Any other use probably signals trouble for the managers, the staff, and the process.

5. DIAGNOSING THE PROBLEM

With step 5, Toni began the team-building process in earnest. Now that the team was in place and had a common understanding of process capability, they were ready to begin looking for causes and solutions to problems. Toni felt that every idea should be given a fair hearing; trouble often comes from small and least suspected sources. Toward that end, the group reviewed the system flowcharts and then conducted a brainstorming session to develop ideas about potential sources of problems and solutions. The following subsections describe the use of these techniques.

Flowcharts

Although flowcharts are often seen as documentation tools, they can also aid in diagnosing problems. One approach to diagnosing a system is to highlight the "go-right" path in the flowchart—i.e., the path in which everything goes right (correctly). With time and patience (or by using a computer program that simplifies the process), one can align the "go-right" path as a straight line down the center of the diagram, as was done with the flowcharts shown earlier in Figures 3.2 and 3.3.

With a straightened-out flowchart, one can examine each branch off the "go-right" path; these branches represent sources of potential errors and extra processing. Toni's team looked at each detailed chart for branches involving special handling and estimated both the frequency and costs of its occurrence. These data led to ideas on how to prevent or reduce the need for special handling. On a detailed chart (not shown) depicting the use of new codes, they found several high-potential opportunities for preventing errors.

Cause-and-Effect Diagrams (Fishbone, Ishikawa)

Brainstorming over possible causes of poor quality can reveal many sources hidden to the manager. Don, in his role as team facilitator, suggested that the group organize their brainstorming using a cause-and-effect diagram. He began by writing the problem on a whiteboard and drawing an arrow pointing to it. He then asked the team to hypothesize causes of the problem. As ideas emerged, Don recorded them as branches off the main arrow. Several ideas were piggybacked on other ideas; Don added those as subbranches off the main branches. After a twenty-minute session, the diagram looked like Figure 3.9.

When it seemed that the group had reached a standstill, Don redrew the diagram, arranging the causes into six main branches—materials (supplies), people (training, personalities), equipment (computers, manuals), procedures, environment, and measurements. This rearrangement provided a chance to relate or combine causes and prompted the team to suggest several additional causes. Figure 3.10 shows the final diagram. (The characteristic branching appearance of this diagram accounts for the name *fishbone diagram*.)

Once these potential causes had been listed, Toni led the group in discussing possible solutions. Some of the solutions could be implemented with minimal effort (e.g., providing each department with a complete listing of valid codes as well as a selected listing of codes most relevant to that department). Some of the solutions were beyond the team's current control (e.g., implementing a purchase-order system, buying new equipment, teaching users the philosophy of the accounting system).

Since time was running out for their meeting, the team agreed to implement several of the easy steps. Joan would continue to measure incoming

Figure 3.9   FISHBONE DIAGRAM FOR A QUALITY-IMPROVEMENT PROJECT IN AP SHOWING MAIN ARROW AND RANDOM BRANCHES

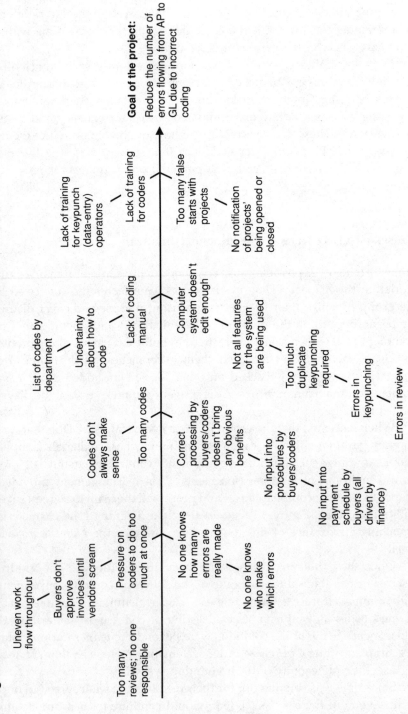

Figure 3.10   COMPLETE FISHBONE DIAGRAM FOR A QUALITY-IMPROVEMENT PROJECT IN AP

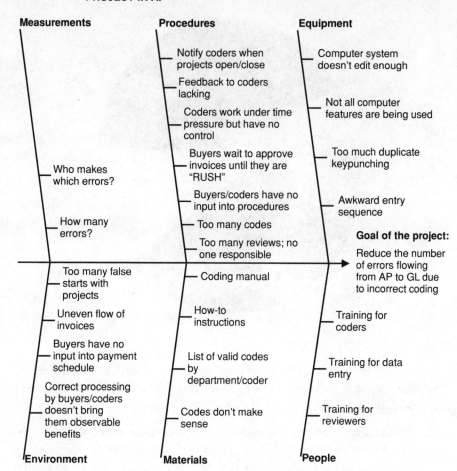

errors. If she discovered out-of-control error rates, she was authorized to act on that information by stopping processing, investigating the source of the problems, and taking corrective actions. Those actions could include contacting coding departments, sending back incorrectly coded invoices, and providing training for anyone in need of coding remediation. Her efforts would also be used to measure the effectiveness of the new procedures. The following is a complete list of planned corrective actions:

1. Provide each buying (and coding) department with a comprehensive list of GL account numbers/descriptions.

Figure 3.11   INCOMING ERRORS BY DEPARTMENT

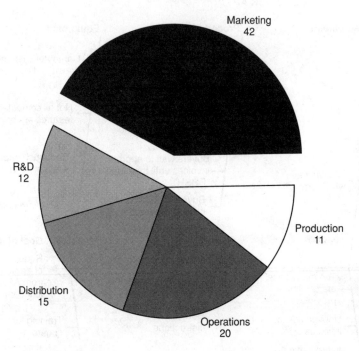

2. Provide each buying (and coding) department with a customized list that includes only the account numbers/descriptions most frequently used by that department.

3. Provide a new list of valid project codes each time accounting assigns a new project code. Include a cover letter that calls the coders' attention to any possible confusion between new, current, and old project codes.

4. Provide feedback by sending a photocopy of any necessary coding corrections to whoever originally coded the invoice.

5. If out-of-control error levels are observed, stop the data-entry process and search out the cause of the errors. In particular, find the people responsible for coding and determine whether something unusual has occurred.

Other Diagnostic Tools

Like flowcharts, PERT and CPM charts can be used for both documentation and diagnosis. Since these tools show time and task dependence, they are particularly useful in project-oriented environments (e.g., construction, consulting, software development, advertising, and engineering). As a diagnostic tool, they show critical dependencies or bottlenecks—those points through which a project must pass before it can proceed.

Although widely used, these diagnostic tools are not the only ones available. Often, the most effective tools are the simplest. A visual representation of the results of a process frequently reveals potential problem areas. Figures 3.11, 3.12, and 3.13 show some common ways of displaying data. (Note: It is possible to prepare all of these diagrams by hand, but they can be produced more easily and accurately with a PC spreadsheet, business graphics package, or statistics package.)

This group of figures illustrates several types of simple data analysis. The pie chart in Figure 3.11 shows that the marketing department produces almost twice as many errors as any other department. Such data can be used to prioritize training efforts. The scatter plot in Figure 3.12 shows that errors in coding accounts do not correlate with errors in coding projects (i.e., project-coding errors are independent of account-coding errors). This means that separate corrective action may be required for each type of error. The bar chart in Figure 3.13 shows the types of errors generated by each depart-

Figure 3.12   SCATTER PLOT OF INCOMING ERORS: PROJECT ERRORS VERSUS ACCOUNT ERRORS

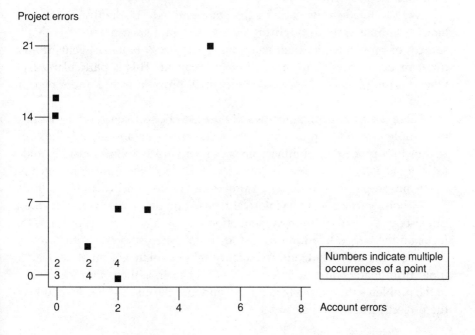

Figure 3.13   INCOMING ERRORS BY DEPARTMENT, BY TYPE OF ERROR

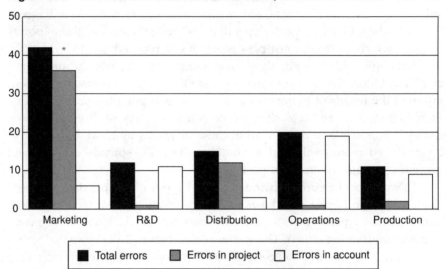

ment. Marketing and distribution make the most errors when coding projects; operations, research and development, and production have more problems with account codes but little trouble with project codes. By preparing and reviewing these simple displays, Toni's team quickly learned a lot about the problems in the process.

As was noted in the earlier subsection entitled "1. Identifying the System," a simple walk-through or review of a system can reveal both the sources of problems and their solutions. Fresh eyes often see events from a different perspective than those directly involved. This is particularly true when training has been sparse or when new procedures are under consideration.

These are some of the most widely used and effective tools for diagnosing simple systematic problems. Diagnostic efforts should always look upstream in a process to eliminate errors and reduce variance, just as Toni's team looked to the source to correct coding problems. Problems created upstream propagate throughout a process and often find ways to multiply.

Although Toni's team has not yet focused on downstream results, these can also guide quality-improvement efforts. Looking downstream keeps the focus on the target. In addition, customers can often suggest useful ways to produce what they need, and the quality-minded manager must be open to input from many sources. Since Toni, as controller, is the primary customer of the problems that ripple through AP and into the GL, she has helped keep the project focused on her target.

6. TESTING THEORIES IN THE WORKPLACE

After measuring process capability and diagnosing potential causes of problems, a quality-improvement team develops theories about how to correct the causes. The next step is to test those theories to see whether changes have positive effects. A general form exists for this step. It is called, among various names, the Shewhart cycle, PDCA (plan, do, check, act), the experimental cycle, or the scientific method. The process is the same regardless of the name; we shall call it the experimental cycle (see Figure 3.14).

The first step is to develop a theory or set of hypotheses about the cause-and-effect relationship that may be at work in the process. The AP team then translated their diagnosis into a plan for changing the system. (Both these steps were discussed in the preceding subsection.)

Since those changes were simple and did not dramatically alter the system, they were implemented without a pilot project. When major changes are contemplated, pilot tests are recommended. Limiting the exposure of a production system to disruption allows inputs and processes to be manipulated while the regular business continues. Often, small-scale tests permit greater control over unexpected inputs as well. In cases where a pilot program is not feasible, contingency plans should be prepared for "falling back" or readjusting the process should unexpected negative results occur.

Figure 3.14   EXPERIMENTAL (PLAN-DO-CHECK-ACT) CYCLE FOR TESTING THEORIES

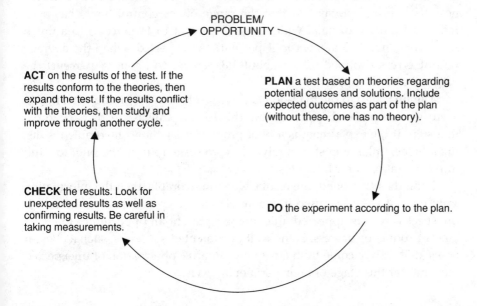

PROBLEM/
OPPORTUNITY

ACT on the results of the test. If the results conform to the theories, then expand the test. If the results conflict with the theories, then study and improve through another cycle.

PLAN a test based on theories regarding potential causes and solutions. Include expected outcomes as part of the plan (without these, one has no theory).

CHECK the results. Look for unexpected results as well as confirming results. Be careful in taking measurements.

DO the experiment according to the plan.

The next step is to check the outcomes. Because process capability was determined before any changes were made, those same measurement techniques should show whether the results have improved (or degraded). If illusory results are to be avoided, it is essential that the same measurement techniques and criteria be used in performing before and after measurements. Changing a measurement technique can yield a changed result in the absence of any actual change in process characteristics.

Measurement problems are more prevalent and subtle than one might think. Take, for example, the following well-documented phenomenon involving precise physical measurements: A single person using a single device (say, a caliper) to measure a single object (say, a metal wire) following a single procedure will get a distribution of results if he or she makes a hundred measurements. That distribution will look like a sample from a normal distribution. The average and variance will depend on the device used, the operator, the object being measured, and the procedure. Which of these hundred measurements is "correct"? In the case of "interpretive" data, such as consumer-satisfaction scales, measurement problems are multiplied. Consumers have no common scale. The fact that person A gives Crunchos a rating of 10 does not necessarily mean that A likes them twice as much as person B, who gives Crunchos a rating of 5. If the question were asked a hundred times, the answers for A and B would probably follow some frequency distribution similar to a binomial distribution.

Figure 3.15 shows the control chart for incoming errors after the simple improvements had been in effect for a month. Note that the chart contains no out-of-control points and that the range of the control limits has been reduced from the original wide range (3 percent to 11 percent) to a much narrower range (2.5 percent to 4 percent). As expected, when the average rate of errors dropped, (from about 1.8 percent to about .8 percent) the variance also dropped.

The final step in the plan-do-check-act cycle is to act on the outcome. In a process of continual improvement, this last step always leads back to the first step. If the experiment is a pilot program that shows favorable results, then the next planning step involves how to scale up from the pilot to a full implementation (or a larger test).

If, on the other hand, the results were unfavorable, then the information from the test would be used in a new planning step and a new pilot test. If unexpected results appeared, this might represent an opportunity to create a new product or process. Some well-documented successes, such as Post-it notes at 3M, have come from creatively attentive observation of unexpected outcomes at this stage of an experimental cycle.

Figure 3.15   ATTRIBUTE (U) CONTROL CHART AFTER QUALITY-IMPROVEMENT PROJECT

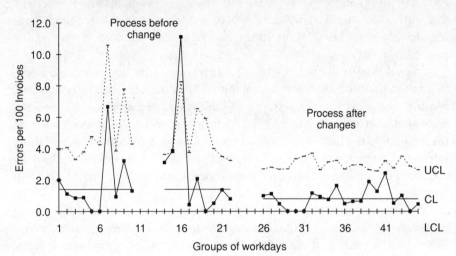

For Toni's group, standardizing the distribution of coding instructions was simple; it became a matter of policy. Their first improvement efforts involved a full implementation. Now they were ready to work on another cycle of improvement. When implementing a new process, the experimental cycle may also be used productively. Implementation should be planned and carried out. After the new process is implemented, its capability should be measured. These measurements can be used to guide adjustments to the process (until it is stable) and then direct the next cycle in the improvement process.

Measuring outcomes can become a fairly sophisticated process, especially when multiple input variables must be manipulated. However, good experimental design and analysis result in more in-depth knowledge of quality-control factors. Although a detailed discussion of experimental design and measurement is beyond the scope of this book, Appendix C lists several excellent sources of information on these topics.

7. QUANTIFYING AND MAINTAINING RESULTS

When Joan's records before and after the changes were compared, a measurable improvement could be observed. Toni was confident that by continuing the measurements and supporting Joan's new authority, the process would be monitored for sustained improvement. Joan had taken her new authority and responsibility quite seriously. She plotted the incoming errors each day and therefore knew when out-of-control problems arose. Since she was authorized to take corrective action, she felt responsible for the incoming mistakes. Within a short time, the AP system showed a very stable pattern of errors.

In addition to the before-and-after measures, Toni had compiled documentation that included training (obtained both from Don and from books), meeting notes, experiments attempted (failures as well as successes), and the estimated cost of the project. This documentation provided evidence that the project was efficient and effective. She now had something to show interested parties, such as her own staff, other staff members within the department, managers of other departments, executives, customers, and suppliers.

By monitoring the results of improvement efforts, Toni sent two strong messages to her staff: (1) Quality improvement is important; (2) Improvements can be made and measured. Having achieved a documented success, Toni was now prepared to build quality-improvement momentum and her SOI.

8. PUBLICIZING AND EXPANDING QUALITY IMPROVEMENT

Since Toni's success was neither huge nor likely to show up in observable cost savings in the near term, she chose to defer public acknowledgment. She hoped that after several successful projects, she would have sufficient evidence and support to "go public" with announcements of her program. But because the improvements were measurable and could clearly be attributed to the team's work, Toni decided to provide at least a modest acknowledgment of that effort.

Her priority at this stage was to build support within her SOI. She sent a letter of thanks to Bob's boss (copying Bob, of course), citing his contributions to the project's success. In a departmental meeting, she reviewed the project documentation—especially, the results—with the entire department. She thanked each of the team members at that meeting, citing their individual contributions. She also asked each of them to comment on how the process had worked. When Joan indicated that she wanted to see more changes like the ones they had implemented, both Toni and the rest of the department were impressed.

With this type of effort, Toni was able to build internal department commitment and experience. After the meeting, several employees requested the opportunity to make improvements in their work areas. With

Susan also acting as a team leader (and Don acting as facilitator for both teams), the accounting department was able to conduct two projects simultaneously. Since the teams were created at the request of the staff, they were asked to select their own projects. Not only did the teams now "own" their projects, but team members were able to use their individual SOIs to extend the effectiveness of the projects undertaken.

Gradually, the projects produced good results. Word of mouth, Toni's subtle lobbying, and her documentation of success expanded her SOI. Several natural team leaders emerged from the AP projects. As other departments started asking for Toni's help in conducting similar quality-improvement projects, she was able to "loan out" these staff members. In so doing, she expanded both her SOI and that of her staff. Everyone gained in the process.

Toni knew she had caught the attention of the executive suite when her boss, Steve, asked whether she could help prepare him for a board meeting. The board was considering authorizing a companywide quality-improvement program. During her months of conducting successful quality-improvement projects, Toni had built a reference library; she had just the right materials for Steve, including books; schedules of training classes and seminars; names of respected consultants; and names of staff members who could lead and facilitate groups and who had special skills, such as flow-charting and control charting.

Moreover, Toni had documentation from each of her projects, which proved quite helpful to the board because it gave board members a concrete idea of the costs and results they could expect in undertaking a quality-improvement program. Toni's documentation showed them:

1. The capability of the preimprovement process, including an estimate of the cost of poor quality

2. A list of team members, the training they received for the project, and team activities (meetings, trips, experiments)

3. A list of tools and documentation of their use (sample diagrams, the lists from brainstorming sessions, charts, plots, etc.)

4. The plans, schedules, and results of experimental cycles

5. The capability of the new process and the cost of the current (i.e., improved) quality level

6. Estimates of the cost of conducting the projects

This documentation built a case for quality improvement. In some instances, the cost improvements were compelling. Even when they were not, the information gathered from each project proved useful in planning subsequent projects. Every documented project provided a road map for future projects and for others who would become interested in quality improvement. The documentation was especially important in dealing with naysayers—those who find fault with all new and unfamiliar efforts. Data, especially cost-reduction data, are often the most effective weapons against negative opinions.

SUMMARY

The tools and techniques described in this chapter by no means exhaust the possibilities. The chapter attempted to keep the focus on managers, especially managers who are new to quality improvement. The materials presented here should be viewed as a starting point; with experience, success, and learning, managers will naturally be led to other, more advanced techniques.

The suggested form of project, process, and staff development allows a manager to build a base of support and interest without drawing negative attention. It forgoes a grand-rollout, sloganeering approach for one based on positive results. Through successful improvement projects, staff, peers, and superiors will come to think and speak well of the quality-conscious manager and support his or her efforts.

The general road map and tools for conducting initial quality-improvement projects include the following:

1. Define and document the current system using flowcharts and narratives.

2. Identify and select projects using brainstorming, Pareto cost analysis, and estimates of the likelihood of successful improvement and expected cooperation within the manager's SOI.

3. Select and train a project team.

4. Assess the capability, capacity, and stability of the current process through the use of control charts. If the process is unstable, focus attention on eliminating special causes of variation before attempting to change the process.

5. Diagnose potential causes of problems, especially looking upstream for sources of variance and downstream for shifting the target product. Brainstorming, cause-and-effect diagrams, flowcharts, PERT and CPM charts, and other tools help in this step.

6. Use experimental techniques to test theories about the causes and effects of process factors. Try pilot projects and use designed experiments when possible. Expand pilot projects using the same techniques.

7. Stabilize the project and publicize its results. Collect case documentation from the project to support both the current project and future projects.

8. Extend the improvement efforts by conducting other projects, offering training and education, and developing resources that can be made available to others.

Although the case presented in this chapter is a simplistic and partly fictitious compilation, each element in it is based on a real situation. The case effectively illustrates how to make specific improvements and is meant to show how to create a quality-improvement program from within an organization. Lacking leverage from the executive suite, a manager must work incrementally. Building expertise and a track record provides the manager with the best possible defense—no one complains about success.

References

Deming, W. E. 1986. *Out of the Crisis*. Cambridge, Mass.: MIT Center for Advanced Engineering Studies.

Duncan, A. 1986. *Quality Control and Industrial Statistics*. 5th ed. Homewood, Ill.: Irwin.

Ishikawa, K. 1990. *Guide to Quality Control*. White Plains, N.Y.: Quality Resources.

Juran, J. M. 1989. *Juran on Leadership for Quality*. New York: Free Press.

Main, J. 1990. "How to Win the Baldrige Award." *Fortune* (Apr. 23): 101–116.

Miller, D. 1990. *The Icarus Paradox: How Exceptional Companies Bring About Their Own Downfall*. New York: Harper Business.

Miller, D., and Friesen, P. H. 1980. "Momentum and Revolution in Organizational Adaptation." *Academy of Management Journal* 23 (no. 4): 591–614.

Nadler, D. A., and Tushman, M. L. 1990. "Beyond the Charismatic Leader: Leadership and Organizational Change." *California Management Review* 32: 77–97.

Schaffer, R. 1989. *The Breakthrough Strategy: Using Short Term Successes to Build the High Performance Organization*. Cambridge, Mass.: Ballinger.

Scholtes, P. R. 1989. *The Team Handbook*. Madison, Wis.: Joiner Associates.

Scholtes, P. R., and Hacquebord, W. 1987. "A Practical Approach to Quality." Madison, Wis.: Joiner Associates.

Schuler, R. S., and Walker, J. W. 1990. "Don't Waste Time Planning—Act: The Development of Human Resource Strategy." *Organization Dynamics* (Summer 1990): 5–19.

Tushman, M. L., and Romanelli, E. 1985. "Organizational Evolution: The Metamorphosis Model of Convergence and Reorientation." *Research in Organizational Behavior* 6: 171–222.

Tushman, M. L., Virany, B., and Romanelli, E. 1985. "Executive Succession, Strategic Reorientations, and Organization Evolution." *Technology in Society* 7: 297–313.

Chapter 4

QUALITY ENHANCEMENT, THE MANAGER, AND THE HR FUNCTION

Launching and sustaining quality-enhancement and quality-improvement programs is easier with the support of top management. Managers would certainly want to know that the executive suite is fully behind the idea. There have been many instances, however, in which this has not been the case, and the progress in achieving total quality reflects this lack of commitment. Roger Smith's comments (made in *Business Monthly*) about his participation in a quality-improvement program at General Motors conveyed to both management and the work force a lack of commitment at the top. Here is a question, together with Roger Smith's answer, during an interview about GM's participative program:

> **Q:** Some 2,500 senior executives have gone through GM's Leadership Now program—a five-day intensive training in participative management. Are you the only one who hasn't taken it?
> **A:** I'm not the only one. If I had two weeks off, I'd spend the first week fishing and the second week in Leadership Now. (Simmons 1989: 79)

These half-hearted endorsements by top management often make for tough sledding for managers during the implementation phase of a quality program. Current CEO Robert Stempl by contrast appears to be more involved in the quality programs at GM.

More typically, however, it is top management pointing the finger at middle management as being the real impediment in quality programs:

> The most resistance usually comes from the middle-manager and supervisory levels. For many of these people, management by quality seems a threat to their authority—if not their jobs. Shop-floor workers are usually eager to assume responsibility for the quality of their work. But for middle managers, says George E. D. Box, director of research for the Quality and Productivity

Improvement Center (QPIC) of the University of Wisconsin, 'it's a different game from the one that they learned.' They must function less like bosses and more like football coaches, relying on powers of persuasion rather than "do-this" directives.

Hewlett-Packard's Walter admits that despite clear signals from President John Young that quality is a top priority, the quality thrust hasn't gone without hitches. 'Even with HP, some people are risk-takers and pioneers, and not others.' At Ford, too, some middle managers are still struggling to accept the idea that costs really do head down when quality perks up. But Ford's quality gains have already produced telling evidence: Last year its fattened profits exceeded those of General Motors Corp. (Bluestone 1989: 134)

Thus, top-management support is important, and middle-management involvement is critical, although it often means that middle managers must assume new roles. Indeed, if success is to be achieved in total quality management, all the organization's employees must participate actively. According to Chairman John Marous, one of the basic lessons learned by Westinghouse (a 1988 winner of the coveted Baldrige Award) is that:

Everybody—*everybody*—has to be involved. You just can't have one person doing it. This is how you get the contribution from the guy who knows his job better than you'll ever know it and therefore knows how to improve it better than anybody else. (Main 1990: 103)

NEW ROLES FOR THE MANAGER

Typically, managers demonstrate resistance when total quality programs are "installed" without their active participation. This resistance is understandable, given that total quality programs require substantial skill and role changes for and from these managers. Jan Carlzon, president and CEO of Scandinavian Airline System (SAS), described the airline's efforts at implementing a quality customer-service program:

Change rarely is accomplished without some difficulty and resistance—and the revolutionary restructuring at SAS was no exception. Although the organization's new philosophy has allowed employees on the front line to grow and thrive as never before, some of the company's other employees—in particular, its middle managers—have found the changes somewhat threatening.

Carlzon explained that in the traditionally structured organization, 'top management hands down orders to middle management, which fine-tunes and interprets them according to the rules and regulations, and then passes them on down to be implemented. Basically, middle managers are messengers for top management.'

However, at the new SAS, this 'messenger' role has been rendered obsolete. Carlzon noted that by creating a freer, less hierarchical structure—in which front-line people have their own information, power, and responsibility—'you undermine middle management in a terrible way. You may not say so, but you question their raison d'être.' (Wagel et al. 1988: 32)

But as the messenger role is being discarded, new roles for managers are appearing. Commenting on SAS's successful change to quality customer service, Carlzon indicates how important middle managers are:

In fact, middle management's new raison d'être—providing support for the 'front-line troops'—is crucial to the company's success. Yet, as Carlzon noted, 'middle managers' role of serving those who used to report to them won't go over too well back at the pub when they're asked to explain what their new jobs are.' Carlzon is confident, however, that middle managers can and will adapt to their new roles. 'One should not discount the possibility of personal growth,' he said. 'In an ideal world, creative people would eventually lose their fear of a highly structured workplace, and the law-and-order people would stop being afraid of free-form entrepreneurship. This may never happen. But we are not bees who are biologically programmed to play a particular role in the hive; our behavior is not genetically determined; and we are all capable of learning to adapt.' (Ibid.: 32)

Middle managers' jobs have also changed at Motorola. According to plant manufacturing vice president Scott Shamlin, with Motorola's quality-enhancement efforts:

'My role has gravitated to being a cheerleader,' he says. 'People don't need a lot of management anymore. They just need leadership to keep their enthusiasm up.' (Murray 1989: 39)

These role changes involve substantial attitude and behavioral changes. If middle managers were not included in designing the quality-improvement program in the first place, and if they are then neither trained adequately nor offered sufficient incentives to change, they can be expected to resist the change process. As for incentives not to change, these managers, faced with a quality program that they do not fully understand and for which their input was not sought, are likely to view the program as resulting in employment loss, not in gain of any kind. And since many quality programs do in fact operate with fewer employees at all levels, including middle and lower managers, middle managers' perception that quality programs result in job loss is not without some foundation. Companies have successfully addressed both this perception and the reality by letting middle managers know that they're valued and that change in their leadership style can be achieved and will be supported. Conveying this attitude to all managers—in fact, to all employees—is important in any organizational quality-improvement program. Also important is changing the effectiveness with which employees are managed. This is occurring as line managers assume more of the human resource function.

TRANSFORMATION OF THE HUMAN RESOURCE FUNCTION

When companies help prepare middle and lower management for quality programs, they address the issues of role changes and employment loss directly. This is done by identifying the new role requirements for these managers. Once it is clear what the new roles are and what training will be provided to assist the managers in performing these new roles, resistance diminishes.

The new managerial roles include:

- Leader
- Coach
- Motivator
- Resource gatherer
- Facilitator
- Negotiator
- Team builder
- Organizer
- Trainer

Middle managers quickly come to realize that performing these roles will involve a great deal of work (i.e., there will be much for them to do)—which means that jobs need not be lost, just transformed.

The magnitude and significance of this transformation, however, are not to be downplayed. This is in fact a major transformation, and one that is consistent with another major transformation in organizations today. This second transformation is nothing less than revolutionary, for we are witnessing the movement of human resource management functions from the human resource department and the HR manager to the line managers

(Schuler 1990). This movement is timely because it supports the efforts of all managers to implement successfully and to sustain quality programs.

THE LINE MANAGER AS HR MANAGER

Even in companies with the most advanced HR departments, the line managers are increasingly involved in human resource issues and management. As these advanced HR departments become more strategic, they move away from, not toward, operational and managerial human resource activities. As a consequence (because both the line and HR managers agree to it), line managers actually perform some of the human resource functions, as illustrated by the example of Jerry Goodman, a vice president in the international operations of Swiss Bank Corporation in New York City.

The international division of Swiss Bank Corporation has a staff of about eighty-four people, about half of whom are sales representatives (marketers). As the world has gotten more competitive and margins have gotten a bit slimmer, making more efficient and effective use of the sales force's time has become critical. Jerry, his boss (Bill Mont, senior vice president), and two other line managers started examining the sales representatives' call sheets and noticed that they couldn't determine the status of a relationship with a potential customer by looking at the sheets. They also discovered that the reps were having a hard time closing deals and that they were not always prepared to negotiate with senior managers. The reps had fallen into bad habits—a situation that had to change or else they would continue losing business. The costs of doing nothing were great.

The conclusion was that Swiss Bank Corporation had a training problem (identified in the late summer of 1988). The required training related to negotiating skills and the completion of call reports (furthermore, the reports themselves didn't request all the necessary information).

The managers then contacted the Richardson Group (in the meantime, just informing the HR personnel of what they were doing). This group came in and tailored the bank's programs. Jerry and the others actually wrote the case studies and the materials used in the role-play exercises. In the late fall of 1988, they were able to accommodate all forty-eight marketers in four training sessions. One member of the top-management group attended each session to answer questions, demonstrate support, and so forth. The results of this effort were as follows:

1. The marketers all learned to speak the same negotiating language.

2. They had a product built for them.

3. The call-report form was made more explicit, so the line managers could use this form to determine the exact status of a call and assess the likelihood of a hit, which, in turn, enabled them to make an informed decision to stop if the likelihood was low.

4. Marketing efforts were better focused.

5. Travel and expenses were now better managed.

6. The marketers experienced more win–win situations.

The bottom line: improved customer service and lower costs.

In part, this whole scenario arose because of Swiss Bank Corporation's new strategic mission of high-quality, relationship-oriented banking and the highly competitive environment and because the HR department had repositioned itself to provide high-quality services and products to its internal customers (Schuler 1988). See Appendix B for more details on this project.

Increasingly, this type of scenario is likely to result in line managers' gaining a greater awareness of the importance of human resources and being evaluated in terms of how well they manage their people. For example, at Merck:

> . . . [L]ine managers are starting to address the needs of organizational and individual performance, e.g., they know why every job exists in the organization, the people in those jobs and how competent they are; and they know it is important to keep their skills updated. There is a saying at Merck that goes like this, 'human resources are too important to be left to the HR department.' Fully one-third of the performance evaluation of line managers is related to people management. (Bluestone 1989: 139)

Thus, with the complete transformation of the human resource function, we see that the HR manager is a member of the executive management team and that members of the HR department (if one exists at all) are out in the line divisions. This transformation, which appears to be in the best interests of both the line managers and the organization, forces line managers to actually do what they have always been responsible for: manage their people.

Because the successful execution of quality programs depends on effective people management, line managers have a greater stake in human resource management issues, policies, and practices. The difference this time, however, is that the line managers may actually have the time to do this. Their old roles are gone, and their new roles are basically focused on managing human resources: training, motivating, team building. If we add to these the roles of selection, compensation, performance review, safety, and labor relations, we have the entire set of traditional personnel practices in the hands of the line managers. However, those traditional activities (e.g., payroll processing) have many components that line managers have neither the time nor the skill to do. Thus, there is still plenty for the traditional HR department to do, although the department is smaller (vacated by people who have perhaps moved into line-manager positions).

THE VICE PRESIDENT OF QUALITY

This shift of human resource functions and activities to the line managers as part of quality-improvement programs is being accompanied by another phenomenon in middle management, this one involving the creation of a new position: vice president of quality.

> Last week, for example, the Whitman Corporation, formerly IC Industries, which grew out of the Illinois Central Railroad, named a vice president to head its new corporate office of quality. At Whitman, now a highly diversified Chicago-based conglomerate with four operational units, the job went to William C. Naumann, who will report directly to the chairman and chief executive, Karl D. Bays.
>
> In addition, each of the company's four subsidiaries has a new vice president in charge of quality who will report to the chief executive of the unit. Mr. Naumann, who is 50 years old, called the new stress on quality 'a pervasive attitudinal approach.'
>
> 'Our focus on quality now is broader,' he said. 'In our definition, quality has two dimensions. Internal quality involves everything we can do inside, including cutting the number of rejects and improving job satisfaction. The second dimension—external quality—is really a perception involving what customers and the community think about us. That is harder to measure.'
>
> Mr. Bays said: 'We have restructured Whitman in the last year and a half. Quality is our top priority and it will be the glue that holds everything together.' (Fowler 1989: D12)

Thus, most, if not virtually all, quality programs are being headed by folks outside the HR department. This being the case, the shifting of human resource activities to line managers is likely to be even more acceptable to those managers.

The key question this scenario poses, of course, is, "What do I, as a line manager, have to know about human resource activities and human resource management in order to increase the success of my quality-improvement program?" The following section provides part of the answer to that question; the next chapter provides the balance of the answer. Both portions of this discussion are based on the assumption that human resource management practices are critical to the success of quality programs and that line managers are becoming increasingly responsible for these practices. Even in cases where they are not formally responsible, these managers still need to know what human resource practices should be in place to encourage quality because they are still responsible for the success of quality programs. This knowledge can then help them convince their HR departments of the need to examine existing HR practices to see whether they fit the quality strategy. Whether or not they fit is the subject of the next several pages.

SYSTEMATIC HUMAN RESOURCE MANAGEMENT

The new role for the line manager in a quality-enhancement program is really a human resource role. Therefore, the line manager, at any level, needs to be current on human resource management practices. A critical aspect of contemporary human resource management is that it can be approached systematically, which means that it can be practiced by all managers. And because being close to the action enables a manager to tailor human resource practices systematically to the needs of the business, *the line manager is in an ideal position to be the analyzer, developer, and implementer of many key human resource practices.*

To facilitate this human resource management role, it is useful to present a framework that any manager can employ in systematically managing human resources. This discussion melds human resource management and the quality-enhancement program. It also examines how a quality-enhancement strategy impacts human resource management and contrasts that with how the strategies of cost reduction and innovation impact HR management.

TO BE OR NOT TO BE SYSTEMATIC

Companies have two main options for how to manage their employees, and increasingly, their choice determines the companies' success and even their viability. The first option is to be unsystematic: to let human resource policies and practices evolve from what's been done in the past or to adopt whatever practice is currently in fashion in the industry. This choice is obviously relatively simple to make and easy to implement. It also gives the appearance of having a human resource department that is right on top of the latest trends. What often happens in this situation, however, is that the company ends up with a staffing policy that doesn't fit its training policy and a compensation policy that doesn't fit its performance-appraisal policy! Yet this is due in part to the fact that even human resource departments become so specialized that the staffing group doesn't talk with the training group and the compensation folks don't talk with those in charge of performance appraisal. But it is also due to the fact that there is no overriding vision or philosophy guiding the development and articulation of the policies and practices used to manage the company's most valued asset—its human resources. The company's ability to deliver its products and services to its customers is doubtless somewhat impaired, and even its ability to survive can be jeopardized if its competitors have a more coherent and consistent set of human resource policies and practices.

To avoid this scenario, companies can choose the second option in managing their human resources—i.e., they can decide to be systematic in the development of human resource policies and practices. Being systematic means selecting and implementing policies and practices that are consistent with and coordinated with each other. Although initially, this approach is perhaps not as easy to implement as the unsystematic approach, once the manager decides to be systematic, it becomes relatively easy to determine whether or not it is in the company's best interests to continue with an established policy or to adopt one of the latest fashions. The decision to be systematic should also result in improved employee performance as well as an enhancement in the company's effectiveness and competitive position.

BEING SYSTEMATIC

When managers consider adopting the systematic approach, two critical questions arise:

1. Why does being systematic in the selection and implementation of human resource policies and practices work?

2. How do managers go about being systematic; what steps are required?

When human resource policies and practices are consistent with each other and coordinated with each other, a consistent message is communicated to employees. A performance-appraisal system that evaluates employees based on the attainment of long-term goals coupled with a compensation system that rewards employees based on the attainment of long-term goals send employees a consistent message. A human resource policy stating that employees are the company's most valuable resource coupled with such practices as constant layoffs and inadequate training send employees conflicting messages. Being consistent across all human resource policies and practices results in consistency and clarity regarding what is expected, what is rewarded, and what is important. Having consistency and clarity regarding all three of these issues is an absolute must if an organization is to use its human resources effectively and achieve organizational effectiveness.

Clarity and consistency regarding what is expected, what is rewarded, and what is important result from the systematic selection and implementation of human resource policies and practices. Being systematic means packaging human resource policies and practices that fit together and send the same message. The availability of such a wide variety of human resource policy and practice options makes this an enormous task, however, and it can take considerable time for an organization to identify and correctly package those policies and practices that send the same message. This, in itself, is the major reason why companies would rather continue doing what they have always done or do what others are currently doing. Fortunately, the dimensions of this task can be substantially reduced by applying human resource management philosophies.

HUMAN RESOURCE MANAGEMENT PHILOSOPHIES

Philosophies are the basis on which policies and practices guiding a company's or unit's behavior can be developed and implemented. Having a philosophy enables an organization to articulate a vision of what it stands for and where it is going. Philosophies also provide an understanding that guides managers' decision making.

At the level of human resource management, philosophies are the basis for HR management policies and practices. A single philosophy assembles thoughts and ideas, policies and practices, that are consistent with each other. Human resource management philosophies package policies and practices that are consistent with each other and that can send the same message to employees. Central, then, to being systematic in human resource management is selecting a human resource management philosophy.

There are three major philosophies of human resource management from which to choose. Each represents a consistent package of policies and practices for managing human resources. Because these three philosophies are essential to the systematic management of human resources, we describe each of them in detail in the following subsections.

Accumulation

The first major philosophy of treating and managing people in organizations is called accumulation. In brief, this philosophy translates into policies and practices designed to attract many good candidates very carefully and very consistently, often more on the basis of personal fit than technical fit. The technical skills that are lacking can be provided by in-house training programs. Although this approach takes a longer-term view of human resource management (training costs a great deal, and many of its benefits are likely to be reaped only after several years), it makes good sense in a constantly changing world in which new skills are needed all the time.

In this scenario, even if a person initially has the necessary technical skills, those skills will eventually become outdated and require change. A policy predicated on constant change makes it easier for the organization to provide training and for employees to adapt to change and retain their flexibility. This policy, in turn, facilitates the practices of lifetime employment and seniority. If these two practices are to be followed and the organization is to be effective, employees must have current skills as well as experience in the company. Current skills and experience can be achieved through the practices of job rotation and internal promotion, with many employees starting at the bottom and working their way up through the ranks.

Because accumulation rests on a policy of long-term (possibly lifetime) employment, many employees will be around for a long time, and there will be a mix of younger and older workers. Practices that complement this policy include relative egalitarianism among workers, slow rates of promotion, salary based on job level and seniority (with groups receiving more attention than individuals), and respect for older workers. Examples of egalitarianism among workers include having a small differential (e.g., 7:1) between the salaries of top management and entry-level workers, common perquisites such as insurance benefits or a single cafeteria, and removal of class distinctions such as reserved parking spaces. Taken together, all of these practices make team activities (such as quality circles) work more smoothly and effectively. Aiding this approach is the practice of extensive management–employee cooperation.

Utilization

The second major philosophy of treating and managing people in organizations is called utilization. In keeping with this philosophy, individuals are generally selected with attention to technical skills (job-relevant skills, knowledge, and abilities), although personal characteristics are still important. Consequently, once hired, new employees can begin their work with relatively little training. This shorter-term view of human resource management saves on training costs and allows organizations to put individuals into vacant positions with relatively little long-range planning. In this respect, the practice of hiring on the basis of technical fit is very efficient and allows for rapid response and adjustment (relatively speaking). It also supports the concept of employment at will (those with currently relevant skills survive) and allows employees to be moved into positions almost anywhere in the organization almost anytime. Consequently, at all levels, there is a lot of external recruitment and a lot of external placement.

Because utilization rests on the policy of employment at will, relevant skills, and organizational need, employees are not always sure how long they will be around. "Here today, gone tomorrow" is truer than ever. Practices that complement this policy include individual-based compensation, preferably with a substantial incentive component. Consistent with this approach are relatively high salary differentials among employees (e.g., 20:1) and rapid rates of performance evaluation and promotion. In fact, employees at different job levels tend to distinguish themselves by wearing different clothing, even when differences in attire are unrelated to actual job requirements. All these practices, taken together, make it possible to reward individuals for outstanding achievement and result in a lack of egalitarianism. Aiding this policy is the relatively modest amount of collective or team-oriented behavior on the part of employees at all levels.

Facilitation

The third major philosophy of treating and managing people in organizations is called facilitation. This philosophy holds that although individuals must have technical skills, it is important that they be able to work together in close reciprocal interaction. Employee development and enhancement are valued, but the organization will facilitate the acquisition of new knowledge and abilities rather than directly providing for their acquisition. This approach then places the responsibility for learning on the individual employees, albeit the organization will assist by providing financial and non-financial resources. Individuals are relied on to develop information networks both inside and outside the organization. This practice, however, results in employees' having one foot inside and one foot outside the organization in order for them to possess and create state-of-the-science knowledge.

Individuals working under the facilitation philosophy become valuable both to the organization and to themselves. They also become valuable to other organizations, especially competitors. Consequently, organizations that adhere to the facilitation philosophy seek to wed their employees to the organization but do so in a very noncoercive manner. Offering employment security has little impact, and practicing employment at will is counterproductive. Instead, what is offered is organizational attractiveness. An environment that stimulates, enriches, and rewards is what drives the compensation system.

Accordingly, facilitative organizations provide opportunities for intensive, free-flowing interaction with colleagues. Chains of command and lines of hierarchy are given little weight. Groups are entrusted with responsibility for staffing because only they can be sure that they can work with a new individual and that the new individual possesses the knowledge they need. Beyond entry-level positions, external recruitment is used in order to tap potential sources of new knowledge.

In essence, the facilitation philosophy is based on new knowledge and the creation of knowledge, whereas the utilization philosophy is based on minimal commitment and high control, and the accumulation philosophy is based on maximum involvement and skilled execution.

CHOOSING A HUMAN RESOURCE MANAGEMENT PHILOSOPHY

How do companies and their managers go about choosing one of these three human resource management philosophies? Certainly, the preferences of top management are important in selecting a human resource management philosophy. Having consistency across all areas of the business is as essential as having consistency across human resource policies and practices. Top management's involvement in the selection of the human resource philosophy can help ensure that this consistency is achieved. The answers the following two questions, then, hold the key to making the decision:

1. What mind-set do you want your employees to have?

2. How do you want them to behave as they go about their jobs?

Alternative Mind-Sets

Each of the three philosophies of human resource management has a distinct impact on how employees think in their work environment and how they think about their jobs.

The accumulation philosophy conveys an expression of caring and concern for the employees, who respond in kind by experiencing an enhanced sense of commitment to the company and to their jobs.

The utilization philosophy focuses employees' thinking on efficiency. It highlights the importance of the short term and of doing things as expeditiously as possible. It conveys to employees the importance of avoiding unnecessary expenditures and cutting costs as quickly and drastically as possible. The employees respond by developing a mind-set of efficiency and doing everything possible to save—whether it be time, money, or other resources.

The facilitation philosophy has a substantially different impact on employees than either of the other two philosophies. It conveys the message that it is important to be creative, to be different, to be willing to think things that have never been thought before. The company gives its employees the freedom to explore and to succeed or fail. The employees respond with a creative mind-set.

Alternative Behaviors

Although the three human resource philosophies and their accompanying policies and practices elicit many specific behaviors from employees, these behaviors or behavioral inclinations tend, in general, to fall into three broad categories.

Under the accumulation philosophy, employees are inclined to behave more intelligently. Reflecting their mind-set of commitment, they are willing to think about how their jobs can be done better for the benefit of themselves and their company. Because they know that the company is committed to them, employees tend to be forthcoming with ideas, even if the implementation of those ideas would result in the elimination of their present jobs. In this organizational environment, doing things right is paramount.

Consistent with the mind-set of efficiency, the utilization philosophy induces the behavior of working harder (faster). Because of the short-term orientation of this philosophy, it becomes imperative that jobs be done as rapidly as possible. A major focus here is maximizing speed and efficiency.

In contrast, the facilitation philosophy induces employees to behave differently. It stimulates and rewards such behaviors as looking for new products and services or new ways of producing existing products and services (even though the attempt might result in failure) rather than merely repeating exactly what was done yesterday.

Now back to the question posed at the start of this subsection: "How do companies and their managers go about choosing one of these three human resource management philosophies?" Based on the foregoing, the answer is, "It depends on what employee mind-set and behaviors are desired." Because the word *desired* may imply choosing a human resource philosophy based on personal preference rather than on the needs of the company, the response here might better be that the selection of the human resource philosophy depends on what the company needs from its employees.

COMPETITIVE STRATEGIES: BEATING THE COMPETITION

Determining what is needed from employees in terms of mind-sets and behaviors becomes the critical task of a company seeking to be systematic in effectively managing its human resources. Although companies traditionally define what they need from employees in terms of their technical skills and abilities to do the job itself, selecting a human resource management philosophy requires defining what is needed from employees in more generic, more encompassing terms. More broadly stated, *what is needed from employees depends on the company's competitive strategy.* For companies to succeed in today's extremely competitive environment, they must develop a strategy that will overcome their competitors and establish a position of competitive superiority. Pursuing a competitive strategy enables them to achieve this and, in so doing, makes it hard for any of their competitors to reestablish themselves as the leader in the industry. This will become more apparent as the three possible competitive strategies are described in the following subsections.

Cost-Cutting Competitive Strategy. The cost reducer strives to produce goods and service more cheaply than competitors. This type of organization stresses having efficient-scale facilities, pursuing cost reductions, and minimizing the expenses of production, services, selling, training, and advertising. Cost leaders try to supply a standard, no-frills, high-volume product. The structure is only moderately differentiated because the emphasis throughout is on following programs and plans. Integration is effected mainly through these programs. Power rests in the hands of the top executives and the designers of work-flow processes.

Quality-Enhancement Competitive Strategy. The quality enhancer attempts to produce and deliver goods and services with the highest possible quality. Because this type of organization recognizes that quality is a product of the total process, quality-enhancement efforts are targeted toward suppliers and customers as well as toward the organization itself. Suppliers are brought into the picture to ensure that they know how to produce quality products. If a particular supplier doesn't know how, then the organization itself trains the supplier in methods that will ensure high quality. The organization also solicits information from customers regarding what they want. It is the customers' desires and needs that drive the quality targets for the products or services the organization delivers.

For example, in manufacturing, quality targets will likely include fit and finish requirements and specifications unique to the customer. In this way, manufacturing organizations become like service organizations: They listen to what customers want. Conversely, nonmanufacturing organizations pursue quality enhancement through the same practices as do manufacturing organizations—by working on the quality of inputs and processes and by obtaining feedback from customers.

Regardless of the type of organization, then, quality enhancement depends on close cooperation not only among all segments of the organization but within the industry chain in order to ensure that the desired products and services are delivered to the customer, when the customer wants them, and that they meet the customer's specifications. In many respects, with quality enhancement, the distinction between manufacturing and nonmanufacturing organizations becomes very blurred.

Interestingly, American managers are learning that the best way to reduce cost is by pursuing a quality-enhancement strategy. According to George Fisher, CEO of Motorola:

> 'Americans used to fall into the trap that high quality costs more. . . . But high quality and low cost go hand in hand.' That's because good quality reduces the so-called hidden plant: people, floor space, and equipment used for nothing but finding and fixing things that should have been done right the first time. This typically represents 25% to 35% of total production costs.
>
> This lesson hit home for Fisher in 1982, when he directed a pivotal push to crack the Japanese telecommunications market, then rigorously protected. His team developed a pager that met the exacting demands of Nippon Telegraph & Telephone Corp. It was produced to quality standards at least five times better than Motorola's U.S. pager. But it turned out to be more profitable. Motorola now holds a leading share of the Japanese paging market. (Therrien 1989: 114)

Innovative Competitive Strategy. In the innovative organization, groups of highly trained specialists from a variety of areas typically work together intensively to design and produce complex and rapidly changing products. Representatives from the research, marketing, and production departments collaborate face-to-face and, via mutual adjustment, coordinate their contributions. A high degree of differentiation prevails as people with different skills, goals, and time horizons work together. Frequent meetings, the integration of personnel, committees, and other liaison devices are used to ensure effective collaboration. Power is decentralized because much of it resides with the technocrats and scientists responsible for innovation. Authority is thus situational and based on expertise. There are few bureaucratic rules or standard procedures since these are too confining and would in any event rapidly become obsolete. Sensitive information-gathering systems are developed for analyzing the environment, and vertical and horizontal communications are open and frequent.

MATCHING PHILOSOPHY WITH COMPETITIVE STRATEGY

From the descriptions of these three competitive strategies, a philosophy of human resource management can be selected. The manager bases the choice on what mind-set and behaviors are needed from the employees.

The accumulation philosophy is a good choice for companies pursuing the quality-enhancement strategy. The success of this approach depends on employees' doing the right things right. Because in many cases, employees are the ones who are most knowledgeable about their own jobs, quality-enhancement benefits from the ideas of employees who are working smarter and are committed to the company.

The utilization philosophy is a good choice for companies pursuing a cost-cutting competitive strategy. The success of this strategy depends on minimizing costs. Not spending money on training and development and being able to lay employees off at will also help to minimize human resource management costs.

Because of the characteristics of the facilitation philosophy, it is a good choice for companies pursuing an innovative competitive strategy. The success of this strategy depends on employees' generating new ideas and working and thinking differently. Companies that hope to pursue successfully a strategy of innovation must make it a practice to assure their employees that occasional failure is to be expected and will not be punished. Creating an atmosphere in which employees constantly think creatively helps guarantee a steady flow of new ideas for products and services.

Table 4.1 shows the mind-sets and behaviors that are elicited by the three philosophies of human resource management as well as the relationships between these philosophies and the three competitive strategies.

Table 4.1 Fitting Philosophies of Human Resource Management with Competitive Strategies

Human Resource Philosophy	Employee Mind-Set	Employee Behavior	Competive Strategy
Accumulation	Commitment	Working smarter	Quality enhancement
Utilization	Efficiency	Working harder	Cost cutting
Facilitation	Creativity	Working differently	Innovation

SUMMARY

With this general introduction to systematic human resource management, the line manager is ready to select the appropriate human resource practices. In keeping with the focus of this book, the next chapter addresses only the quality-enhancement strategy.

References

Bluestone, M. 1989. "Quality Means a Whole New Approach to Manufacturing." *Business Week* (June 8): 131–143.

Fowler, E. W. 1989. "A New Post: The Office of Quality." *New York Times* (June 15): D12.

Main, J. 1990. "How to Win the Baldrige Award." *Fortune* (Apr. 23): 101–116.

Murray, T. J. 1989. "Rethinking the Factory." *Business Month* (July): 39.

Schuler, R. S. 1988. "Personnel and Human Resource Management: Choices and Organizational Strategy." In *Personnel and Human Resource Management,* ed. R. Schuler, S. Youngblood, and V. Huber, 24–39. St. Paul, Minn.: West Publishing.

Schuler, R. S. 1990. "Repositioning the Human Resource Function: Transformation or Demise?" *Academy of Management Executive* 3 (no. 3): 49–60.

Simmons, J. 1989. "The Painful Reeducation of a Company Man." *Business Monthly* (Oct.): 76–79.

Therrien, L. 1989. "The Rival Japan Respects." *Business Week* (Nov. 13): 112–116.

Wagel, William H., Feldman, D., Fritz, N. R., and Blocklyn, P. L. 1988. "Quality—The Bottom Line." *Personnel* (July): 30–42.

Chapter 5

CHOICES IN HUMAN RESOURCE MANAGEMENT

Once the overall philosophy of human resource management is chosen (based on whether the organization is pursuing a competitive strategy of cost cutting, quality enhancement, or innovation), the line manager needs to select a more specific set of human resource practices. Doing this requires further refinement of our systematic approach to human resource management. Because quality enhancement is our focus, the remainder of our discussion applies primarily to practices that complement the quality-enhancement competitive strategy.

LINKING HUMAN RESOURCE PRACTICES WITH COMPETITIVE STRATEGY

Managing human resources by the type of competitive strategy the organization is pursuing is the essence of "linking human resource practices with competitive strategy." And central to this approach is the fact that different competitive strategies require different employee behaviors and attitudes, which means that the line manager must pay close attention to the selection of human resource management activities because different activities are likely to elicit different employee behaviors and attitudes. This assertion is based on two premises: (1) human resource management activities are basically cues, stimuli, and reinforcements for employees; and (2) individuals (factoring out any limitations on their abilities) act on and respond to information, cues, reinforcements, and rewards (or punishments) in the environment. Thus, line managers must know the different employee behaviors and attitudes that are required and then manage accordingly.

In the following section, we identify the different behaviors and attitudes needed to pursue a quality-enhancement competitive strategy and then match them with the different human resource practices. Doing this requires that we examine the various types of human resource practices associated with each human resource activity. After this, we consider in detail what it means for a line manager to manage human resources systematically for quality enhancement.

QUALITY ENHANCEMENT AND REQUIRED ROLE BEHAVIORS

At Xerox, former CEO David Kearns defines quality as "being right the first time every time." The implications for managing people are significant. According to James Houghton, chairman of Corning Glass Works, his company's "total quality approach" is about people. At Corning, good ideas for product improvement often come from employees, and in order to carry through on their ideas, Corning workers form short-lived "corrective-action teams" to solve specific problems. For example:

> Employees [also] give their supervisors written 'method improvement requests,' which differ from ideas tossed into the traditional suggestion box in that they get a prompt formal review so the employees aren't left wondering about their fate. In the company's Erwin Ceramics plant, a maintenance employee suggested substituting one flexible tin mold for an array of fixed molds that shape the wet ceramic product baked into catalytic converters for auto exhausts. (Wiggenhorn 1990: 74)

At Corning, then, quality improvement involves getting employees committed to quality and continual improvement. Although policy statements emphasizing the "total quality approach" are valuable, they are also followed up with specific human resource practices: Feedback systems are in place, teamwork is permitted and facilitated, decision making and responsibility are a part of each employee's job description, and job classifications are flexible.

As described in Chapter 2, quality improvement often means changing the processes of production in ways that require workers to be more involved and more flexible. As jobs change, so must job-classification systems. At Brunswick's Mercury Marine division, the number of job classifications was reduced from 126 to 12. This has permitted greater flexibility in the use of production processes and employees. Machine operators have gained greater opportunities to learn new skills along with training in quality-improvement techniques. They inspect their own work and perform preventive maintenance in addition to running the machines. It is because of human resource practices such as these that employees become committed to the organization and hence are willing to give more. This is the essence of the accumulation philosophy and the employee mind-set needed to implement a quality program, as described in Chapter 4. But we must now move beyond the necessary employee mind-set and examine the employee behaviors required for quality improvement.

The profile of employee behaviors necessary for companies pursuing a strategy of quality enhancement consists of:

1. Relatively repetitive and predictable behaviors

2. A longer-term or intermediate focus

3. A high amount of cooperative, interdependent behavior

4. A high concern for quality of output

5. A modest concern for quantity of output

6. A high concern for process (how the goods or services are made or delivered)

7. A low level of risk-taking activity

8. Commitment to the organization's goals

Because quality enhancement typically involves greater employee commitment and effectiveness, fewer employees may be needed to produce the same level of output. As customers perceive quality rising, demand may also rise, yet this demand can be met with proportionately fewer employees than previously. Thanks to automation and a cooperative work force, Toyota is producing about 3.5 million vehicles a year with twenty-five thousand production workers—about the same number as in 1966, when it was producing 1 million vehicles. The size of the work force is reduced not only because workers are more effective but also because fewer workers are needed to repair the rejects resulting from poor quality.

TYPOLOGY OF HRM PRACTICES

When deciding what human resource practices they should use to execute the quality strategy, line managers can choose from six human resource practice "menus." Each of the menus concerns a different aspect of human resource management (Schuler 1988): planning, staffing, appraisal, compensation, training and development, and labor-management relations. All of these are practices over which line managers have varying degrees of influence and control.

These menus are summarized in Figure 5.1. Readers should note that each of the choices runs along a continuum. We describe these practices in the following subsections; then, in the next section, we identify which practices help implement quality enhancement.

PLANNING MENU[1]

The line manager can make several planning choices. The first choice in the planning menu is the extent or degree of formalization. This ranges from informal to formal. The more formal the planning activity becomes, the more attention and concern shown to explicit planning procedures and activities for human resource management. One result of formal planning is Hewlett-Packard's willingness and ability to state and support its human resource policy of "not to be a hire and fire company."

A second choice in the planning menu is the degree of tightness. A tight rather than a loose link between the human resource planning and corporate planning facilitates formal planning. The articulation of this necessity is most evident in the recent discussions of corporate strategic management and human resource management. However, since organizations can choose not to have a tight link between corporate planning and human resource planning, the degree of tightness is another critical choice in planning.

A third choice is the planning time horizon. Companies can choose to plan only for the very short-term human resource needs or to extend themselves further into the future. Longer-term time horizons are preferred, since a company's human resource characteristics may be slow in changing. Nevertheless, since a company's environment may be volatile, short-term responses and adjustments by the company may be required. Thus, companies may benefit from some long-range planning considerations with shorter-range flexibility.

The next two choices relate more directly to job analysis and job design. A critical choice in job analysis is choosing the degree of explicitness. On the one hand, job dimensions and requisite skill and behavior requirements can be detailed precisely, and on the other hand, they can be described in general terms and with more emphasis on the results expected of the job incumbent.

---

[1]This section is adapted from R. S. Schuler, "Human Resource Management: Choices and Organizational Strategy," in *Readings in Personnel and Human Resource Management*, Third Edition, edited by Randall S. Schuler, Stuart A. Youngblood, and Vandra L. Huber. (St. Paul, Minn.: West, 1988), 24–39. Used by permission.

Figure 5.1   HUMAN RESOURCE MANAGEMENT PRACTICE MENUS: FACILITATING COMPETITIVE STRATEGIES

Planning Choices

Informal <————> Formal
Loose <————> Tight
Short-term <————> Long-term
Implicit job analysis <————> Explicit job analysis
Job simplification <————> Job enrichment
Low employee involvement <————> High employee involvement

Staffing Choices

External sources <————> Internal sources
Narrow paths <————> Broad paths
Single ladder <————> Multiple ladders
Explicit criteria <————> Implicit criteria
Limited orientation <————> Extensive orientation
Closed procedures <————> Open procedures

Appraisal Choices

Loose integration <————> Tight integration
Behavioral criteria <————> Results criteria
Purposes: development, remedial, maintenance
Low employee participation <————> High employee participation
Short-term criteria <————> Long-term criteria
Individual criteria <————> Group criteria

Compensation Choices

High base salaries <————> Low base salaries
Internal equity <————> External equity
Many perks <————> Few perks
Standard, fixed package <————> Flexible package
Low participation <————> High participation
No incentives <————> Many incentives
Short-term incentives <————> Long-term incentives
No employment security <————> High employment security

Training and Development Choices

Short-term <————> Long-term
Narrow application <————> Broad application
Emphasis on productivity <————> Emphasis on quality of work life
Spontaneous, unplanned <————> Planned, systematic
Individual orientation <————> Group orientation
Low participation <————> High participation

Labor-Management Relationship Choices

Traditional <————> Nontraditional
Adversarial <————> Cooperative

Job design focuses on the degree of breadth of the jobs. With breadth ranging from very narrow to very broad, companies have a great deal of choice in designing their jobs. More broadly designed enriched jobs provide for more employee autonomy, skill usage, and identification with the product itself. More narrowly designed simplified jobs limit these employee/task attributes.

A final choice in planning is choosing the degree of employee involvement. Employees can be involved in many workplace decisions ranging from making quality improvement suggestions to deciding on their own benefit packages.

STAFFING MENU

The line manager can make several staffing choices. The first choice on the staffing menu involves the source from which to recruit applicants. At one extreme, candidates are chosen internally, from other departments in the company and other levels in the organizational hierarchy; at the other extreme, external sources (employment agencies, schools, etc.) are used. The options are limited for entry-level jobs, but this decision is very important for other jobs. Recruiting internally means a policy of promotion from within. Although this policy serves as an effective reward, it commits an organization to providing training and career-development opportunities to ensure higher performance. Companies such as UPS, McDonald's, and Procter & Gamble strongly believe that their promotion-from-within policy is a key to their success.

A second choice focuses on the breadth of career paths. The broader the paths that are established, the greater the opportunity for employees to acquire skills relevant to many functional areas, gain exposure in more parts of the organization, and possibly, get promoted. However, the time frame for the acquisition of many skills is likely to be longer than would be required for the acquisition of a more limited skill base; thus, promotion may be quicker under a policy of narrow career paths, although an employee's career opportunities may be limited over the long run.

Another staffing choice facing managers is whether to establish one or more promotion ladders. Having multiple career ladders increases the opportunities for employees to be promoted while allowing them to stay within a given technical specialty without their necessarily having to assume managerial responsibilities. Establishing only one promotion ladder enhances the value of promotions and increases the competition for them.

The criteria used in deciding whom to promote are part and parcel of a promotion system. The choice is whether the criteria for promotion are explicit or implicit. The more explicit the criteria, the less adaptable the promotion system is to exceptions and changing circumstances. What the company loses in flexibility the individual may gain in clarity. With implicit criteria, there is greater flexibility to move employees around and to develop them more broadly.

The socialization process is also important to the staffing of organizations. With minimal socialization, organizations establish few rules or procedures designed to immerse individuals completely in the organizational culture and practices. Although this approach is probably easier and cheaper than providing for maximum socialization, it is likely to result in more limited psychological attachment and commitment to the organization.

A final choice involves the degree of openness in the staffing procedures. With more open procedures, there is more likely to be job posting for internal recruitment, self-nomination for promotion, and involvement in assessment centers for promotion. With less open and more secretive procedures, employee involvement in selection decisions is more limited but the decisions are made faster.

APPRAISAL MENU

Because the performance-appraisal system has many components, the first choice on the menu involves deciding on the degree of integration of these components. This integration includes the following factors:

1. Establishing the link between job analysis and the performance-appraisal forms and criteria

2. Identifying who can provide relevant appraisal data regarding the identified criteria

3. Developing and coordinating the appraisal forms for the desired purpose

4. Gathering and combining the various sources of performance data as expeditiously as possible

5. Communicating the results to the employees in a timely fashion, thus allowing an opportunity for appeal

6. Ensuring that the results are utilized for their intended purposes (such as compensation) and are still relevant (valid) for the employees and jobs

Point 6 brings the process full circle with continual monitoring and adjustment as necessary. When companies do not engage in continual monitoring and adjustment, they establish a loose integration; if they do, the integration is much tighter.

Another appraisal choice is whether to evaluate behaviors or results. Appraisal of behaviors focuses on "how" things are done, whereas appraisal of results focuses on "how many" things are done. Appraisal forms often reflect these focuses: Behavioral-anchored rating scales (BARS) focus on behaviors, and management by objectives (MBO) focuses on results. However, it is possible to use both formats with equal emphasis.

The third choice involves identifying the general purpose of the appraisal. Appraisal can be used to develop employee performance (DAP), maintain it (MAP), or improve it (RAP). DAP (developmental performance appraisal) is future-oriented and focuses heavily on spotting employees who are likely to do well in more challenging jobs and providing developmental opportunities to help ensure their success. In contrast, RAP (remedial performance appraisal) is more present-oriented and seeks to spot current performance deficiencies, analyze the reasons for them, and then design programs to eliminate them. MAP (maintenance performance appraisal) is concerned with maintaining current levels of employee performance.

A fourth choice centers on the degree of employee participation in the performance-appraisal process. Companies can choose to have employees involved in all the components of the system, only some of them, or none. For example, line managers can involve employees in writing their own job descriptions, identifying critical job dimensions, and then developing examples of effective and ineffective performance in each of these dimensions. Conversely, employees can be excluded from active participation in any of these tasks.

Another choice for companies in appraising employees is whether to emphasize short- or long-term criteria. Short-term criteria are defined as having a time horizon of twelve months or less.

A final choice is whether the appraisal process should give more weight to individual criteria or group criteria. For instance, if collective action is required to get results, group criteria are more appropriate in appraising employees' performance.

COMPENSATION MENU

As with the preceding human resource functions, the compensation menu offers the manager many choices. One of the first of these involves determining the level of base pay. Companies must decide on an hourly or a salaried base, and they must focus on internal or external equity. Another critical choice involves the number of perquisites.

Companies can also choose to offer either a standard package of direct and indirect compensation or a total compensation package consisting of a mix of components of different values, such as is found in flexible pay programs. By offering more flexibility in compensation, companies are determining the degree of employee participation in that compensation. Because employees are the best judge of what they value, permitting a high level of employee participation and considerable flexibility makes a great deal of sense. Employees can also participate in other aspects of compensation, job- or skill-based evaluations, and salary-increase decisions. If participation is allowed, however, the company must be prepared to furnish relevant pay information and abandon the practice of pay secrecy.

Another compensation choice is whether to provide incentives and, if so, whether they should be short- or long-term-based. For example, companies can offer cash or stock to reward the achievement of short-term goals (i.e., goals having a time horizon of twelve months or less) based on such criteria as output, sales, or return on capital. In contrast, they can offer incentive stock options (ISOs) or stock appreciation rights (SARs) to reward the achievement of long-term goals.

A final choice in compensating employees involves whether to offer guarantees regarding employment security. This choice is perhaps one of the most critical and one that some highly successful companies seem to favor. It appears that employment security encourages employee suggestions for improvement, a longer-term orientation on the part of employees, and greater loyalty and commitment to the company.

TRAINING AND DEVELOPMENT MENU

As with the other human resource functions, the training and development menu also contains many options from which the manager can choose. The first menu choice involves the extent to which programs focus on the employees' short- versus long-term needs. To the extent that emphasis is on the short term, there will be more training programs and fewer development programs.

Although training may be short-term-oriented, it can be offered to improve employees' skills for their present job or to enable them to learn skills more relevant for other jobs in the organization. Similarly, the choice with development involves the breadth of the program. This choice is influenced by whether the company focuses its human resource management effort primarily on its need for improved quality of work life or improved productivity. Although the two are not mutually exclusive, where the primary emphasis is placed constitutes a training and development choice.

Another critical choice involves the degree to which the training and development activities are planned, formalized, and systematically linked to the other human resource functions. At issue here is whether training and development are delivered to individuals as individuals or as members of a cohort group. Membership in a cohortlike group can facilitate both the socialization process and the training and development activities. It can also buffer individual members against company stress and time pressures as well as encourage improved performance.

A final choice in training and development involves the extent of employee participation. For example, managers can allow employees to identify their preferred career paths and goals as well as their own training needs (which employees might ordinarily be unwilling to identify), or they may choose to limit participation in training and development activities. We suggest that the choice in this case (as well as in the case of all the other human resource practices) can be made based on the employee characteristics needed by the organization, in keeping with its strategy.

LABOR-MANAGEMENT MENU

The major choice in the labor-management menu involves the extent to which a manager chooses to have a traditional, adversarial relationship with the union(s) representing the employees or a nontraditional, cooperative relationship. Increasingly, organizations such as Ford Motor Company recognize that a cooperative union-management relationship is essential to their pursuit of quality.

HUMAN RESOURCE PRACTICE CHOICES FOR QUALITY ENHANCEMENT

Now that we have presented the human resource practice choices and the employee behaviors needed for quality enhancement as a background, the following subsections offer a detailed discussion of the most appropriate choices for the line manager to make.

PLANNING PRACTICE CHOICES

As discussed in Chapter 4, it is very important for managers to be systematic in the implementation of human resource practices. Since all the human resource practices send important signals and reinforcements to the employees, these signals and reinforcements must be consistent in order to help align employees' behaviors with the quality-enhancement effort. Rarely is this consistency attained merely by using common sense, and rarely is it attained without a carefully considered plan. Because human resource planning is really the activity that mobilizes, articulates, and coordinates the rest of the human resource practices, human resource planning for quality enhancement must be systematic and well thought out. It must be formalized by managers so that the right practices are put in place in order to influence the desired behaviors. The planning practice choices consistent with a quality-enhancement strategy include some degree of formality, a longer-term framework, explicit job analysis, some job enrichment, and a high level of employee involvement.

The rationale for these choices is that: (1) the process of systematically aligning human resource practices with a quality-enhancement strategy takes time and depends on the resources and skills involved; (2) a longer-term mind-set is required of employees if they are to perform effectively in a quality program; and (3) employee commitment comes from the organization's establishing a longer-term relationship with employees. Thus, the human resource planning process is longer-term-oriented.

Achieving quality means doing the right things correctly over and over. It also means having everyone doing this. To facilitate this process, clear and explicit task descriptions can be written to convey task duties and processes. In turn, developing explicit task descriptions can facilitate the process of job rotation. With explicit task descriptions, employees can move from job to job (learning the entire system and enjoying some job variety) and quickly know what is expected. To facilitate an even greater degree of understanding and enhanced employee commitment, the employees can be involved in the preparation of the task descriptions. To ease the manager's job of assigning employees to different tasks, organizations reduce the number of job classifications, which, in turn, minimizes the issue of having better- and higher-paying jobs and eliminates the status differences (and pay differences) that come with having numerous job classes and titles.

Consistent with this theme of employee commitment and involvement are job enrichment and the opportunity to own a greater part of a total job. Job enrichment offers more skill variety, task identification, significance, autonomy, and feedback. Employees respond with greater satisfaction, dedication, and involvement. They are successful in these newly enriched jobs to the extent that they have been trained adequately and then selected for the enriched jobs on the basis of their skills and ability to perform the work. Job enrichment is not always necessary to get employee commitment, however. McDonald's illustrates that other human resource practices, such as orientation and clear and extensive job descriptions, can elicit high-quality service and that commitment can be achieved by selecting employees who are at either the beginning or the end of their careers (Tansik 1990; Schneider 1990).

STAFFING PRACTICE CHOICES

The staffing practice choices consistent with a quality-enhancement strategy include an emphasis on internal sources of recruitment, narrower job-progression paths, multiple ladders of career progression, explicit criteria for job analysis and selection, extensive orientation, and relatively open procedures for recruiting and selection. Together, these practices create a mind-set of commitment and loyalty as well as a desire to improve the quality of the service or product. As such, they are part of the proper staffing system so critical in quality enhancement.

> According to Marcia Hyatt, director of staffing and employee development, at Minnegasco Inc., a utility company in Minnesota, two major components in the creation of a quality service system are proper selection and orientation of front-line employees.
>
> Minnegasco's front-line employee selection program is based on KSA analysis—i.e., identification of the knowledge, skills, and abilities workers must possess to perform their jobs well. To identify essential KSAs, Hyatt says, employers should study those front-line workers who are already excellent service providers. Once the necessary KSAs are identified, job interviewers should apply them in their hiring decisions.
>
> Proper orientation gives new service providers a structured transition into their new work environment, and instills a positive attitude that they will pass on to customers, Hyatt maintains. Moreover, she adds, a proper orientation allows the company an opportunity to impart its service philosophy.
>
> To make orientation a success, Hyatt recommends that employers:
>
> • Plan in advance. Orientation activities such as a benefits review, introductions to co-workers, and training in basic job tasks should be listed on a checklist. Managers should check off each activity as it is accomplished to ensure that orientation is complete.
>
> • Communicate expectations. Tell new workers how the company expects them to interact with customers, explain how much decision-making authority the worker has when solving service problems, and review customer expectations.
>
> • After employees have spent some time on the job, hold a one-day orientation workshop where top executives can communicate company values, such as quality service and teamwork. ("Cultivating Quality Service," 1989: 392)

Another important component of quality staffing is employee participation and employees' ability to select themselves into or out of the program if it involves a change in the way things have been done. A critical aspect of implementing quality-enhancement programs, as with any change effort, is the realization that not all employees will want to make the change. (Lack of ability on the part of many of the employees is to be expected, and this becomes a training concern.) Thus, the organization needs to allow employees to select themselves *out* of the program (and thus perhaps out of the organization as well). Everyone on board must be an active participant in the quality program. Self-selection out of the organization is an important event and is facilitated by the aggressive use of outplacement. This helps foster the commitment mind-set of the remaining employees and conveys to them that change is not something to be feared because of job loss or other punitive actions on the part of the organization.

For job applicants who have yet to be selected, clear and explicit job descriptions, as mentioned by Marcia Hyatt at Minnegasco, are useful. They provide potential employees with specific information about the job, which will facilitate self-selection. They also provide the manager with information on what to ask or look for in interviewing applicants. Although selection tests could be developed based on these job descriptions, it is more consistent with a quality program and with an attitude of employee trust and loyalty to select applicants primarily on the basis of how well they fit with the company rather than with the job itself. Any lack of ability can be overcome by training. If testing is done, it might involve a job sample to see whether applicants like both the job and the work environment. Testing can also give the manager and the other employees an opportunity to see whether applicants are motivated to work (do they have the desire and the right mind-set to be committed to the work and to constant improvement?). Having current employees recommend their friends and/or relatives may also increase the likelihood of success in selection. But even in the best-case scenario, a manager should be happy to achieve an overall success rate of 70 percent with his or her job hires.

Employees who are unlikely to be successful must be identified early (within an initial ninety-day period of employment at will). Once this time period has elapsed, employees should be dismissed only by a jury of their peers. Selection out of the organization (involuntarily) can best be done by the employees themselves. An example of this approach comes from Ensoniq, a two-hundred-person company west of Philadelphia that makes high-quality musical keyboards and hearing aids. At Ensoniq, rules covering dismissals and reprimand punishments are unambiguously and rigorously applied; peers enforce the rules and handle all appeals/exceptions. Employees at Ensoniq no longer say, "The manager fired X." They say, "X fired himself [or herself]." This reflects trust in the employees' judgment and responsibility on the part of both management and the employees and enhances the employees' level of commitment and feelings of ownership in the company. (Appendix A presents a more complete description of the role of managers in Ensoniq's change to high quality.)

PERFORMANCE-APPRAISAL PRACTICE CHOICES

In the area of performance appraisal, the major practice choices that facilitate quality enhancement were presented earlier in the chapter, in Figure 5.1. These choices include an emphasis on behavioral criteria as well as on skills development and improvement, employee participation in the design and administration of reviews, a focus on short- and longer-term criteria, and an emphasis on individual and group criteria. Together, these choices create a mind-set of commitment and loyalty as well as a desire to provide quality products and services and to improve on quality continually. Some examples may serve to illuminate the rationale for these choices.

Quality often results from employees' performing in ways that have been identified as being good examples of effective, high-quality behavior. Particularly in the service business, where the customer is the consuming and paying public, certain behaviors can be identified as embodying the essence of customer (quality) service. In this situation, managers must be sure that employees are aware of these behaviors and repeatedly engage in them with each customer—an outcome that can be facilitated by the development of detailed examples of desired behaviors and performance-appraisal forms that indicate the value of different levels of these behaviors (this enables the manager to use the results of appraisal for development and even for making compensation decisions).

When National Car Rental decided to improve customer service as a marketing strategy to gain competitive advantage, it changed to a very detailed performance-appraisal form that shows behavioral examples. These examples are developed with extensive input from employees, and in National's case, this activity was performed entirely by line managers. Figure 5.2 illustrates the behaviors that reflect various levels of quality for an office representative providing customer service.

This National Car Rental behavioral example of effective customer-service performance illustrates what many organizations, especially larger ones, do in implementing a quality-enhancement strategy. Having a detailed

Figure 5.2   OFFICE-REPRESENTATIVE APPRAISAL: DEALING WITH CUSTOMERS

TASK: CUSTOMER SERVICE

(The job of customer-service representatives [CSRs] is to build customer relations through the concern extended to customers, which recognizes them as individuals and makes their lives more pleasant by resolving their problems and making them more comfortable and at ease. It is the behavior demonstrated by CSRs that influences how positive customers feel about National Car Rental. It is also how we present ourselves and convey our excitement about our work and our confidence in both ourselves and our coworkers in delivering the best car-rental service possible.)

CSR name: _____   Task weight: _____%

In the space provided below, please describe your observations of the CSR you are evaluating. Be certain that what you write are descriptions of what you have observed the employee doing during the performance period. Use words such as *enters, smiles, inserts, orders, puts,* etc., to describe CSR actions. Once you have documented your observations, compare your documentation with the five rating levels below and, on the rating scale at the end of the form, check the rating that best indicates the employee's level of performance.

Documentation: _____

_____

_____

_____

_____

_____

5. **Well above standard:** Greets customers with a smile while making eye contact; anticipates customers' problems and provides whatever is necessary to make customers more comfortable and coworkers more effective; asks customers what they need and tells them that we are there to serve them; checks with customers to determine whether the car was satisfactory and makes a note of problems with the car to give to service; makes the best possible presentation of self—uniform is neat, clean, and tidy; explains rental processing procedures to customers in detail; quickly communicates positive feedback to coworkers and discusses concerns in private; keeps his or her composure even when customers are irate with the CSR and the company; tells customers about the organization and what makes it a good place to work.

Figure 5.2 (*Cont.*)

4. **Above standard:** Acknowledges customers by using a greeting when they are standing in line behind the customer being served; makes eye contact upon greeting; recognizes changes and/or contributions of coworkers and follows up with specific compliments; checks to be certain that customers have been heard accurately by saying, "Did I understand you to say that . . . ?"; makes positive comments about the organization and its employees to customers; tells people over the phone what he or she is going to do for them before putting them on hold; makes certain that customers understand what is expected before an activity/procedure is to begin by asking them whether they fully understand before proceeding; makes suggestions or initiates methods to improve organizational performance; encourages the work of coworkers by letting them know when they have done a good job; works with coworkers to ensure cooperative, not competitive, efforts; makes time to help train new CSRs in rental processing.

3. **Standard:** Listens to customers' needs; apologizes for car problems and lets customers know that the CSR will do his or her best to respond to their needs; greets customers over the phone by telling them to whom they are talking and asking how the CSR may be of help; says "please" and "thank you" when interacting with customers; is well groomed and careful about person hygiene; wears clean clothing that meets dress-code standards; gives directions by using a map to show customers how to get to where they wish to go; explains to customers specifically what is in the rental agreement in ways that they can understand; uses customers' name (with "Mr.," "Mrs.," or "Ms.") when addressing them; demonstrates respect for property and equipment by ensuring that equipment is properly taken care of and public areas are clean and tidy; greets customers before customers greet them; asks customers what problems they may have had with the car; makes suggestions about ways to improve customer and service performance; tells coworkers when they have done a good job.

2. **Below standard:** Does not greet others or attempt to make them feel good about our organization; does not ask how he or she may be of help or service to the organization; does not address customers by name when talking to them; hair is neither clean nor well groomed; does not tell others when they have done exceptional work; is not specific with customers in explaining the cost of coverages or the effect and coverage of waivers; does not use a greeting when answering the phone; puts customers on hold without telling them that they will be put on hold or why they are being put on hold.

Figure 5.2 (*Cont.*)

1. **Well below standard:** Does not listen to others—interrupts customers; closes the station with customers waiting; does not greet others with a smile or make eye contact; hair is not clean; makeup is overdone; uniform is soiled or does not comply with the dress code; makes unfavorable comments about the organization to customers or coworkers; does not support the efforts of coworkers; does not monitor the work area to ensure counter is clean and equipment is well maintained, does not explain rental procedure to customers or call them by name; discusses customers' problems in public; does not make positive comments when possible; puts people on hold without telling them why this is being done or hangs up on customers; complains about the organization to improve the situation; discusses coworkers problems' with customers; takes credit for others' work; uses abusive language with customers; criticizes coworkers for providing excellent customer service.

RATING:

☐	☐	☐	☐	☐
Well below	Below	Standard	Above	Well above

Source: Adapted from R. W. Beatty, "Competitive Human Resource Advantage through the Strategic Management of Performance," *Human Resource Planning* 12, no. 3 (1989): 185–186. Used by permission.

written description of the desired behaviors makes it easier to convey the organization's expectations to many employees.

This entire approach, however, is in contrast to the Deming approach to quality and performance appraisal. Using the Deming approach to quality management, managers may focus on the relationship between the employee and the production system. "Appraisal," as such, becomes a determination of whether the employee is performing within the system or outside the system. (See Chapter 2 for a discussion of "within the system" versus "outside the system.")

In the case of employees performing outside the system on the low end, the review process is an opportunity to uncover the special causes of that poor performance. If the poor performance cannot be attributed to the work system, then remedial action is called for. This could include counseling, training, and if necessary, reassignment or outplacement. In the case of employees performing outside the system on the high end, the review process is an opportunity to learn. These employees are consistently "beating the system." Hence, learning their personal system may provide clues as to how to improve both the overall organizational system and the quality of output of all employees. This is no time to rein in such high performers.

For the vast majority of employees functioning within the system (this category should include 99 percent of the total), the review becomes an opportunity to exchange views on the work system as well as to review performance and plan for personal growth and career development. Employee feedback on managerial behaviors and system problems/opportunities can flow from these reviews, and managers can probe employees for ideas while also coaching them on expected behaviors and areas needing improvement.

Although a form like the one used by National Car Rental (Figure 5.2) might prove helpful in coaching desired behaviors, Deming would argue against using it for determining rankings or compensation, on the grounds that review sessions should be divorced from compensation discussions and should never involve ranking employees. Others agree that it is most important to separate the specter of quantitative evaluation from the process of appraisal for the purposes of reward or punishment. When management shows its trust, employees will do their best and respond responsibly. If they are falling short, it is because of problems in the system, which can be solved for everyone's benefit. Performance-appraisal sessions then become an opportunity to spot systems problems and to identify the employees' development needs. An example of a performance-appraisal form that follows the Deming approach is the one used by Ensoniq (see Figure 5.3).

Figure 5.3   ENSONIQ CORP.: HOURLY AND SALARIED REVIEW FORM

Employee: _____

Supervisor: _____

Employee's social security number: ___ ___ ___ - ___ ___ - ___ ___ ___ ___

Department/position: _____

Review due: _____ Date reviewed: _____

The following are things you have done well:

_____

_____

_____

_____

_____

_____

The following are areas where improvement would help your overall position in the company:

_____

_____

_____

_____

_____

_____

_____

Employee comments: _____

_____

_____

_____

_____

_____

_____

Figure 5.3 (*Cont.*)

Employee's signature: _____ Date: _____

Supervisor's signature: _____ Date: _____

Manager's signature: _____ Date: _____

PERFORMANCE-REVIEW DEFINITIONS

Use the following list as ideas to generate appraisal topics for discussion.

- **Analytical ability**: To what extent does the employee develop and consider alternatives and relevant factors, demonstrate and evaluate skills, utilize available data and information, divide problems into elemental parts and reason from a perception of the parts and interrelations of a subject, and assess the probable impact?

- **Attitude**: How does the employee represent Ensoniq in his or her approach to assignments?

- **Commitment**: To what extent does the employee strive to do a good job, with concern for the company's well-being?

- **Communication**: Does the employee openly exchange information in a timely manner, know whom to keep informed, listen and understand, use confidential information with discretion, and write and speak in a clear and concise manner?

- **Cost awareness**: To what extent is the employee aware of costs, waste, and proper utilization of financial and human resources?

- **Creativity**: To what extent is the employee imaginative and original?

- **Customer responsiveness**: How well does the employee meet the needs of the customer or potential customer?

- **Decision making/judgment**: To what extent does the employee understand what decisions he or she can and cannot make? Are the employee's decisions reasonable and sound?

- **Flexibility**: How effectively can the employee adjust to something new and different?

- **Focus**: Does the employee focus his or her efforts and activities?

- **Initiative**: To what extent does the employee predict and act rather than react to circumstances and events? Does the employee have the ability or instinct to initiate and follow through with a plan or task?

- **Motivating**: Does the employee recognize performance problems and give support to subordinates, and encourage self-development and recognize individual differences?

- **Leading**: Does the employee make effective decisions, initiate action, resolve conflict, take advantage of opportunities, take appropriate risks, accomplish objectives, and use his or her influence and power wisely?

Figure 5.3 (*Cont.*)

- **Organizing:** Does the employee define responsibilities, authority, and work relationships effectively; staff and train properly; delegate authority; and arrange and systematize in a coherent form?

- **Output:** What quantity of high-quality work does the employee produce? Is his or her work thorough? Does the employee check his or her work for mistakes?

- **Persuasiveness and sales ability:** How effective is the employee's influence on others, both within and outside Ensoniq? To what extent can the employee handle conflict and achieve agreement and acceptance?

- **Planning:** Does the employee define and analyze opportunities? Does the employee establish schedules, plans, and budgets and set goals? Does he or she have a specific aim or purpose in mind?

- **Resource management:** How well does the employee develop and manage forecasts and budgets? Does the employee select the right people for the right job? Does he or she utilize equipment for maximum output and effectively maintain and/or replace equipment as necessary?

- **Teamwork:** How well does the employee work with others, both within and outside Ensoniq? Does he or she support company and departmental plans, programs, policies, and procedures?

- **Technical capability/job knowledge:** To what extent does the employee know the what, how, and why with respect to the requirements for his or her position?

- **Training:** Does the employee provide effective on-the-job training?

- **Vendor relations:** How well does the employee work with vendors?

- **Tolerance:** To what extent does the employee recognize and respect the opinions, practices, and behaviors of others?

Other topics discussed:

_____

_____

_____

_____

_____

_____

_____

_____

Source: This form is adapted and used with permission from the Ensoniq Corp.

The Deming approach, however, need not be restricted to small to medium-sized companies such as Ensoniq. According to Donald E. Petersen, former chairman of the board of Ford Motor Company:

> Dr. Deming's influence continues to be strongly felt at Ford Motor Company and our commitment to improved quality is absolute. . . . His philosophy reflects our customer-driven approach to quality. . . . We meet with Dr. Deming at least once a month, and I personally discuss our progress on the quality front with him several times each year. . . . We are moving toward building a quality culture at Ford and the many changes that have been taking place here have their roots directly in Dr. Deming's teachings. (Serlen 1987: 19)

At both National Car Rental and Ensoniq, the focus of performance appraisal is on the long term as well as the short term. In the short term, employees need to exhibit the right behaviors. They must know, however, that doing so will promote their longer-term interest in having a job. Thus, it is important that performance appraisal be linked to the organization's overall strategy. Because quality enhancement is a central strategy, coordinating performance appraisal with it serves both the short- and long-term interests of the employees and the organization.

In these two companies, the focus seems to be on the individual rather than the group. A closer examination, however, suggests that they recognize the importance of group efforts and teamwork. In these examples, jobs are designed more around the individual than around teams. However, the employees are aware that their own success and that of their company depends on cooperation and teamwork. Thus, a mind-set of cooperation and teamwork prevails. If the technology facilitates a true team approach to job design, even the appearance of conflict between the individual and group focus disappears.

COMPENSATION PRACTICE CHOICES

As was illustrated in Figure 5.1, there are many compensation practice choices. In general, high base salaries are not essential to achieve high quality. What has a far greater impact on quality are such considerations as feelings of internal equity, relatively fair distribution of compensation from top to bottom, employment security, some incentives to make longer-term contributions, some participation and flexibility in the provision of benefits (to indicate a recognition of the importance of individual needs), and roughly equal treatment when it comes to perks. Again, these practice choices, taken together, help form a mind-set of commitment and loyalty as well as a desire to improve the quality of the product or service.

Although high base salaries may not be essential for quality, generous incentives may be:

> One customer service manager motivated his representatives with incentive pay. Every month, a customer service representative in his department typically handles between 100 and 200 calls. The manager calls every customer who registered a complaint, problem, or request and asks each a series of questions. The questions are scored for each customer's representative. The reps receive a monthly score, averaged over a quarter. Their quarterly scores then determine extra incentive compensation they receive over base salary, which could mean as much as an extra 25%. The result? The customer service representatives have a powerful incentive to take calls, be polite, and provide the customers with what they need. In this case, the ability to earn more than weekly pay was the most powerful incentive. (Wagel et al. 1988: 33)

But without the necessary training and company commitment to quality, even generous incentives may not be sufficient:

> A major ingredient in Nordstrom's success is the quality of the salesclerks. They are paid about 20% better than those of competitors, and they are well trained and encouraged to do almost anything within reason to satisfy customers. 'Nordstrom's motivates people, not just by paying them well but by congratulating them and encouraging them.' (Russell 1987: 56)

In both these cases, the organization does not simply offer a compensation incentive for outcomes. Rather, the compensation incentive is combined with specific and extensive training on how to produce those outcomes and how those outcomes will be measured. In the first case, outcomes are very specific and apparently under the direct control of the customer-service representative; here, the bonuses might not distort the system. In the Nordstrom case, the outcomes are much less under the control of a salesclerk (i.e., the overall system dominates the outcomes); here, individual bonuses would seem capricious, since the system rather than the individual determines the outcomes. Nordstrom has resorted to higher salaries to raise overall motivation. In general, the more the system dominates the outcomes, the more individual bonuses and incentives will distribute rewards capriciously (randomly) and introduce distortions into the work flow as individuals compete to beat the compensation system.

Beyond compensation, providing for some employment security appears to be crucial. It seems crucial because of an anomaly in the quality-enhancement strategy—an anomaly captured quite nicely in the following quote:

> At many U.S. companies, executives still aren't thinking about it in the right way. They regard quality improvement as merely a cost-cutting tool or a way of keeping customers happy. Those it is, but it can be much more. When the goal of raising quality infuses an organization, it makes employees happier and more productive, leads to product innovation, and often increases market share. The good news for the U.S.: Now that the quality obsession is taking hold, it should spread fast. When executives in part of a company realize the benefits, they like to tell colleagues. Competitors are spurred to learn about quality fast. Suppliers find they had better shape up too. In that sort of environment, no one can afford to be left behind. (Dreyfuss 1988: 88)

The anomaly—i.e., the fact that quality enhancement results in innovation—occurs because quality improvement not only means repeating the same things (things that have been determined to be linked both to quality and to the organization's strategy), it also means improving and thus changing. Recognizing the apparent contradiction, companies like Ensoniq say to their employees, "Yes, do what you've been taught in training, but try to improve on those methods; you know your job best. If you spot a way that you think is better, though, please tell the engineers and production supervisor first." The company then tests out the new way through experimentation, as discussed in Chapter 3, and if the experiments are successful, incorporates the improved approach into all the relevant systems. But in order to get employees to suggest improvements, they must first be assured that their suggestions will not result in their being put out of work.

Contributing new ideas and identifying improvements are also facilitated by a feeling that everyone shares in the benefits. Having a fairly egalitarian compensation system and compensation based on internal equity helps. This does not mean, however, that all employees are paid the same. But it may mean that there are relatively few job classes and that within each class, there are few wage distinctions. At Ensoniq, there are only two job classifications in manufacturing (other than managerial); each class has only two wage distinctions. All employees receive an entry-level wage for the first ninety days. After that, all employees within a class receive the same pay (with some minor distinctions for seniority that mirrors the learning curve).

Aiding the spirit of all employees' benefiting equally is companywide profit sharing. This incentive system combines the motivation to focus on the good of the company with the philosophy that everyone is in it together and everyone shares the good and bad times.

Financial compensation is often thought of as the primary mover and shaper of employee behavior, but this may not always reflect reality. Federal Express operates on the premise that employees want and need job security, justice, an understanding of what's expected and what's in it for them, and knowledge of where to go if they have problems. Although compensation certainly plays a role in satisfying these wants and needs, so also do praise, recognition, celebration, task-oriented feedback, and systems for soliciting employee suggestions and participation.

TRAINING PRACTICE CHOICES

Facilitating a quality-enhancement strategy are the training and development practices that were presented in Figure 5.1. Training and development are focused on the intermediate term, and their scope is relatively narrow (the immediate job) but has applicability to several jobs (thereby facilitating job flexibility). The training, which emphasizes improving both productivity and quality of work life, is planned and is tightly connected to the needs of the organization and the jobs being done.

Although the training may be conducted for a specific individual for a specific job, it is aimed at improving the skills of all the workers in order to enable them both to perform more than one job and to work cooperatively. The concept of working cooperatively applies equally to employees performing jobs designed at the individual level and to employees performing jobs designed at the team level. As employees are grouped in teams, either to handle job assignments or to solve problems, training for group skills becomes more extensive. As with the other practices, high levels of employee participation in designing and implementing training programs and in identifying training needs become typical. This enhances employee involvement and ownership and also increases the probability that the training program will be appropriate for the company's needs. Together, these choices help increase employee loyalty and commitment and strengthen the desire to improve quality. This is particularly true when top management is strongly committed to training and when it is done in extremely large doses:

Meantime, while other companies were ordering massive layoffs and plant shutdowns to counteract the threat from abroad, Galvin had the foresight to realize that nothing less than top-to-bottom employee education and retraining was needed to compete effectively. His pioneering steps were gradually expanded into one of the largest and best corporate training programs in the nation. This attention to training has been well worth the time and expense, he says; besides enhancing individual on-the-job performance, it also has engaged employees more closely and pridefully in the pursuit of corporate goals. Indeed, Galvin believes that all Motorola employees now take pride in the quality of their work. (Murray 1989: 37)

The extent of the commitment that Motorola and Galvin have to the training and development of their employees is best described by the following quote:

> To instill its far-flung work force with the new corporate goals, Motorola has launched a massive educational drive for all 105,000 employees. Some courses explore global competitiveness and risk-taking. Others hone practical skills in statistical process control or ways of reducing product cycle times. Workers and managers alike are now expected to keep their noses in books throughout their careers. This type of commitment doesn't come cheap: In 1989, the company spent $60 million on education. (Ibid.: 38)

Applying training broadly across many different levels of employees rather than focusing primarily on the employees on the firing line seems very important for quality-enhancement programs. It is important because it conveys the message that quality is everybody's job and responsibility and that no one is above the need for retraining. And because managers are closest to the action, they are often the ones in the best position to develop and deliver the training programs:

> The service strategy at Good Samaritan Hospital in Cincinnati, Ohio, is two-fold: train all employees from physicians on down in the basics of good service, and encourage employees and departments to offer better service as a team, says Carol Belmont, director of guest relations at the 750-bed acute care hospital.
> Since some employees were resistant to the idea of customer service training, Belmont notes, 4,500 hours of training were made a condition of employment for hospital staff. In addition, 13 doctors were designated 'physician leaders.' These MDs were given a one-day training session so that they, in turn, could conduct 4-hour training sessions in customer service for other physicians. The hospital trained 900 doctors using this system. ("Cultivating Quality Service," 1989: 392)

Training and development can be aimed at improving the level of skills and knowledge that employees need to do their immediate job, and this helps by enabling them to do that job over the near term as it changes incrementally. In the longer term, though, a job can change substantially and/or unpredictably, thus making long-term training difficult. Therefore, the application of the training and development typically spans several jobs. This is because employees usually operate under some system of flexible job assignments (consistent with quality, however), and a great deal of the training is generic to several jobs (e.g., statistical control):

> To help them reach higher quality standards, Bretz's staff trains their production people in statistical process control methods and works with the engineers on redesigning components to simplify them or substitute less expensive materials. By cramming more electronic circuits into less space, for example, Pitney Bowes cut by two-thirds the number of assembly boards in its postage meters. (Richman 1988: 12)

Illustrating further that training is generic to many jobs in organizations pursuing high quality is the practice of Motorola's and others to teach their employees a common language of quality. Juran echoes this need in calling for a common language for quality. In his book *Juran on Leadership for Quality* (Juran 1989), a recommended reference, he provides a quality glossary.

Enhancing quality calls for employee commitment and loyalty. An important ingredient in eliciting these is communicating to the employees that the organization cares for them as people, not just as instruments of production (that's also in part why job security is necessary in quality programs). Training efforts can help attain this mind-set by focusing on improvements in quality of work life as well as in productivity. This means having training programs directed at career improvement, stress management, teamwork, and participation skills as well as programs on statistical control processes.

As emphasized in Chapter 3, training programs having a group orientation are important in quality enhancement. Quality depends on everyone's working at it themselves and being able to count on everyone else's doing their jobs correctly. This is true regardless of whether employees produce their products by working in groups or individually. Training programs delivered to groups of employees as groups go a long way toward developing this feeling of group orientation. Further expanding this feeling are other complementary practices:

> To foster more team spirit, Motorola is tearing down the traditional walls that isolate various departments, such as design, manufacturing, and marketing. Now, people from each discipline get involved in new projects early on, so products are designed from the outset to be cost effective to build and to provide the features that customers want. (Murray 1989: 39)

Finally, to enhance employee involvement and commitment even further, why not involve employees in the design *and* delivery of the training and development programs?

LABOR-MANAGEMENT PRACTICE CHOICES

The final human resource management practice presenting the manager with choices is the labor-management relationship. The use of the term *labor* is meant to convey representation of employees by a union. The decision here is between two alternatives: (1) adopting a newer, cooperative relationship (and if so, to what degree?) or; (2) continuing the more traditional, adversarial relationship. This decision influences the entire collective-bargaining arrangement as well as such related issues as employee voice and participation, grievance and due-process procedures, and flexible job assignment and classification. In the present context, the choice consistent with the mind-set of loyalty, commitment, and quality improvement is the newer, cooperative relationship.

The newer, cooperative approach results in a union-management relationship that focuses on including the workers, giving them a voice and greater involvement in the work processes. And in large part because this new relationship grows out of the need to be more competitive internationally (and primarily in manufacturing), it focuses on improving quality. Proponents of this cooperative relationship, sometimes referred to as employee involvement (EI), believe that it improves a company's ability to compete (because the major competitors are winning on the basis of quality), which, in turn, improves job security for the union membership. Unions that support this relationship include the United Auto Workers (UAW), the Oil, Chemical and Atomic Workers union (OCAW), and the Amalgamated Clothing and Textile Workers (ACTW).

The General Motors–Toyota joint venture in Fremont, California, is perhaps most widely known for taking a plant that had been producing low-quality cars and turning it into one that produces cars that receive the highest customer-satisfaction ratings of any GM products. This turnaround was accomplished through the cooperation of the UAW and the management of Toyota and General Motors. This cooperative arrangement resulted in the institution of flexible job classifications, worker retraining, the switching of supervisory roles from watchdog to coach and trainer, employee involvement and participation, and greater employee control of the workplace pace. Of course, other systems of manufacturing, such as inventory control through just-in-time methods, are also part of this new cooperative arrangement. No single aspect of a plant can improve quality; it takes all the systems working together.

The movement toward a cooperative relationship thus impacts managers directly. It often means sharing power and decision-making authority and working with the employees as equals: Earned respect, not formal authority, influences workers and the way work is done. The movement toward a cooperative relationship is facilitated when top management supports the effort and exhibits a willingness to shift its fundamental philosophy of organization and management. Described by Lawler and Mohrman as "characteristics of the new management," this shift results in the organizational characteristics shown in Table 5.1.

A careful review of Table 5.1 suggests that the new management is consistent with quality enhancement. Thus, the new cooperative relationships between unions and companies that have adopted the new management are on track to improve quality. This is further illustrated by how Jan Carlzon, president and CEO of Scandinavian Airline System (SAS), describes union-management relations and the company's quality customer-service program:

> As a new management philosophy has emerged at SAS, a new relationship with the unions has also developed. As Carlzon described it, 'The challenge is to make the unions your partner in establishing the overall direction of the company.' Carlzon conceded that the unions cannot be expected to abandon

Table 5.1 Characteristics of the New Management

Philosophy	• Shared values, trust
Organizational structure	• Flat • Light on staff • Self-contained organizational units responsible for product or customer • Decentralized decision making
Job design	• Individually enriched jobs or teams • Flexible job duties • Cross-training • Responsible for "doing" and "improving"
Employee voice	• Participative work teams • Task forces
Information systems	• Business data widely shared
Performance standards	• Goals and standards participatively set • "Stretch" goals emphasized
Reward systems	• Variable rewards share in business gains • Linked to skills and mastery • Team rewards
Personnel practices	• Developed participatively

Source: E. E. Lawler III and S. A. Mohrman, "Unions and the New Management," *Academy of Management Executive* 1, no. 2 (1987): 295.

'their traditional role of being your opponents in cutting up the cake. But the sharing of the cake is done with greater insight and cooperation if the union has been your partner from the outset.'

Is it realistic for managers to attempt to form a partnership with the unions that have always been their adversaries? Carlzon pointed out that although they traditionally regard themselves as rivals, management and the unions share a single overriding goal: the success of the organization. 'It is therefore vital,' he said, 'that the unions be involved in the strategic decisions that affect our common destiny. The purpose of these decisions is, of course, to develop and safeguard the corporation, making its future as successful and secure as possible.' (Wagel et al. 1989: 32)

It might also be suggested that resistance to shifting toward a new style of management might bring neither improved cooperation nor improved quality. At USX Corporation, executives are mounting a management-driven effort to build worker involvement outside the union contract, a strategy antithetical to cooperative principles and the spirit of new management. According to Lynn Williams, president of the United Steelworkers Union (USW):

By rejecting such 'co-management,' USX wants to have it both ways. While it's asking employees to work with managers, USW officials say that the company continues to violate the union contract by subcontracting work to outside, non-USW suppliers.

This was the major issue that led to the work stoppage. Worker involvement won't succeed with 'a management-controlled process where the company does just what suits them,' says Williams. (Miles 1989: 151)

The cooperative relationship between union and management is often reflected in enhanced group processes and group programs. Quality circles is one such program that is group-oriented and relies on the contributions of employees in groups to help solve quality problems. Although many of these group efforts are ongoing, groups can also be formed for more single-purpose tasks, such as deciding on the purchase of a new machine or meeting with suppliers. Perhaps the most advanced form of group programs is those resulting in self-managed teams, in which workers make the decisions and basically operate as independent units. In this case, management often shifts from the role of controller to that of facilitator.

PUTTING IT ALL TOGETHER

It is important to emphasize here that when selecting human resource practices from the menus discussed, all the menus must be utilized. To ignore or overlook one menu may result in unintended employee behaviors. This could happen if, say, a compensation practice were implemented unsystematically, in such a way as to send the employees signals that conflict with the signals they are getting from all the other practices. When the human resource practices are put together systematically, though, the results can indeed be powerful. Ford and Motorola, for example, have had outstanding success in their quality-enhancement efforts. Here's how the human resource choices came together and impacted the quality efforts of the producer of Honda, America's best-selling car in 1990 and 1991:

We can identify those human resource practices that facilitate product quality by examining Honda of America's Marysville, Ohio plant. With a current workforce of approximately 4,500, this plant produces cars of quality comparable to those produced by Honda plants in Japan. Although pay rates (independent of bonuses) may be as much as 30–40% lower than rates at other Midwest auto plants, Honda has had fewer layoffs and lower inventory rates of new cars than its competitors. How is this possible?

One possible explanation is that Honda knows that the delivery of quality products depends on predictable and reliable behavior from its employees. In the initial employee orientation session, which may last between 3 and 4 hours, job security is emphasized. Employees' spouses are encouraged to attend these sessions, because Honda believes that spouse awareness of the company and its demands on employees can help minimize absenteeism, tardiness, and turnover. Of course, something so critical to quality as reliable behavior is not stimulated and reinforced by only one human resource practice. For example, associates who have perfect attendance for four straight weeks receive a bonus of $56. Attendance also influences the size of the semiannual bonus (typically paid in spring and autumn). Impressive attendance figures also enhance an employee's chances for promotion. (Honda of America has a policy of promotion from within.)

In addition to getting and reinforcing reliable and predictable behavior, Honda's HRM practices encourage a longer-term employee orientation and a flexibility to change. Employment security, along with constant informal and formal training programs, facilitate these role behaviors. Training programs are tailored to the needs of the associates (employees) through the formal performance appraisal process, which is developmental rather than evaluational. Team leaders (not supervisors) are trained in spotting and removing performance deficiencies as they occur. To help speed communication and remove any organizational sources of performance deficiencies, the structure of the organization is such that there are only four levels between associates and the plant manager.

At Honda, cooperative, interdependent behavior is fostered by egalitarian HRM practices. All associates wear identical uniforms with their first names embossed; parking spaces are unmarked, and there is only one cafeteria. All entry-level associates receive the same rate of pay except for a 60-cents-an-hour shift differential. The modern health center adjacent to the main plant is open to all. These practices, in turn, encourage all associates to regard themselves collectively as 'us' rather than 'us' versus 'them.' Without this underlying attitude, the flexible work rules, air-conditioned plant, and automation wouldn't be enough to sustain associate commitment and identification with the organization's goal of high quality.

The success of Honda's quality-enhancement strategy goes beyond concern for its own HRM practices. It is also concerned with the human resource practices of other organizations, such as its suppliers. For example, Delco-Remy's practice of participative management style, as well as its reputation for producing quality products at competitive prices, was the reason why Delco was selected by Honda as its sole supplier of batteries. (Schuler and Jackson 1987: 212)

Of course, quality enhancement involves more than just putting together all the appropriate human resource practices, as we suggested in Chapters 1 and 2. At American Express, improving quality and continually motivating employees has been an integral part of the company's culture since its founding 150 years ago. According to Mary Anne Rasmussen, vice president for worldwide quality assurance at Amex (American Express) Travel Related Services Co., the organization's quality-enhancement process has seven basic elements, the first six of which are:

- Quality assurance organization in every operation worldwide.

- Extensive quality tracking system.

- Heavy market research on customer satisfaction.

- On-site reviews that incorporate the practice of "managing by walking around."

- Employee education and involvement encompassing employee training, development, recognition, rewards, and communications programs.

- Company leaders committed to the culture of high quality and employee motivation. (Farish 1989: 23)

Again, emphasizing the importance of top-management support for any successful quality-enhancement effort, Rasmussen cites CEO Jim Robinson's support and philosophy (the seventh basic element):

Robinson is a believer. I know it and feel it. Every employee knows it and is both inspired and motivated by the depth and sincerity of his commitment. . . . The commitment of Robinson and senior management is a key reason why quality has become a company obsession, why every employee takes it seriously. (Ibid.)

SUMMARY

This chapter provides an overview of a broad menu of human resource practices and discusses which ones are consistent with a quality-enhancement strategy. The suggested choices evolve from the human resource philosophy of accumulation. In keeping with the concept of making systematic choices regarding human resource practices, the menu selections are presented as complementary and mutually required. If choices are inconsistent with one another, they will conflict among themselves and result in suboptimal performance.

Managers reading this book now have an understanding of quality, some ideas about how to begin quality-improvement projects, and a framework for making the most effective use of their most valuable tool—human resources. The next and last piece of the total quality picture involves relationships external to the manager's sphere of influence—namely, the new approaches to suppliers and customers that are required in keeping with the new thinking about quality.

References

"Cultivating Quality Service." 1989. *Bulletin to Management* (Dec. 7): 392. Reprinted by permission from Bulletin to Management (BNA Policy and Practice Series), Vol. 40, No. 49, p. 392 (December 7, 1989). Copyright 1989 by The Bureau of National Affairs, Inc. (800-372-1033).

Dreyfuss, J. 1988. "Victories in the Quality Crusade." *Fortune* (Oct. 10): 80–88.

Farish, P. 1989. "HRM Update." *Personnel Administrator* (Mar.): 23.

Juran, J. M. 1989. *Juran on Leadership for Quality.* New York: Free Press.

Miles, G. L. 1989. "Suddenly USX Is Playing Mr. Nice Guy." *Business Week* (June 26): 151–153.

Murray, T. J. 1989. "Rethinking the Factory." *Business Month* (July): 34–39.

Richman, L. S. 1988. "Why Inflation Is Not Inevitable." *Fortune* (Sept. 12): 122.

Russell, G. 1987. "Where Customer Is Still King." *Time* (Feb. 2): 56–57.

Schneider, B. 1990. "Alternative Strategies for Creating Service-Oriented Organizations." In *Service Management Effectiveness,* ed. D. Bowen, R. Chase, and T. Cummings, 126–151. San Francisco: Jossey-Bass.

Schuler, R. S. 1988. "Personnel and Human Resource Management: Choices and Organizational Strategy." In *Personnel and Human Resource Management,* ed. R. Schuler, S. Youngblood, and V. Huber, 24–39. St. Paul: West Publishing.

Schuler, R. S., and Jackson, S. E. 1987. "Linking Competitive Strategies with Human Resource Management Practices." *Academy of Management Executive* 1, no. 3: 207–219.

Serlen, B. 1987. "W. Edwards Deming." *NYU Business* (Fall) 15–20.

Tansik, D. A. 1990. "Managing Human Resource Issues for High-Contact Service Personnel." In *Service Management Effectiveness*, ed. D. Bowen, R. Chase, and T. Cummings, 152–176. San Francisco: Jossey-Bass.

Wagel, William H., Feldman, D., Fritz, N. R., and Blocklyn, P. L. 1988. "Quality—The Bottom Line." *Personnel* (July): 30–42.

Wiggenhorn, W. 1990. "Motorola U: When Training Becomes an Education." *Harvard Business Review* (July-Aug.): 71–83.

Chapter 6

QUALITY FROM EXTERNAL RELATIONSHIPS

We have identified quality and defined it as producing the right product with little variation from a single effort, such that it generates loyalty and support from customers (and from consumers if they are not direct customers). Thus far, though, we have paid little attention to two groups that have a great impact on defining and delivering quality. First, customers define what is "right" and provide loyalty and support; quality improvement calls for treating customers as more than an arm's-length feedback mechanism. Second, suppliers have considerable impact on variation and the ability to produce correctly from a single effort; traditional adversarial or competitive relationships with vendors will undermine all attempts to achieve quality. With the advent of new thinking on customer and supplier relationships, a manager must be prepared to act on all fronts to improve quality.

EXPANDING THE DEFINITIONS OF CUSTOMER AND SUPPLIER

Quality improvement depends on effective external relationships. The customers, in this view of quality, define the quality of a product or service. Their experiences, expectations, perceptions, and support (or lack thereof) are the final word on whether a product is a success or failure. Suppliers, to a large extent, set minimum bounds on variation and on the percentage of products and services that can be delivered correctly through a single effort (i.e., without defects). Accordingly, improving relationships with customers and suppliers becomes critical to the success of any quality-improvement process.

Who are these customers and suppliers? As discussed earlier and illustrated in Figure 6.1, customers and suppliers cannot be defined in terms

Figure 6.1   SOME CUSTOMER-SUPPLIER RELATIONSHIPS FOR A PURCHASING DEPARTMENT

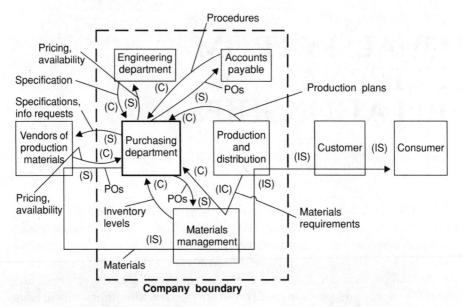

(C) = purchasing department acting as direct customer

(S) = purchasing department acting as direct supplier

(IC) = purchasing department acting as indirect customer

(IS) = purchasing department acting as indirect supplier

of organizational "walls." Customers and suppliers include subunits of the main organization as well as external organizations. Any entity that provides inputs to a process is a supplier, and any entity that receives outputs (both intended and unintended) is a customer. As the case in Appendix B illustrates, some of the greatest improvements in quality can flow from recognizing customers and suppliers within an organization.

Many participants, especially in service activities, share both supplier and customer roles, as illustrated in Figure 6.2. Buying departments function as suppliers to accounts payable when they send in purchase orders (POs) and coded invoices; yet they act as customers when they receive operating procedures, forms, and vendor invoices. When they rely on accounts payable to provide a service—paying invoices that maintain relationships with outside vendors—the buyers are indirect customers. Those outside vendors are also suppliers (submitting invoices) and customers (receiving payments) of accounts payable. Virtually any subunit of an organization will contain similarly complex relationships.

An expansion of this idea might suggest that every person/unit/organization that interacts with a manager's processes and products should be treated as both customer and supplier. For example, L. L. Bean, the legendary leader of quality in the mail-order business, had $82 million worth of goods returned from customers in 1988, which amounted to 14 percent of total sales. Rather than just treating those returns as a cost of doing business, employees at Bean realized that they had fantastic market-research data; 62 percent of the returns involved wrong sizes. As a result, size information in both catalogs and order takers' computers has been changed to reflect changes in consumer preferences and to help increase ordering accuracy. For L. L. Bean, consumers are not only customers but also suppliers of order data and market-research data (Phillips et al. 1990: 94).

RELATIONSHIPS

Although, as noted, participants play the roles of both suppliers and customers, it is more convenient in the present context to analyze those roles separately. We begin with suppliers.

SUPPLIERS

According to Douglas P. Lansing, quality-improvement manager at Boeing Company:

Figure 6.2   EXAMPLE OF MULTIPLE CUSTOMER-SUPPLIER RELATIONSHIPS

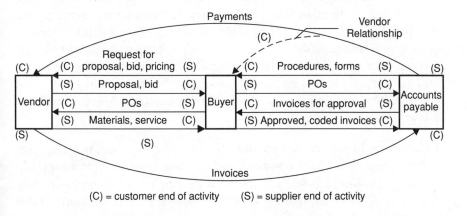

(C) = customer end of activity   (S) = supplier end of activity

Our thinking has evolved from 'Find the guy with the lowest bid and monitor him so he doesn't screw up,' to, 'Find the guy who makes the best product and make him part of the process.' (Deutsch 1990: F25)

This is the lesson being learned over and over again by companies around the world—it is more important to have better-quality supplies than low-cost supplies. The really good news comes when a supplier–customer relationship leads to better quality *and* lower costs. This is often the case when the relationship involves trust and cooperation on both sides. Suppliers must be willing to work with customers to improve quality, reduce costs, and increase timeliness. Customers must be willing to allow suppliers a fair profit, work with them to improve quality, listen to their suggestions, and provide stable ordering patterns. The following suggestions lead to this type of environment:

1. Suppliers and customers should work together, sharing ideas, capabilities, and expertise to improve the overall quality of output. For example, Xerox will send its own team of specialists to train suppliers. "We'll do anything to help Xerox-certified suppliers become truly world-class companies," says Ray C. Stark, Xerox's vice president of materials management, design, and manufacturing (Deutsch 1990: F25).

2. Relationships should be long-term, though they need not be governed by contracts. Colgate-Palmolive illustrates this point in its relationships with its advertising agencies, Foote, Cone & Belding and Young & Rubicam. Colgate has maintained those relationships for over seven years, showing long-term commitment through such actions as giving stock to every agency employee working on its account and granting unasked-for rate hikes when it appeared the agencies were not getting a fair profit. In return, the agencies have agreed to operate in every country where Colgate wants to sell, even if it means acquiring foreign companies. Says Reuben Mark, Colgate's chief executive, "The agencies know they are not in danger of losing our business. That means that when there is a problem, we can sit down and fix it together, without fear" (Deutsch 1990: F25).

3. Each item being ordered should always come from a single supplier. This is one of the most prevalent and quickest ways to improve quality. Between 1983 and 1988, Xerox reduced its suppliers from approximately 4,500 to 450. During that same period, incoming defects dropped from 8 percent (typical for most U.S. companies) to .03 percent. Several sup-

pliers have not shipped a single defective part for three years (Main 1990)!

4. If lower costs are required, then the customer should work with the supplier to reduce the supplier's costs rather than beat the supplier down on price. One year after Harley-Davidson sent two of its employees to a supplier as consultants and provided the supplier's employees with Harley training, their relationship changed dramatically. The supplier, whose deliveries had originally tended to be late and of low quality, became a top-quality producer, whose parts now routinely arrive on schedule and go directly to Harley's production line without inspection. With Harley's support, the vendor learned how to reduce labor costs by two-thirds while improving quality. It is now more profitable while Harley has a lower-cost, more reliable supplier (Reid 1990: 185).

5. Key suppliers should be involved early in design processes in order to alert them to impending changes, take advantage of their expertise, help contain costs, and provide accurate estimates while ensuring proper quality. When Artco (an alias for a recently studied arts and media company that wished to remain anonymous) moved into new offices in Los Angeles, it did not involve its information systems and communication systems experts in the space design. Consequently, Artco had to reopen walls to run wires and also introduce unplanned (and sometimes orphaned) technology to accomplish what could, with proper planning, have been done through simple, low-cost installations during remodeling. Having learned its lesson, Artco involved its experts with the architects, engineers, and contractors when designing its New York offices. As a result, the cost of designing Artco's New York offices was substantially less than half the cost of retrofitting its L.A. offices. Furthermore, the New York design allowed connections for telephones, network stations, and mainframe computers to be moved in minutes instead of the normally required three days to two weeks.

6. If possible, ordering patterns should be stabilized so that suppliers can plan for and provide reliable deliveries. Ensoniq Corp. (see Appendix A for a more detailed discussion of this case) moved to a "materials-as-needed" program with its main suppliers. The organization now has standing orders for regular deliveries (weekly to daily, depending on the product). Paperwork and ordering time are reduced for both Ensoniq and its suppliers. Furthermore, because Ensoniq has dependably maintained its orders (and has also implemented the preceding five points

on this list), it has seen its suppliers give preference to Ensoniq's ship-
ments when supplies of raw materials have been short and the parts
market has been very tight.

The foregoing points work best when practiced together. The following
example illustrates this combined effect:

> Other companies are discovering what the Japanese manufacturers have
> known for years: Paying attention to quality, along with streamlining produc-
> tion and making it more flexible, yields outsized cost savings. Pitney Bowes
> materials manager Robert Bretz calculates that it costs his company an average
> of $600 to identify, fix, and replace a component that goes on the fritz anywhere
> from the time it arrives at the assembly line to post-sale warranty repair. To
> end costly waste, Pitney Bowes three years ago concentrated its orders on
> fewer, better suppliers.
>   Some 150 of the company's 750 vendors supply nearly 70% of its purchases,
> versus just 35% in 1985. In exchange for bigger orders on longer-term contracts,
> Pitney Bowes requires suppliers to invest in cost-efficient product technologies
> and take over final quality control. They also help their suppliers by providing
> training and engineering services. (Richman 1988: 122 © 1988 Time, Inc. All
> rights reserved.)

These kinds of relationships create competitive advantages from lower
costs, higher quality, and frequently, quicker product introductions. Although each of the success stories described above cites some gains, a simple
table (see Table 6.1) illustrates how the gains accrue. The first line in this
table shows the cost of old-style final inspection for quality control. The
second line shows the cost savings associated with incoming inspection. The
third and fourth lines show the benefits from reduced incoming errors. The
fourth line shows a savings of 4.8 percent over the old-style quality control.
Savings like these and more are the goal of improved vendor relations.

Table 6.1 Cost of Production Comparing Incoming Inspection with Outgoing
Inspection

Defect Rate	Parts Required for 100	Price per Part	Unit Cost Incoming Inspection	Unit Cost Added in Production	Unit Cost Outgoing Inspection	Total Unit Costs	Total Costs	Finished Cost per Unit
5%	105	$100		$10	$2	$112	$11,760	$117.60
5	105	100	$1	10		111	11,605	116.05
1	101	100		10	2	112	11,312	113.12
1	101	100	1	10		111	11,201	112.01

Figure 6.3   MIXED INPUTS FROM VENDORS

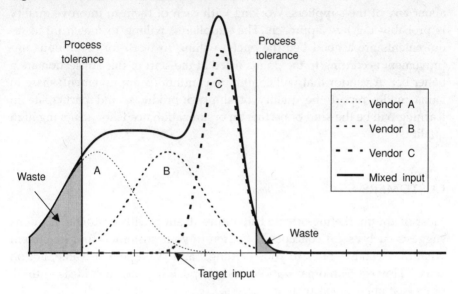

It should be noted that Table 6.1 does make some broad simplifying assumptions: (1) all tests are nondestructive, but defective materials are scrapped; and (2) no additional errors are generated during production. Destructive testing, the creation of defects during production, rework of defectives, and other factors will influence the total cost of finished products. In general, though, most modifications of this simple example will show even greater benefits flowing from reduced incoming errors and earlier testing (if, indeed, testing is even needed).

Moving to a new supplier relationship may be neither simple nor quick. Figure 6.3 shows a situation in which three suppliers provide an input (part or service). The process has some tolerance for input variation (process tolerance). When the inputs are mingled (as shown by the bold line), significant waste occurs. More important, mixing inputs hides the source of the waste. Only by segregating inputs can each supplier's performance be measured.

The three distributions—A, B, and C—show the segregated input from the three vendors. If the manager of this process wants to slim down to a single supplier (as suggested), which supplier should be chosen? Should it be supplier C, which has the lowest variance, under the assumption that C can change its target? Or would supplier B make a better choice, based on its having a closer match on the process target (and hope for reduced variation)?

The answer is not that simple, since no assumptions should be made about any of the suppliers. Working with each of them to improve quality is probably the best approach. The supplier(s) willing to match input requirements are a good bet; the one(s) willing to work for continuous improvement according to the points listed at the start of this subsection are a better bet. A vendor that will commit to continuous improvement, share in gains made, report the quality of shipped products, and participate in learning will be the kind of partner an organization needs for achieving high quality.

CUSTOMERS

Most of the marketing-oriented literature dealing with customer relations suggests such useful concepts as "Listen to your customers and give them what they want," "Stick to your knitting," and "Compete on value, not on price." However, an organization needs to push beyond such ideas to think of its customers as partners in success.

Certainly, customers are more than a necessary evil; they are, quite simply, the reason for being. Customers want high-quality goods and services; they want value for their money (time, energy). Just as relationships with suppliers will improve and become more profitable when they are involved and accorded trust, so, too, will relationships with customers improve when they are accorded trust and respect. Customers can often provide guidance, suggestions, technical assistance, and support in developing and delivering products.

Before much can be done, however, an organization must know its customers. This requires two steps. First, all those downstream in the value-added process, down to and including the final consumer, must be identified. They are all customers according to the new thinking. Then, once the customers have been identified, their "voice" needs to be analyzed. For example, unanalyzed feedback from customers might reveal a relationship between the voice of the customer and the voice of the process similar to that shown in Figure 6.4. Here, the match does not seem very good (poor quality).

However, if the customers are separated into groups (A, B, and C), it can be seen that one group, B, can experience high quality. Let's say for the moment that these three groups are the shipping companies (A), the retailers (C), and the final consumers (B). The consumers can be happy with the product, but the retailers and shippers are not. In this case, products may never reach the consumers because of problems in the chain of distribution.

Figure 6.4   MIXED CUSTOMER VOICE SEEN AS THE SUM OF SEPARATE CUSTOMERS

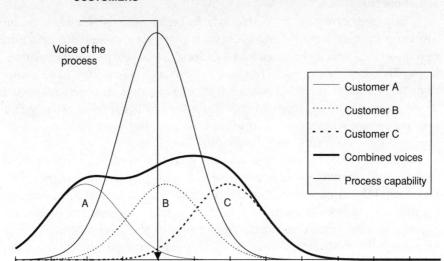

When this type of situation occurs, it is probably because shippers and retailers are unhappy with some dimensions of quality, as discussed in Chapter 2. They may want a change in packaging, service, support, or some other dimension. Meanwhile, the consumers' expectations match the product's capability. To add value for all customers in the chain, the manager must investigate which dimensions fall short and which dimensions satisfy. Hopefully, changing dimensions to satisfy intermediate customers (on the way to the final consumers) will both overcome this problem and increase (or at least not disrupt) the consumers' satisfaction.

On the other hand, the three customer groups shown in Figure 6.4 might all be at a similar level in the distribution chain. Let us now say that they are three retailing groups. The manager still needs to investigate which dimensions of quality satisfy which group and which need changing. In this case, however, it is less likely that a change designed to accommodate one group will necessarily be viewed favorably by another group. Then, the manager's task would be to create two new products (services) to match each group of customers. This is the essence of niche marketing and product customization.

For high-value sales, efforts must be made to match production output to the expectations of all three customers. In addition to changing production output, the manager may be able to match the customers to the process through education and marketing. Most certainly, selling what cannot be delivered will assure a mismatch between customer expectations and the actual output.

Customers can play an active role in improving the match between process output and their desires. Often, a customer can suggest, or teach, new processes and techniques to a vendor. Just as with supplier relationships, discussed in the preceding subsection, each party may have something to learn from the other when it comes to quality. Customers may have an edge in technology, production, distribution, or some other activity that they may share with a valued supplier. Like selecting good vendors, selecting good customers can improve quality.

One way to help secure good customers is by demonstrating high quality. For example, providing a customer with process run charts for all products shipped may eliminate the customer's need to perform incoming inspections. As shown earlier (in Table 6.1), this can result in significant savings for the customer, which adds value to the relationship without increasing the customer's costs. A partnership arrangement calls for the party with more knowledge and ability to share with the other party for the benefit of both.

DIFFERENCES BETWEEN INTERNAL AND EXTERNAL RELATIONSHIPS

Not all suppliers and customers are equal. There are important distinctions between internal suppliers and customers and external ones. The two primary differences involve the explicitness of transaction costs and the option to change suppliers or customers. In the case of internal suppliers, the manager striving to improve quality may have less leverage for effecting change; being a captive places strains on relationships.

Because internal transactions do not ordinarily involve explicit monetary exchanges, internal supplier-customer changes must be negotiated in the currency of the organization—power, influence, mutual advantages, exchanges of work loads, etc. When executives mandate quality improvement, these exchanges may come more readily (assuming the executives are prepared to back up their mandates). The SOI (sphere of influence) again enters the picture, since exchanges are often easier with those in the manager's SOI.

Internal supplier-customer relationships often benefit when all concerned keep in mind that most internal suppliers are also customers. By explicitly playing to these multiple relationships, or "expanding the pie" when negotiating, a manager may increase the chances of implementing changes. For example, the information systems (IS) department in most organizations functions as a customer of other departments, even when developing (supplying) software. The IS department requires inputs in the form of requests and specifications. The consuming department must supply those inputs as well as human resources for testing and implementation.

In the partnership approach, the IS department, recognizing its future role as a customer, might train client departments on how to prepare systems requests and specifications; this reduces variance in the IS department's incoming products and improves its incoming supplies. The payback to the client department is a better-designed and -developed system that is delivered more quickly. The partnership thus benefits both parties.

If a manager is in a position to mandate changes within an SOI, then some sharing and cooperation may be imposed. For example, William J Sheeran—vice president for engineering, production, and sourcing at General Electric—unified two Balkanized engineering departments: design and manufacturing. By changing procedures and organization design, he ended a long, troublesome handoff problem between the two groups. This was one factor contributing to a 60 percent reduction in direct-labor costs and a 75 percent reduction in overhead for GE's circuit-breaker manufacturing (Vogel 1989: 100).

Another tool available to managers to encourage cooperation and interaction is to shift the focus of reviews and compensation to group outcomes. Profit sharing, group bonuses, gain sharing, and the like emphasize interdependencies, leading to an environment conducive to cooperative problem solving and quality improvement. Including group and cross-departmental outcomes in the review and coaching sessions emphasizes and reinforces the importance of cooperation.

For a manager positioned in the center of an organization, working through other departments as customers and suppliers is the most effective way to help the organization. The Swiss Bank case, discussed in Appendix B, illustrates a very complete program of changing supplier-customer relationships for the bank's human resource department. This shows how much can be accomplished by treating other areas like customers—a process called "customerizing." In a case like this, improvements in service, working conditions, and corporate stature accrue to the manager and his or her reports.

SUMMARY

Quality improvement is a critical, ongoing process. Any organization that cannot produce high-quality products and services exposes itself to the risk of competitive extinction. After Harley-Davidson fought its way back from the precipice, its executives offered the following warning: "Don't delay. Get started now overhauling your systems and preparing your managers while you still have time to do it right" (Reid 1990: 186).

As the examples and quotes in this chapter suggest, quality improvement does not happen by fiat or slogan. In every instance, improvement comes through changing activities, attitudes, and conditions. Each gain is achieved by deliberate efforts, which link cause and effect. If success or improvement seems to appear independently of any change process or apparent cause, it is probably not true success or lasting improvement; more likely, it is random variation, which will soon disappear.

What has been offered here is not a complete solution to quality. It is only a beginning. The suggested format for improvement projects is just that—a suggestion to be tried, improved on, and advanced beyond; it is a starting point. So, too, are the suggested tools; much more sophisticated tools for analyzing product features, customer requirements, and intersecting points for quality improvement can easily be found. But the tools presented here provide a starting point for the novice and can enable him or her to begin developing a frame of mind that will become increasingly receptive to the quality process. And despite their simplicity, these tools can make significant contributions toward solving the big and easily identified quality problems.

Similarly, the observations on human resource management and customer-supplier relationships only point the way toward quality. Different managers will have different degrees of freedom to act with respect to human resources and customer-supplier relationships. Different organizations will have different sets of circumstances and different levels of receptiveness to this message. However, by knowing the required direction and having a plan, the manager will be prepared to act when opportunities arise.

The prepared manager is aware of alternatives and understands the interactive nature of processes as systems that make suppliers into customers and customers into suppliers. Given this awareness, together with an understanding of variation and how it affects quality, the high-quality manager looks both upstream and downstream in the production cycle. Rooting out sources of variation and focusing more clearly on target products creates quality. Systematic human resource management and the application of appropriate tools make improvement projects possible.

This, then, is the culminating message of our book: Prepare and begin. As Dr. Deming asserts: Significant advances, perhaps all true advances, come from the application of profound knowledge—the combination and interaction of knowledge about variance, systems, individual and group psychology, and learning. Although this book does not claim to present profound knowledge, it does provide a beginning, which can lead to the accumulation and application of profound knowledge. By applying the principles outlined here, managers can reap amazing benefits, not just in the workplace but in education, government, and personal life. May the ending of this book be the beginning of your success in managing quality!

References

Deutsch, C. H. 1990. "Just in Time: The New Partnerships." *New York Times* (Oct. 28): F25.

Main, J. 1990. "How to Win the Baldrige Award." *Fortune* (Apr. 23): 101–116.

Phillips, S., Dunkin, A., Treece, J., and Hammonds, K. 1990. "King Customer." *Business Week* (Mar. 12): 88–94.

Reid, P. C. 1990. *Well Made in America: Lessons Learned from Harley-Davidson on Being the Best.* New York: McGraw-Hill.

Richman, L. S. 1988. "Why Inflation Is Not Inevitable." *Fortune* (Sept. 12): 122.

Vogel, T. 1989. "Big Changes Are Galvanizing General Electric." *Business Week* (Dec. 18): 100–102.

Appendix A

THE CASE OF ENSONIQ CORP.: APPLYING DEMING QUALITY IMPROVEMENT IN A SMALL BUSINESS[1]

Ensoniq Corp., a privately held company founded in 1982, manufactures professional-level electronic musical instruments—synthesizers, digital samplers, and electric pianos. Its products have been highly successful and include two of the best-selling keyboards in the world. It is currently establishing a new division for hearing aids.

Ensoniq's revenues for 1989 were roughly $25 million and it was mildly profitable. Approximately two hundred people work in the company's single facility in Malvern, Pennsylvania, a suburb northwest of Philadelphia. Because Ensoniq designs all its own products, the work force ranges from engineers to blue-collar manufacturing staff. None of the staff is unionized.

Ensoniq did not begin with the Deming philosophy. This approach was introduced three years after the company's inception, when the need for quality became apparent to Bruce Crockett, president and co-owner, and Roy Thomas, operations manager. Keyboard manufacturing is a worldwide business, and Ensoniq's major competitors include Japanese companies famous for high quality: Yamaha, Casio, Korg, and Roland. Although Ensoniq quickly developed a reputation for innovative features, high-quality sound, and good feel (all critical measures for electronic keyboards), its reputation for manufacturing quality, reliability, and durability was not competitive. Furthermore, Ensoniq's Japanese competitors were much larger and better financed; they could afford to reduce the price of their keyboards if customers balked at the quality/price ratio of a particular model. Ensoniq did not

[1]Adapted from R. S. Schuler and D. L. Harris, "Deming Quality Improvement: Implications for Human Resource Management as Illustrated in a Small Company," in *Human Resource Planning* 4, no. 3 (1991): 191–208. The case material presented in this appendix comes from a series of interviews and visits with Ensoniq executives and staff in January, February, March, and September 1990. Because the company is privately held, some confidential information is either withheld or given here in approximate form. Used by permission of the Human Resource Planning Society.

have that option; its survival required that its products be better than its competitors' products on most measures and equal on the others, and that those products be delivered at low cost.

Searching for a solution, Crockett and Thomas attended a Deming seminar, which led them to the realization that attaining world-class quality requires a systematic approach to management. As Deming (1991) says, "Experience by itself means nothing; look at the United States." Although the seminar stimulated Crockett and Thomas, they believed they needed a real-life model to emulate.

Following the seminar, Ensoniq staff visited a Harley-Davidson Corporation plant in Pennsylvania. Harley-Davidson was going through a successful transition to quality management and faced world-class competitors from the same nations as Ensoniq (Reid 1990). The learning experience at Harley-Davidson provided important insights into manufacturing and supplier relationships as well as the Deming's treatment of systems and variation.

Crockett and Thomas also began a reading program. They cite a book by Keki R. Bhote, *World Class Quality* (1988), as being particularly helpful. Among other things, the book explains experimental design in corporate settings.

In the last three years, Ensoniq has employed the Deming philosophy, variations learned from Harley-Davidson, and its own now-systematic learning to improve quality. Although quality is often viewed as comparative (see Garvin 1987; Juran 1989; Ernst & Young 1990; Peters and Waterman 1982), and showing comparative gains can be difficult, Ensoniq offers convincing evidence that its efforts are paying off. Returns on the company's latest model have dropped by around 50 percent from previous models.

Although no standard industry figures are available, estimates show Ensoniq gaining 3 to 4 percentage points in market share during the last year (in a shrinking market). Bruce Crockett offers the following comments on this gain in market share: "Changing a reputation for poor quality takes a very long time. We expect it will take two more high-quality product releases to really change our dealers' attitudes about our products." A large New York dealer echoed this sentiment: "They are supposed to be getting better. Their latest product looks good. We'll see over the next couple of releases." Since the dealers strongly influence the end market, improvement in market share is a very positive indicator of progress.

In addition to the aforementioned external indicators, a number of internal indicators signal improvement. Productivity (manufacturing work-hours required to produce a finished product) has improved 33 percent. Costs have dropped in a similar fashion. Employee turnover is below 2.5

percent per year. Employee complaints have dropped dramatically. And as discussed below, Ensoniq enjoys a high level of employee cooperation in the quality-improvement effort.

Although Ensoniq believes it still has much to accomplish (indeed, its managers agree with Deming that the pursuit of high quality is a never-ending process, since competitors are always improving as well), its experience illustrates Deming's philosophy in action. We are therefore using the Ensoniq case to demonstrate the application of the principles discussed in this book.

EXAMPLES OF PROJECTS

The purchase of printed circuit boards illustrates the change in Ensoniq's vendor relations. Before the change, Ensoniq had entered into a series of very detailed contracts with its suppliers. Every time a board was modified (perhaps three or four times per year), the contract(s) would be renegotiated, the price adjusted, delivery schedules revised, and in some instances, vendors changed. The process was time-consuming, required Ensoniq to buy and take delivery in large quantities, and provided no process for improved vendor cooperation. Each purchase was a contest to see who could get the best deal.

After the change, Ensoniq decided to negotiate a long-term arrangement (though not a contract) for its boards. The primary focus shifted to scheduled deliveries (once per week), quality of incoming materials (with processes for providing feedback to the vendor), and flexibility regarding design changes. After an extensive search, Ensoniq found a vendor that would agree to weekly deliveries, making design changes with four weeks notice, pricing by the square inch (eliminating the need for constant renegotiation), and committing to improving quality of incoming products. Although the nominal price per board was slightly higher than it had been with the negotiated contracts, direct savings from reduced inventory and reduced contracting costs more than made up the difference. Moreover, the immeasurable benefits of high-quality supply and quick responsiveness probably overshadowed all direct cost implications. The vendor benefited by having a partner in improving its output and a predictable, consistent source of revenue.

Ensoniq has invested little in the way of new equipment. Instead, it increased maintenance and worked to improve existing equipment. Its wave soldering machine is a prime example. Under its old system, Ensoniq could not get the machine to perform to the vendor's specifications (1,500 to 3,500 bad connections per million). Instead of buying the next level of technology (an investment of about $110,000), Ensoniq assessed process capability using control charts and conducted a series of industrial experiments. Over a period of several weeks, a team (made up almost entirely of line workers) reduced the error level to 1,000 per million—better than the vendor's specifications—simply by adjusting temperature, speed, setup, etc., and measuring the outcomes. Emboldened by their success, the team decided to experiment further. After including the board-design engineers in the effort, they made a small design modification that resulted in a further reduction of the error level to 100 defects per million—ten times better than the vendor's specifications! The team's new goal is 10 defects per million.

This project did not receive a lot of notice until the team had achieved success. Frankly, both the employees and the manager were initially skeptical of the project's potential. But now that the changes have been made and the results are apparent, everyone involved is proud to tell of his or her part in the project. Other groups and projects now have a model to emulate.

In similar fashion, Ensoniq has revamped its entire manufacturing process, but at little extra expense. Fundamental to achieving these improvements are HR practices such as training, hiring, compensation, discipline, and performance reviews. Training in statistical analysis and experimental design provides employees with the tools and know-how to analyze problems and measure the effectiveness of changes. Freedom from numerical quotas and performance-based pay gives workers time to make improvements. An egalitarian environment is conducive to cooperation between engineers and line workers. Clearly, the HR practices are vital to quality improvement!

ENSONIQ'S HUMAN RESOURCE PRACTICES

Two of the most significant HR management implications of the Deming approach involve compensation and performance appraisal. Two of Deming's principles in particular affect Ensoniq's appraisal system: (1) eliminate numerical quotas for the work force and numerical goals for management; and (2) eliminate the annual rating or merit system. Numerical quotas and compensation goals (such as MBO or performance bonuses) limit management's willingness and capability to produce. If a production manager has a monthly quota of 1,000 units to produce and that quota is met on the twenty-fifth of the month, very little output is likely to be produced during the balance of that month, and whatever output there is will be stockpiled to meet next month's quota. Such goals drive management (and workers) toward their objectives blindly, without regard for the company's well-being.

These plans rarely exceed their objectives and suboptimize other functions at the expense of achieving their goal. If the production manager is short of the 1,000-unit bonus level, he or she will speed up the production line regardless of any effects this action might have on the quality of output.

Returning to the example of the wave soldering machine, the improvements we described would not have occurred in an environment dominated by traditional work quotas and production bonuses. If the workers or managers had received a bonus for numeric production, they would have resisted spending the time required to experiment with the machine. This example also shows the potential for limiting improvement. If the work force had been given a goal of meeting the vendor's specifications (which would have been all that management could reasonably have expected), they would have reached that goal and stopped, never realizing what dramatic additional improvements in quality they could have achieved.

Some argue that the problem is not the existence of goals but the fact that goals are poorly defined. Unless goals are open-ended, constantly changing, or extremely short-term (in which case, they will present enormous problems in evaluation), they cannot possibly overcome the inherent conflict between specific goals and changing company needs. Nor can even the best-defined goals overcome their own inherently limiting force. Even offering bonuses for quality improvement, as some organizations try to do, creates problems: Who will be given the opportunity to participate in quality-improvement projects? Will workers in a very low-quality area receive greater bonuses because they have so much more room for improvement? Who authorizes the production stoppage that will be required in order to conduct experiments?

PERFORMANCE REVIEWS

Deming blasts annual rating or merit systems as destroyers of a work force. Ranking and rating rarely demonstrate more than statistical artifacts (e.g., about half the workers must be above average and about half below). For those ranked below average, the loss in motivation, morale, and even self-respect can have a devastating effect on their performance, creating a self-fulfilling prophesy.

In accordance with Deming's teachings, Ensoniq believes that compensation and what it calls "performance reviews" should *not* be linked and that employees should be informed of their pay scales. (Following Deming's suggestion that even using the term *performance appraisal* might unintentionally bestow legitimacy on ranking or merit-based systems, alternative terms are used. Ensoniq employs the term *performance review,* and in other places, we have employed the term *formal feedback.*) The company has made this philosophy the cornerstone of its review process for both hourly and salaried workers. As Ensoniq states in its salary-administration guidelines: "Reviews and salary administration are totally separate. The purpose of the performance review is to provide a dialogue between the employee and supervisor, whereby the employee's performance can be enhanced. The performance reviews are not used to determine the employee salary" (Ensoniq "Personnel Policies Handbook," effective November 10, 1989). Both hourly and salaried employees at Ensoniq are reviewed every four months.

For both types of employees, there is *no* emphasis on quantitative measures. As Roy Thomas, Ensoniq's manager of operations, points out: "We used to have standards. Then we realized they never made a bad person good; but they sure made good people mad!" Furthermore, workers use control charts and other statistical measures of production extensively, so they obtain immediate and direct quantitative feedback from the system. If an employee's output at a workstation falls outside the system for that workstation, the employee or his or her supervisor initiates an investigation into the causes of that deviation. ("Outside the system" typically means that performance measures are more than three standard deviations from the average performance or that a consistent pattern is revealed for seven or more consecutive measurements [such a pattern may involve all measurements' being above or below average, all moving in one direction, or measurements' alternating between above- and below-average]. The use of such measures requires only a rudimentary knowledge of statistics. The curious reader is directed to Deming [1986, pages 109–115, 256–266, and 321–327] and, for complete coverage, to Duncan 1986). Discovery of the source of the anomaly leads to corrective action. If the employee is responsible, that action might include additional training, counseling, or reassignment, as conditions warrant. If machinery or tools are malfunctioning, they receive maintenance. If supplies are defective, production is halted until good supplies can be obtained.

Formal reviews focus on a worker's overall effectiveness in terms of communication skills, leadership, adaptability, and initiative. The reviews are designed to be interactive, and their structure strives to create regular, constructive communication between employee and supervisor. An example of an Ensoniq review form was shown in Chapter 5 (see Figure 5.3).

Because the reviews are highly qualitative, the potential for favoritism— or at least the perception of it—exists, but because the review process excludes salary considerations, the issue rarely arises. Ensoniq managers also try to avoid this pitfall by maintaining an open-door policy for all workers. Managers know about problems before they show up on the review. "[A supervisor] can't say a person has poor quality without someone else already knowing about it," says Personnel Director Terry Carter. Publicly displayed production data contribute to shared awareness of how everyone is doing.

Ensoniq encourages people to talk to managers in their department, the personnel director, or the company's president if they are dissatisfied with the response to a complaint. And says Carter, "Co-workers stick up for one another, but anybody who's not toeing the line sticks out like a sore thumb."

Ensoniq's size contributes to the success of its innovative review program. All the workers know each other, and many of the salaried workers have risen through the hourly ranks themselves. "Everyone is for the company because they know it's in their interests . . . so they're looking out for each other," Carter says. "Of course, as we get bigger and bigger, that will be harder and harder." The company projects growth from $25 million in sales to $75 million in five years, so Ensoniq will soon be facing those challenges.

COMPENSATION

Deming's position on compensation is one of the most difficult for American businesses to accept. Merit raises, bonuses for accomplishing numerical goals, and pay for performance are deeply ingrained in management thinking and in American culture at large. When Deming insists on abolishing these practices, he cuts at strongly felt values. Why would Deming suggest so fundamental a change?

Workers rarely control the resources that truly influence output. They cannot buy new equipment. They are not allowed to change procedures. They do not assign territories or accounts. They do not buy the materials they use. These factors and more, along with the workers, determine output. Ascribing full responsibility, and hence reward or punishment, to the workers for the variance of the entire system can only be capricious.

If differential pay systems are to be eliminated, what will take their place? Ensoniq has two approaches—one each for hourly and salaried employees. Hourly employees advance by seniority in grade, by grade advancement, and by grade adjustments made in response to labor-market conditions. Publicly posted schedules of advancements and grades reveal a flat pay structure (there are typically only two grades in a work area, with employees reaching the top of a grade in two years or less).

Initially, employees resisted this open, egalitarian approach. They would say, "If I am producing twenty-two boards a day while Joe is only producing eighteen boards a day, why am I not getting paid more?" Management's response: "We made a contract with you. We pay you a fair wage, one you have accepted. You have agreed to put in a full day's work, putting forth your best efforts. We have the same contract with Joe. Our agreement does not specify comparing you and Joe, nor do you and Joe have a contract with each other."

Equity theory would suggest that the employee producing twenty-two boards per day would adjust his efforts (slack off) to create a more "equitable" situation (Pinder 1987; Mowday 1987). Ensoniq overcomes this equity pressure in two ways. First, the gestalt of quality helps. Managers have credibility; employees see through repeated, consistent action that management is not out to take advantage of them. So, employees listen to managers and think. Managers also provide repeated explanations of the effect of the overall system. When necessary they may make demonstrations of the system. For example, two employees might be asked to chart their production for a month, and then switch workstations and chart production for another month. Almost always, comparing the two reveals dominance of the workstation over the employee. The employee then begins to understand why differential pay for "performance" often has little to do with their performance.

For salaried workers, the situation is a little different. Greater competition for skilled employees forces Ensoniq to adjust to the market. Although annual raises are given at employment anniversary, more significant adjustments occur when the employees and management become aware of an imbalance between the employees' skills and the labor-market valuation of those skills. Both employees and management read job ads and salary surveys, participate in employment interviews, gather information from many sources, and discuss that information in coming to an estimate of employees' market worth. Because of the trust built into the system, employees seem willing to discuss options and offers from others with Ensoniq management before committing to those alternatives.

Besides receiving wages, all employees participate in a quarterly profit-sharing plan. A portion of the profits is distributed pro rata to all staff, based on regular salary. Because of high research and development expenses associated with starting a new product line and division, payouts from the profit-sharing program have been very small in the last two years.

Strong evidence of the effectiveness of these HR policies can be seen in Ensoniq's low turnover rate. Only one person has left the salaried ranks (which total over eighty people) in the last eighteen months. Turnover in hourly employees is less than 2.5 percent per year.

TRAINING AND DEVELOPMENT

The employee side of quality depends on employees' knowing what to do and having the ability to perform. Extensive orientation provides the former, and extensive training provides the latter. As conditions change (e.g., technology and methods), retraining prepares employees for new tasks and enables an organization to maintain its current work force. It also supports employees who develop new and improved ways to perform their tasks, thereby enhancing quality even further. If their suggestions result in technology change, employees know that training will be available and that a policy of employment security will be followed.

At Ensoniq, Bruce Crockett estimates that employees in the plant receive between 100 and 160 hours of training per year. All of this training is on-the-job (or at least very near the employees' jobs). This compares with industry and association (e.g., the American Society for Training and Development) estimates of between 25 and 30 hours of training per year for the average production worker. Thomas and Crockett view Ensoniq's 33 percent improvement in productivity and costs and its 50 percent to 60 percent reduction in returns as evidence that the company's training in tasks, statistics, and experimental design is paying off.

STAFFING

In building a work force dedicated to quality, offering the current employees opportunities for promotion and new job assignments rather than seeking people from the outside fosters loyalty and commitment. This policy, aided by internal job posting, creates a viable internal labor market. Having employees systematically move through different jobs provides newness, change, and an opportunity to grow. This, of course, requires concern for employee job readiness.

Ensoniq builds job rotation into some positions and, through internal job postings, makes rotation available to all employees. Moreover, Ensoniq allows employees the opportunity to move or advance and, if the new position does not work out, return to their former position. Employees are not fired or transferred merely because they try something different and discover they are not suited or ready for it. Furthermore, some employees have left Ensoniq in pursuit of other opportunities, only to rejoin the company (for whatever reasons). When their past performance has been satisfactory, Ensoniq has welcomed these returning employees.

Another aspect of staffing is the initial hiring of individuals from the outside. Dedicated and committed employees can be good sources of referrals, and it is in their personal and professional interests to refer candidates who are likely to be acceptable to the organization. Regardless of whether candidates are referred, staffing procedures consistent with building employee commitment tend to minimize task-specific fit and instead accentuate fit with the organizational culture. Consequently, the selection process focuses on allowing enough time for each applicant to view the work environment and for the organization to see whether the current employees react favorably to the potential hire. Formal testing is minimal, particularly for production jobs that require skills that can be readily provided by on-the-job training.

For managers and technicians, job differences are greater and job-related skills more extensive and critical. Hence, references, samples of work, demonstration of skills, work experience, and field of specialty in college aid in selecting candidates. This, in turn, makes it very difficult to fill skill gaps with quick training programs.

At Ensoniq, staffing works very much this way. For production workers, Ensoniq "hires" a candidate for a day. For a day's pay the candidate receives an overview and works side-by-side with existing employees, receiving a realistic preview of the environment. Existing employees get to meet candidates and assess their likely "fit" in the group and the task environment; this assessment becomes part of the hiring decision. The success rate for production worker applicants is about 75 percent. Engineering and other candidates go through multiple interviews including an occasional team interview. While production work applicants are readily available (most based upon referrals), mechanical-design engineers rarely match Ensoniq's requirements.

A third component of staffing is the discipline and removal of employees. In an environment dedicated to quality, any practice that threatens employees must be applied consistently and fairly. Deming demands that organizations drive out fear; threats of capricious or politically influenced dismissal create persistent fear in an organization. Ensoniq addresses the issues of consistency and fairness by making workers enforce rules. Except for egregious offenses (e.g., arriving at work drunk, fighting at work, bringing weapons to work) and during an initial ninety-day probation period, managers do not dismiss employees. Peers handle all employee discipline, removal, and appeals according to rules established by management.

Since quality production at Ensoniq allows little buffering between work stations, the primary cause of dismissal involves exceeding the attendance boundaries specified in the "Personnel Policies Handbook." Ensoniq calls these rules "No Fault Absence" because they define attendance, absence, and tardiness independently of the reason for absence. An employee accumulates points for various forms of absence, as shown in the following list:

Type of Offense	Points
1. Late 1 to 12 minutes	1
2. Late more than 12 minutes with prior notice	1
3. Late more than 12 minutes without prior notice	2
4. Absent up to 8 hours with prior notice	2
5. Absent up to 8 hours without prior notice	3
6. Absent more than 8 consecutive hours	3
7. Absent without calling in or prior notice	4

These points accumulate during a floating ninety-day period. The following list shows the sanctions imposed for the accumulation of various point totals. An employee's only recourse is to appeal these sanctions to a committee composed of two peers and the HR manager.

Infraction	Sanction
1. Accumulating 9–11 points in a 90-day period	Warning
2. Accumulating 12 or more points in a 90-day period	Discharge
3. Accumulating 3 warnings in a 90-day period	Discharge
4. Being absent for 3 consecutive days without notifying the company	Discharge

Because discipline is based on rules and data, workers perceive it as being consistent. Employee acceptance and the rigor of the peer committee (few win an appeal) attest to perceived fairness. At Ensoniq, employees no longer say, "The manager fired so-and-so"; they say, "So-and-so fired himself [or herself]." And since no excuse is good enough to prevent accumulating points, employees appear less inclined to resort to deception and lying to managers.

Once management directs attention to human resources in pursuit of quality, its focus expands to all areas of HR practices. Ensoniq illustrates follow-through in work environment, health, and safety. The production area is clean, orderly, well lit, and fairly quiet. A clean, orderly work space leads to fewer defects from contaminants. Furthermore, employees prefer to work in good conditions.

Management and staff share responsibility for safety. Management has the main responsibility: equipment maintenance, environment, work flow and pace, and training. Employees are responsible for working within the limits of the environment, monitoring equipment status, and demanding that management address potential safety hazards. Management also establishes dress and grooming rules aimed at limiting the chance of injury from machines. Because Ensoniq does not have numeric quotas or hard production limits, employees are not at odds with management over safety.

Although the first step in the area of employee health is accident prevention, Ensoniq also addresses several more general issues. Its facilities all adhere to a no-smoking policy; no one—executives, managers, hourly workers, visitors—is allowed to smoke inside an Ensoniq building. Employees at all levels receive reimbursement for membership in a health club of their choice. Ensoniq encourages employees to take accrued vacation time. Attention to health appears to pay off for Ensoniq in reduced workers' compensation claims and lower levels of health-related absences.

THE TRANSFORMATION TO QUALITY

Although this catalog of HR practices appears readily understandable, the transition to a high-quality workplace is by no means easy. Before any changes are implemented, upper management must decide not only whether it is willing to take the necessary steps but also whether it is actually capable of taking them. Management must commit to the new philosophy and be prepared to commit resources. As Bruce Crockett explained:

> [Once management thinks it wants to change] people have to go someplace where they are doing what you want to do. You have to make sure it works; don't just read books. After you decide it can work, you have to decide if you are willing to do what they [the model company] did. The path to a new system is long and strenuous.

As mentioned earlier, Ensoniq used Harley-Davidson as its model. Almost all managers and supervisors, plus several line workers, visited Harley-Davidson. They went through every aspect of Harley's transition. Upon their return, the Ensoniq staff agreed that they could copy many of the things Harley had done and that they could change some other things, and they committed to the transition.

Bruce Crockett estimates that the transition to real effectiveness under the new philosophy involved a two- to three-year undertaking. Changing the attitudes of personnel and gaining acceptance of the new policies and work procedures required sustained effort on the part of management. For line workers, accustomed to more traditional American HR practices, the transition brought sometimes painful changes. Some of the pretransition staff left Ensoniq to avoid changing.

SUMMARY AND CONCLUSION

Ensoniq applied the general principles advocated in this book. Although managers like Roy Thomas had support from the executive suite, they still approached their quality-improvement efforts on a project-by-project basis, letting success generate enthusiasm and momentum. Documenting and selling success led to similar projects on each major piece of equipment in the manufacturing process. When personnel policies are changed to reduce antagonism and distrust, employees at all levels become willing to cooperate in the future of the company—in its quality. Perhaps this is the most important lesson: When employees see direct benefits in the form of stable, reliable, rewarding jobs in the future, they find good reasons to cooperate.

This case has attempted to illustrate how Ensoniq has worked toward improved quality by applying Deming's fourteen points (which were listed in Chapter 2) on a project-by-project basis. Although Ensoniq has not implemented every one of Deming's points (e.g., although it would like to provide full support for outside education, Ensoniq cannot afford that step), it *has* addressed some of the more difficult issues:

- Ensoniq no longer applies numerical quotas or ranks employees (points 11 and 12).

- Nowhere at Ensoniq will one find slogans or exhortations regarding goals over which the workers have no control (point 10).

- By eliminating conflicting compensation systems, ensuring that discussions of product or process change consist of data-based (not opinion-based) analysis, and involving all departments in planning change, Ensoniq is removing barriers between departments (point 9).

- Changes in hiring, firing, promotion, reviews, and compensation aid in driving out the fear between workers and management (point 8).

- Because management no longer needs to worry about these issues, it has more time to provide leadership (point 7).

- Ensoniq conducts much more than the average amount of on-the-job training (point 6).

- Management (and workers) have adopted and committed to the goal of long-term quality improvement, with the aim of beating competitors, staying in business, and providing jobs (points 1, 2, and 14).

Ensoniq's approach is not the only possible way to implement a quality-improvement effort, but it does provide evidence that Deming's approach and the approach suggested herein are not culture-specific; the task *can* be accomplished. The effort is neither simple, quick, nor one-shot; quality requires sustained effort and commitment. The steps to quality must include changes in HR practices as well as in supplies, equipment, procedures, and facilities.

References

Bhote, K. R. 1988. *World Class Quality*. New York: AMA Membership Publications.

Deming, W. E. 1986. *Out of the Crisis*. Cambridge, Mass.: MIT Center for Advanced Engineering Studies.

———. 1991. Comments made at annual conference of PACE, Philadelphia Area Council for Excellence, titled "Transformation for Management of Quality and Productivity." Philadelphia, PA, Feb. 19–22.

Duncan, A. J. 1986. Quality Control and Industrial Statistics. 5th ed. Homewood, Ill.: Irwin.

Ernst & Young Quality Improvement Consulting Group. 1990. *Total Quality: An Executive's Guide for the 1990's*. Homewood, Ill.: Dow Jones–Irwin.

Garvin, D. A. 1987. "A Note on Quality: Views of Deming, Juran, and Crosby." Harvard Business School publication 9–687–001, rev. June 1987.

Juran, J. M. 1989. *Juran on Leadership for Quality*. New York: Free Press.

Mowday, R. T. 1987. "Equity Theory Predictions of Behavior in Organizations." In *Motivation and Work Behavior*, edited by R. Steers and L. Porter. New York: McGraw-Hill.

Peters, T. J., and Waterman, R. H. 1982. *In Search of Excellence*. New York: Warner Books.

Pinder, C. C. 1987. "Valence-Instrumentality-Expectancy Theory." In *Motivation and Work Behavior*, edited by R. Steers and L. Porter. New York: McGraw-Hill.

Reid, P. C. 1990. *Well Made in America: Lessons from Harley-Davidson on Being the Best*. New York: McGraw-Hill.

Appendix B

CASE STUDY OF THE HR DEPARTMENT AT SWISS BANK CORPORATION: CUSTOMERIZATION FOR HIGH-QUALITY CUSTOMER SERVICE[1]

The demand for U.S. companies to respond to the needs of customers has never been greater than today. Increasingly, responding effectively to the external customer also requires that units within the organization treat each other as customers. By responding more effectively to the needs of its customers, human resources can become a higher-quality, more customer-service–oriented department. This case describes how one HR department made the transition from performing a traditional HR function to being a totally high-quality, customer-oriented operation.

THE PHILOSOPHY OF CUSTOMERIZATION

In the service business of providing line managers with human resource services and products, high quality results in part from putting the customer first—something easier said than done.

Systematic programs to put the customer first involve changing an extensive set of processes and procedures and creating an "everybody is a customer" mentality. To highlight the fact that what is being discussed here is more than traditional "treating the customer right" or "customerizing for the customer" campaigns, the term *customerization* is used.

A fundamental aspect of customerization as a way of doing business is the recognition and acceptance of the fact that all organizations—even ser-

---

[1]Adapted from R. S. Schuler, "A Case Study of the HR Department at Swiss Bank Corporation," *Human Resource Planning* 11, no. 4 (1989): 241–253. Used by permission of the Human Resource Planning Society.

vice businesses—produce and deliver products. Although these may vary in terms of tangibility, half-life, or customer participation, they are all products nonetheless, and they can be differentiated. It is recognized that services and products are generally treated as different types of organizational outputs. Services are typically distinguished by their intangibility, the fact that they are produced and consumed simultaneously, and the extent of customer participation. Even when services are rendered, however, a product is in fact being transferred. Seen in this light, service becomes a part of the delivery system for a product and, as such, an essential part of customerization. So essential is the quality of the delivery that it is typically used to differentiate products—e.g., Ford cars from GM cars. Thus, customerization incorporates service as an integral part of product differentiation.

ASPECTS OF CUSTOMERIZATION

Although putting the customer first is an integral part of customerization, customerization means a great deal more. Fundamental to customerization is gathering information from and about the customer, responding to the customer, including the customer in the development of responses, and getting feedback that will enable the organization to evaluate, revise, and rerespond.

Essential to customerization is the realization that it requires more effective work from everyone. It requires internal motivation. Customerization programs often result in jobs' being redesigned to increase the level of responsibility and accountability. Although not all employees respond equally, for those who prefer enhanced responsibility, customerization can be energizing and rewarding. For those who regard it as more work, a different job environment may be necessary.

Employees must also be motivated if customerization programs are to succeed. Consequently, such programs typically involve more recognition: more pay for performance, more attendance programs, enhanced performance-appraisal systems that result in fairer evaluation of performance, and more celebrations of success.

Thus, customerization programs typically require new and/or additional behaviors (roles) from employees. Because behavior is commonly a function of ability and motivation, training programs are often offered in conjunction with customerization programs. Outstanding customer service requires a commitment to ongoing training that stresses job-related skills, positive attitudes toward customers and coworkers, and overall company knowledge, according to Robert L. Desatnick, president of Creative Human

Resources and former vice president of human resources at McDonald's. In his book *Managing to Keep the Customer,* Desatnick maintains that comprehensive training programs are the key to successful customer service at many leading companies (Desatnick 1988: 8).

In essence, then, customerization involves both process and content. It depends on every employee, every unit, and the entire organization seeing the rest of the world (internal and external) as customers. It means asking, responding, and revising. It means enhancing the ability of each employee, unit, and organization to respond to the changing demands of others in the environment. And it means adding value by enhancing the quality and uniqueness of the products offered to others. As such, customerization involves a specific set of activities with a highly participative philosophy directed at revitalizing organizations (or parts thereof) so they will be more competitive and respond more flexibly to the changing demands of the environment.

Although customerization programs involve a generic set of activities and a common philosophy, the specifics of their implementation will vary with each unit or organization—e.g., compare Ford's dealer-improvement program with Bell Canada's customer-service program. Nonetheless, examining the specifics of one situation in some detail can offer insights relevant to other applications. Thus, we look at the specifics involved in customerizing the human resource department at the Swiss Bank Corporation (SBC) in the United States (Schuler and Jackson 1988).

THE SWISS BANK CORPORATION

SBC is a $110-billion Swiss universal bank headquartered in Basel, Switzerland, with branches around the world. SBC's U.S. organization has relative autonomy and thus is able to decide how to run its own human resource operation, as long as that operation is consistent with the bank's overall mission and strategy. A new mission statement was officially issued in June 1986. A short time later, all areas of the bank were asked to examine their strengths and weaknesses in relation to the new mission and strategy and to set a course of action to support their findings.

During this time, Michael Mitchell was hired as the vice president of human resources. With his broad business and human resource management background, Mitchell began running the HR department as a business designed to serve other units in the bank. He wanted his department to have credibility and impact with the rest of the bank and knew that the only way to achieve this was by adding value through the creation of a strong customer focus within the HR function. This marked the metamorphosis of the human resource department from record keeper and rule enforcer to facilitator and deliverer of new products and services. In essence, this was the beginning of the customerization of the HR department at SBC's U.S. organization.

CUSTOMERIZING THE HR DEPARTMENT AT SBC

SBC's HR customerization program had four major phases:

1. Information gathering

2. Developing action agendas

3. Implementing the action agendas

4. Evaluating and revising the agendas

Throughout all four phases, a major goal was for the HR department to become more customer-oriented. Prior to Mitchell's arrival in late 1985, the HR department at Swiss Bank Corporation had focused on bread-and-butter activities (record keeping, recruiting, rule enforcement, etc.). Soon, the department was completely reorganized and clearly focused on enhancing the quality and uniqueness of the HR products and services it offered.

PHASE I: INFORMATION GATHERING

The first phase involved a great deal of learning. The HR department diagnosed the environment both outside and within the HR department. HR staff talked with "customers" (employees and managers of the bank) and learned to see the world through their eyes. In effect, the HR department conducted a needs assessment focusing on the requirements of its customers. During this phase, it is important to resist the temptation to *tell* customers "what ails them" and what cures you can offer, according to Mitchell. Instead, you must *listen* to customers and encourage them to tell you how they think you can be of service. Key questions that were asked included:

1. "What do you now get from the HR department?"

2. "What is your ideal of the department?"

3. "How can we begin to change the situation together?"

At Swiss Bank Corporation, Mike Mitchell found informal discussions with line managers and nonmanagers to be a particularly good way to gather information and obtain commitment to change. One line manager who turned out to be a supporter of customerization was Joel Stewart, senior vice president of domestic operations, a twenty-five-year veteran of SBC. Given the new demands from the environment and SBC's new mission statement, Stewart welcomed the opportunity to get assistance from this newly developing HR service group. Such conversations also helped Mitchell identify which of SBC's potential customers would be good first customers for his customerization program, which became known as Operation Phoenix.

Operation Phoenix is a name that might be applied to a secret corporate merger or covert government operations, but at Swiss Bank Corporation, it describes the transformation of the human resources department from a record-keeping cost center to a customer-oriented function integrated with the business and generating revenue (Halcrow 1987: 96).

Information gathering by the HR department did not stop at the company's boundaries. Valuable data were also collected outside the organization. Information about what other companies were doing was obtained by reading news reports, attending conferences, and talking with colleagues. These external sources of information helped the department identify possibilities for new activities and new ways of performing current activities. Learning from competitors has been an institutional practice in a few excellent companies that have sought ideas for initiating new HR programs.

In some organizations, such as Xerox and Motorola, initiatives result from "competitive benchmarking," a process of assessing the best of competitor practices and acting to reduce the competitors' advantage while also building on unique company strengths (Walker 1988).

Finally, information was gathered from the HR department itself. Questions asked within the HR department included:

1. "Who are our customers?"

2. "What is the bank's business strategy?"

3. "How can we best help our customers?"

4. "Are we able to help them?"

5. "Are we motivated to help them?"

The HR department's self-examination and evaluation of its readiness to customerize was a critical process, according to Mitchell.

Before developing action agendas, it was important for the HR department to have a vision of itself in the future. Given the newly acquired information and the state of the HR profession, the department needed to articulate what it wanted to be like at the end of its transformation period and what type of relationship it should have with the rest of the company. It also needed to ask itself two questions: (1) "Will the department's current ways of operating and its current structure suffice to enable it to move ahead?" (2) "Do the department members have all the skills needed to meet future challenges, or are new skills called for?" In response to this self-examination, the HR department developed a mission statement, which read as follows:

> Develop and deliver the highest quality HR products and services that meaningfully support the needs and vitality of our organization and its employees.
> Create a business strategy for our function that challenges the limitations of the HR practice and provides the potential for us to become a successful business enterprise in our own right.
> Be the best at who we are and what we do. ("Operation Phoenix" 1988: 21)

At Swiss Bank Corporation, part of the new vision included changing the HR department from a cost center to a profit center. The department realized that this vision would require that it completely reorganize itself. One interesting aspect of the reorganization was the establishment of a group responsible for long-term planning and new-product development. Significantly, the reorganization helped the HR department respond to its own desire to establish career paths within the department in addition to serving the needs of its customers. The department's overall structure was reshaped from the typical five separate sections—training, employment and salary administration, payroll, benefits, and internal staffing—to three functional units: planning, marketing, and systems and administration.

For the first time, the HR department was a fully integrated whole, not five separate areas heading in five different directions. As a result of the new mission and structure, the HR department:

- Became an integrated player in the business planning of the organization.

- Developed and implemented major new programs including an incentive compensation plan, an upgraded mortgage and benefits program and a new training strategy.

- Developed and piloted a fully integrated HR management program named *Horizon* [described below].

- Set the stage for developing better products and services by establishing a planning function known as the "SBC Resource Management Group." This team does not handle day-to-day transactions and can therefore focus completely on product development, service innovations, and planning for the future. ("Operation Phoenix" 1988: 21)

Although this was an exciting time, it was also a time of considerable ambiguity for most of the twenty-eight employees working in Mitchell's department. According to the employees, Mitchell gave them confidence, support, and training but not always all the answers. Both as a consequence and by design, they became adept at dealing with the environment and modus operandi of customerization. After deciding that the new environment required too much self-directed and self-initiated behavior, eight employees voluntarily left (and their positions were quickly filled). When the company clearly explained what was expected early on, self-selection to leave became a natural outcome. This, of course, is the fairest way to reorganize a group.

PHASE II: DEVELOPING ACTION AGENDAS

Armed with the relevant information and a mission statement, the HR department was ready to develop action agendas. Agendas were drawn up with the intention of reducing the gaps between:

- The HR department's limited knowledge and what was required to become an informed partner

- The line managers' awareness of the products the HR department was offering and what it actually offered

- What the line managers saw as the activities that the HR department was currently carrying out and what they saw as the activities that the department should ideally be carrying out

- What the HR department saw as the current state of the services it provided and what it saw as the actual needs of the department's customers

Agendas were in fact statements of actions to be taken by the HR department to reduce the gaps and be more customer-oriented. Agendas included conducting meetings with line managers and identifying specific actions that could be taken to develop new products. One result was the establishment of an HR hot line (a cordless telephone moved from desk to desk to enable the HR department to respond to any phone inquiry from line customers). With the introduction of the hot-line concept, HR employees were expected to solve customer problems immediately. Neither the problem nor the customer was to be passed on to someone else.

Once the vision started taking shape and action agendas were drawn up, the HR department established a game plan for implementing the agendas. Line approval and support for moving ahead were obtained, especially from those line managers who wished to be the new HR department's first "customers." Due to resource limitations, not all units of SBC could be involved in the customerization program initially. Mitchell selected as the first customers those who were most supportive of the HR department's new services. Joel Stewart was among the first group, as was Jerry Goodman, a vice president in the international division. Both these individuals saw Mitchell's customerization program as something that would help them be more effective and help SBC move into the increasingly deregulated (post–Glass-Steagal) banking era.

PHASE III: IMPLEMENTING THE ACTION AGENDAS

The third phase of customerization involved the HR department's going out and recontacting customers to discuss the agendas. The goal of these meetings was to ascertain precisely how the specific needs of the line managers would be met. When the HR staff and each line manager agreed on what was needed, a formal contract was drawn up to serve as an action plan. The contract specified dates, indicated who was responsible for what, and clarified how the project's success was to be evaluated.

As it carried out these activities, the HR department started gaining new knowledge of the business as well as acceptance by some line managers. The seeds were being planted for the HR department to play a valued strategic role in the business. Joel Stewart came to regard Mike Mitchell as an unofficial adviser on Stewart's compensation strategy and on the selection of outsiders for key management positions. It was at this point that Mitchell realized that in order for the HR department to play a strategic role, he and the department had to know the line managers' business concerns and have their confidence and trust. He also realized that these were the fruits of the customerization process.

This third phase also involved a major marketing effort. As the HR department became more customer-oriented, it quickly began to develop innovative ideas for products based on new knowledge of the strategy, the competitors, and what other successful companies were doing. Because these services were new and unfamiliar to the department's customers, they had to be sold, at least initially. Once these services had proved their worth, however, they generated their own demand. So in addition to implementing the specifically agreed-upon agendas and contracts, the third phase of customerization included developing and selling new products and creating a market demand.

At Swiss Bank Corporation, one of the major new HR products was an HR management program called "Horizon." Horizon was created to address SBC's HR management needs by ensuring the continued success of the bank through the success and growth of its employees. Horizon has four major parts:

1. *Business Planning:* Translates the mission and business plans of the Bank into performance objectives for today and staffing requirements for the future.

2. *Performance Management:* Focuses employees' efforts directly in support of the bank's most important current business objectives.

3. *Human Resource Planning:* Matches employee development plans and aspirations with the Bank's human resource needs. This analysis provides succession plans and identifies recruiting, training, and development needs.

4. *Career Planning:* Provides a more formal channel of communication to discuss employee career aspirations and developmental needs. ("Operation Phoenix" 1988: 19)

Horizon has been so successful that the HR group is considering developing and marketing it, together with software they developed to prepare the department's impressive multimedia "sales presentation" for top SBC management. In other words, the HR department is now expanding its definition of customers to include some that are outside SBC.

PHASE IV: EVALUATING AND REVISING THE AGENDAS

Part and parcel of the agenda-implementation phase was developing contracts that specified what was to be delivered to each customer. The customer then had the right to appraise the work delivered. These appraisals were the means by which the quality of the HR department's work was evaluated. This was not a totally novel approach to improving the quality of products delivered to customers. According to William Eggleston, vice president in charge of quality at IBM:

Throughout IBM you find people setting 'contracts' at the internal customer interface. Each contract contains explicit statements of what the internal customer expects and clear criteria for measuring success in meeting those expectations. We manage directly to the goals established in the contracts. (Labovitz 1987: 8)

Contracts were not the only way to appraise the HR department's work. For example, the HR department also developed a list of criteria for evaluating its own performance. Such criteria included a reduction in turnover due to better selection procedures and an increase in the number of innovative products the HR department developed for its customers. Ultimately, of course, the true test of success is whether customers come knocking on your door to solicit your help, according to Mitchell. Table B.1 illustrates short-term results for the HR department, which, in turn, led to company and departmental effectiveness (see Fitz-enz 1984).

MAXIMIZING THE SUCCESS OF SBC'S CUSTOMERIZATION PROGRAM

Several characteristics of SBC's customerization program contributed to its success:

1. *The program was aimed at the highest level (qualitywise and organizationwise).* It was important that the HR department have as much impact as possible from the beginning.

2. *Early projects were successful.* Mitchell's group initially worked only with the line managers who were most committed to participating in the new program and most willing to work with the HR staff. Following the successes with those managers, the rest of the company could see the benefits and then ask to join in.

Table B.1 Effects of Customerizing the HR Department to Enhance the Quality of Services

Phase of Customerization	Short-Term Results	HR Department Effectiveness	Company Effectiveness
Information gathering	Reorientation New knowledge	New Products Responsiveness	Better selection
Agenda building	Creative insights	Strategic player	Greater utilization
Agenda implementation	Familiarity	Heightened commitment	Increased retention
Evaluation and revision	Acceptance	Internal cohesiveness	Competitive advantage

3. *Customers and HR staff experienced ownership and involvement.* Both customers and the HR department were part of the program's development and implementation from the very beginning. This helped ensure that the products delivered were of the highest quality and met the customers' needs.

4. *The customerization program was marketed.* The HR department named its customerization effort as a means of crystallizing its new image in people's minds. In the case of the Swiss Bank Corporation, as mentioned earlier, the name selected was *Operation Phoenix.*

5. *The HR staff had fun.* Customerization represented a major organizational change that required tremendous energy and new learning. Doing it right involved a great deal of work, and HR employees were stretched to new limits. However, motivation levels were kept high.

Although these characteristics might not guarantee success for customerization programs elsewhere, they do appear to be necessary. Because Operation Phoenix has been in existence for less than two years, however, it is impossible to determine whether these characteristics will prove sufficient in the long run.

IMPLICATIONS OF HR CUSTOMERIZATION FOR SBC MANAGERS

Members of the HR staff were not the only people affected by customerization. Clearly, the customers' old ways of doing business had to change in order for customerization to succeed.

Perhaps the most important change for SBC line managers was that they needed (and wanted) to work closely with the HR department as they gathered information. Line managers had to share their views on the strategy of their business with Mike Mitchell and consider the implications of the strategy for human resource management. As the line and HR staff became partners in the business, the line managers began to play a new role and accepted the new role played by the HR director and department. This adjustment proved to be natural for line managers like Stewart and Goodman. It is also proving natural for line managers elsewhere as they increasingly embrace the concept and importance of customerization:

"Close to the customer" may have become the grand corporate cliché of the Eighties, but it's a cliché that one CEO after another invokes with no apparent sense of embarrassment. To the contrary, they embrace the principle with the fervor of born-again believers. (Keichel 1988: 35)

In addition, the line managers were ready to talk with and listen to Mitchell and his staff as they proposed new programs to improve their chances for gaining competitive advantage through the use of human resources. Line managers accepted some of the responsibility for ensuring that their units were using human resources to their fullest potential.

Finally, line managers worked with the human resource group to appraise the success of the HR efforts. This included developing and using contracts for the new products that the HR staff devised in response to the needs of the line managers as well as providing honest and useful feedback that would enable the HR department to improve its future efforts.

Overall, customerizing the HR department required the line managers to play a much bigger, more active, and more explicit role in the management of human resources. For them, at least initially, this meant a great deal of time, involvement, and learning as well as new behaviors. Fortunately, "customers—individual or industrial, high-tech or low-, science-trained or untrained—will pay a lot for better, and especially *best* quality . . . " (Peters 1987: 54).

SUMMARY

Although customers are willing to pay for high quality, it may not always be easy for companies, HR departments, or any other departments to convince themselves that a quality-improvement program is worth the effort. It's easy to acknowledge that things aren't as good as they perhaps could be, but it isn't always easy to accept this fact, realize the consequences of not acting, and then take the next step of actually changing the situation:

> There is a story that when productivity guru, W. Edwards Deming, gave a speech in Detroit in 1980 lambasting the U.S. auto industry for its shortcomings versus the Japanese, Ford's Donald Petersen was seated on one side and GM's James McDonald was seated on the other. After listening to Deming's diatribe, GM's president issued an edict that no one in GM should ever use Deming's consulting firm. Ford, on the other hand, hired Deming and took his lessons to heart. ("How Ford Turned Around" 1988: 1)

The basic tendency of organizations is to maintain the status quo, perhaps because successful examples of major change are seldom seen. The leadership role goes to those departments that do change, that do so for the benefit of the organization, and that do so successfully—e.g., William Eggleston at IBM and Michael Mitchell at SBC. Assuming a leadership role is itself a significant contribution in this time when change and adaptation are more vital than ever before.

The type of change described in this appendix is very special. It is focused on improving quality, developing new products, enhancing value, staying current, adding excitement, and creating a win–win attitude throughout an entire unit of an organization. These results of HR customerization easily carry over to other areas of a company. As they do, they become the glue capable of binding the organization together. Consequently, the customerization program becomes self-perpetuating. It creates its own energy and excitement, which sustain the customerization process and spread it to other areas. The result: HR departments and organizations that are delivering the highest quality and most innovative products today and are willing to adapt to meet tomorrow's challenges.

For HR departments in particular, the rewards of customerization are substantial. HR departments have the opportunity to become strategic players in organizations. They are typically eliminated from that role (by default), however, because they just don't know the business and don't have a bottom-line orientation. The customerization process requires HR departments to gather data from their customers. As a consequence, they learn about the business, and they come to appreciate the bottom-line orientation. The result: a greater ability to link human resource management practices and concerns with the strategic issues facing the business and an even greater ability to obtain competitive advantage through the skillful application of human resource practices.

The beauty of customerization is that it's integral to organizational survival today. So when it is started in one part of a company, it is likely to spread in response to demand from other areas. Customerization by one department results in at least one other department's becoming more effective (or more embarrassed). Although the SBC example illustrates how this process was handled by an HR department, earlier references to Bell Canada and IBM show that customerization can also be done by other departments.

Organizations in which all areas believe in total customerization, not just in the external customer, will be more successful than those that don't, according to Mitchell. HR departments thus have a tremendous opportunity to make a major contribution.

Customerization results in new and improved products and services. For an HR department, it may result in the department's becoming a strategic player because the process of customerization can lead to new knowledge, creative insights, familiarity, and acceptance. For any department, it is likely to result in heightened commitment, responsiveness, and internal cohesiveness. For the company as a whole, it is likely to result in improved effectiveness, with customerization being one way to gain competitive advantage.

References

Desatnick, R. L. 1988. "Customers for Keeps: Training Strategies." *Bulletin to Management* (Mar. 31): 8.

Fitz-enz, J. 1984. *How to Measure Human Resources Management*. New York: McGraw-Hill.

Halcrow, A. 1987. "Operation Phoenix: The Business of Human Resources." *Personnel Journal* (Sept.): 92–101.

"How Ford Turned Around." 1988. *Board Room Reports* (Feb. 15): 1, 6.

Keichel, W., III. 1988. "Corporate Strategy for the 1990's." *Fortune* (Feb. 29): 35.

Labovitz, G. 1987. "Keeping Your Internal Customers Satisfied." *Wall Street Journal* (July 6): 8.

"Operation Phoenix." 1988. *Crossroads* (an internal SBC journal; winter): 21.

Peters, T. 1987. *Thriving on Chaos*. New York: Knopf.

Porter, M. E. 1985. *Competitive Advantage*. New York: Free Press.

Schuler, R. S., and Jackson, S. E. 1987. "Linking Competitive Strategies with Human Resource Management Practices." *Academy of Management Executive* 1: 207–219.

———. 1988. "Customerizing the HR Department." *Personnel* (June): 36–44.

Smith, F. 1987. As quoted in T. Peters, *Thriving on Chaos* (New York: Knopf), 89.

Walker, J. 1988. "Managing Human Resources in Flat, Lean and Flexible Organizations: Trends for the 1990s." *Human Resource Planning* 11, no. 2: 125–132.

Appendix C

BEGINNING READING LIST IN QUALITY

Note: The works in the following lists are presented in suggested order of importance.

GENERAL QUALITY TOPICS

The First String

Scherkenbach, William W. *The Deming Route to Quality and Productivity—Road Maps and Road Blocks*. Rockville, Md.: Mercury Press/Fairchild Publications, 1990. An excellent and easily read explanation of implementing Dr. Deming's views on quality. Contains excellent examples.

Deming, W. Edwards. *Out of the Crisis*. Cambridge, Mass.: MIT Center for Advanced Engineering Studies, 1982. A seminal (though tersely written) book on all aspects of quality thinking and quality management.

Ernst & Young Quality Improvement Consulting Group. *Total Quality: An Executive's Guide for the 1990's*. Homewood, Ill.: Dow Jones–Irwin, 1990. Presents a good overall view of quality thinking, with practical ideas for implementation and an introduction to some tools and techniques.

Juran, J. M. *Quality Planning* and *Juran on Leadership for Quality*. New York: Free Press, 1988, 1989. Both present broad views on thinking and planning for quality. Both offer full-company, top-down views of quality-improvement efforts. Short on specifics of implementation.

The Second String

Tribus, Myron. "Selected Papers on Quality and Productivity Improvement." Available from G. N. Wright, National Society of Professional Engineers, Washington Engineering Center, 1420 King St., Alexandria, Va. 22314. Each paper focuses on a specific issue, such as selecting vendors or the conflict between MBO programs and quality.

Aguayo, Raphael. *The American Who Taught the Japanese About Quality*. New York: Lyle Stuart, 1991. Provides a schematic for implementing Dr. Deming's philosophy and teachings on quality.

Reid, Peter C. *Well Made in America: Lessons Learned from Harley-Davidson on Being the Best*. New York: McGraw-Hill, 1990. Tells an exciting but challenging story of Harley's transformation. Provides good insights into the difficulty of making a transition.

Peters, T. J., and Waterman, R. H. *In Search of Excellence*. New York: Warner Books, 1982. Eloquently presents the need for and benefits of high quality. Although the prescriptions are a little shallow, the language is persuasive and the examples thought-provoking.

Walton, Mary. *The Deming Management Method*. New York: Perigree Books, 1986. Easy-to follow presentation of Deming's approach to quality, including case studies. Follows the format of Deming's four-day seminars.

Dobin, Lloyd, and Crawford-Mason, Clare. *Quality or Else: The Revolution in World Business*. New York: Houghton-Mifflin, 1991. Companion book to Public Broadcast Service series by same title. Cuts to the heart of issues on quality with simple prose and case studies.

Mann, Nancy R. *The Keys to Excellence: The Story of the Deming Philosophy*. Los Angeles: Prestwick, 1985. Easy-to-read review of the impact of Dr. Deming's teachings around the world.

APPROACHES/TOOLS FOR IMPLEMENTING QUALITY PROJECTS

Scholtes, Peter R. *The Team Handbook*. Madison, Wis.: Joiner Associates, 1989. Practical and theoretical guide to selecting, training, and managing a team. Useful illustrations, forms, etc.

Ishikawa, Kaoru. *Guide to Quality Control*. New York: UNIPUB, 1976. Best-seller in the area of statistical approaches to quality improvement. Although originally written for factory foremen in Japan, it has wider appeal. Good examples, including several extended case histories.

Shingo, Shigeo. *Zero Quality Control: Source Inspection and Poka-yoke System*. Stamford, Conn.: Productivity Press, 1986. Good and early treatment of error-proofing processes (especially applicable to manufacturing but can also be applied elsewhere).

Moen, R., Nolan, T., and Provost, L. *Improving Quality Through Planned Experimentation*. New York: McGraw-Hill, 1991. A clear exposition of how to design and conduct experiments aimed at improving quality.

AT&T. *Statistical Quality Control Handbook*. 2d ed. Indianapolis: AT&T, 1958. The classic book on statistics in manufacturing.

IBM. *Process Control, Capability, and Improvement*. Southbury, Conn.: Quality Institute, 1985. Excellent, concise presentation of control charts, including a clear discussion of the interpretation of charts and appropriate action to take after interpreting them.

Shaffer, Robert H. *The Breakthrough Strategy: Using Short-Term Successes to Build the High Performance Organization.* Cambridge, Mass.: Ballinger, 1989. Good description of improving quality by executing projects, not big programs involving lots of planning. Especially useful for middle managers who may not have the resources, the time, nor the support to undertake large projects.

Wheeler, Donald, and Chambers, David. *Understanding Statistical Process Control.* Knoxville, Tenn.: Statistical Process Controls, 1986. Excellent, current book on statistics for manufacturing processes.

Kane, Victor. *Defect Prevention: Use of Simple Statistical Tools.* New York: Marcel Dekker, 1987.

Imai, M. *Kaizen: The Key to Japan's Competitive Success.* New York: McGraw-Hill, 1986. Similar to the Ernst & Young book presented earlier in this appendix (see "The First String" list under "General Quality Topics") but written by a Japanese scholar and consultant. Some of the examples are quite detailed.

Cochran, W. G. *Sampling Techniques.* 3d ed. New York: Wiley, 1977. One of the most widely used textbooks for teaching sampling techniques in graduate-level statistics courses. A dense but thorough read, even for academics.

VIEWS ON VENDOR-CUSTOMER RELATIONSHIPS

Carlisle, John A., and Parker, Robert C. *Beyond Negotiation: Redeeming Customer-Supplier Relationships.* New York: Wiley, 1989. Not just a "wish it were better" book. Provides cases and examples of model relations, tools and techniques for assessing and improving relationships, and a clear understanding of the challenge.

Fisher, R., and Ury, W. *Getting to Yes: Negotiating Without Giving In.* New York: Houghton Mifflin, 1981. A classic on overcoming verbal and psychological barriers to successful negotiations.

Folger, J. P., and Poole, M. S. *Working Through Conflict: A Communication Perspective.* Useful handbook on overcoming communication barriers that contribute to conflict. Important for team building as well as vendor-customer relationships.

Kohn, Alfie. *No Contest: The Case against Competition.* Boston: Houghton Mifflin, 1986. Goes beyond interorganizational competition, but the concepts presented relate to the problems of vendor-customer relationships.

Quality in Service Environments

Zeithaml, Valarie. *Delivering Quality Service: Balancing Customer Perceptions and Expectations.* New York: The Free Press, 1990. This book focuses on matching delivery of services with expectations among customers. Draws attention to the importance of generating impressions and expectations of deliverable value among customers.

Human Resources Planning Society. *Human Resources Planning, Special Issue—Service Quality and Organizational Effectiveness.* Vol. 14, no. 2, 1991. Six articles linking human resources and quality—especially for service businesses.

Glossary[1]

Note that many of these terms have multiple meanings. The definitions given below reflect the meanings as applied in the text of this book.

Anatomy of processes The structural linkage of the multiple operations (tasks, steps, unit processes, and others) that collectively produce the product.

Assembly tree A process form in which inputs from numerous suppliers converge into subassemblies and assemblies.

Autonomous department A process form that receives various inputs and converts them into finished goods and services, all within a single self-contained department.

Autopsy Analysis of products to determine the causes of deficiencies—literally, to see with one's own eyes.

Big Q A term used to designate a broad concept of quality in which "customers" includes all who are impacted; "product" includes goods and services; "processes" includes business and support processes. For contrast, see *Little Q*.

Brainstorming A process for securing ideas during a meeting of multiple participants.

Breakthrough See *Quality improvement*.

Business process In general, an office process, as distinguished from a factory process. (There is substantial overlap.)

Carryover The utilization of existing product (or process) design features as elements of new products (or processes).

Cause-and-effect diagram Prof. Ishikawa's "fish-bone diagram" for listing theories of causes.

Champion See *Sponsor*.

Charter See *Project team charter*.

[1]Reprinted from Joseph M. Juran, *Juran on Leadership for Quality: An Executive Handbook*. (New York: The Free Press, 1989), 355–364. Reprinted by permission of the publisher.

Check list An aid to human memory—a reminder of what to do and not to do. A form of "lessons learned."

Chronic waste The loss due to continuing quality deficiencies that are inherent in the system.

Cloning The application of remedies, derived from a completed quality-improvement project, to similar problems elsewhere in the company.

Company Any organized entity that produces products (goods or services) whether for sale or not, whether for profit or not.

Competitive analysis Analysis of product and process features and performance against those of competing products and processes.

Concept to customer A term used by the Ford Motor Company to designate the progression of events for creating a new model and putting it on the market.

Conformance A state of agreement between actual quality and the quality goal.

Conscious errors Nonconformance to quality goals resulting from actions knowingly taken.

Consumer An individual who buys for self-use.

Control chart W. A. Shewhart's chart for continuing test of statistical significance.

Control station A quality-oriented activity center for carrying out one or more steps of the feedback loop.

Control subject Any product or process feature for which there is a quality goal. The center around which the feedback loop is built.

Controllability The extent to which a process meets the criteria for self-control, enabling workers to detect and correct nonconformances.

COPQ Cost of poor quality.

Corrective action A change that restores a state of conformance with quality goals.

Cost of poor quality Those costs that would disappear if all products and processes were perfect—no deficiencies.

Cost of quality A term difficult to define because it fails to distinguish the cost of providing product features from the cost of poor quality.

Countdown A list of deeds to be done, in a predetermined sequence.

Craftsman A category of worker qualified by training and experience to carry out a recognized work specialty.

Critical processes Processes that present serious dangers to human life, health, and the environment, or that risk the loss of very large sums of money.

Criticality analysis The process of identifying product features that may be critical for various reasons, for example: essential to human safety, legislated mandates, essential to salability.

Cultural needs Needs for job security, self-respect, respect of others, continuity of habit patterns, and still other elements of what are broadly called cultural values.

Cultural pattern A body of beliefs, habits, practices, and so on which the human population has evolved to deal with perceived problems.

Cultural resistance A form of resistance to change based on opposition to the possible social consequences.

Customer Anyone who is impacted by the product or process. Customers may be external or internal.

Customer needs Those desires of customers that can be met by the product features of goods and services.

Customer satisfaction See *Product satisfaction.*

Data bank A compilation of numerous inputs specially organized to facilitate retrieval. A form of "lessons learned."

Deficiency See *Product deficiency.*

Department Any organization unit that is intermediate between a division (that is, a profit center) and the nonsupervisory work force.

Deployment The process of submitting broad quality goals to subordinate levels to secure identification of the deeds and resources needed to meet those broad goals.

Design review A participative process for securing early warning of the impact of a proposed design on subsequent functions.

Detection A concept of managing for quality based on inspection and test to detect and remove defects prior to shipment to customers.

Diagnosis The activity of discovering the cause(s) of quality deficiencies.

Diagnostic journey Those activities of the quality-improvement process that start with the outward symptoms of a quality problem and end with determination of the cause(s).

Dry run A test of a process, under operating conditions.

Early warning Advanced notification of upcoming problems, derived (usually) from customers' participation in suppliers' planning. "If you plan it this way, here is the problem I will face."

External customers Those who are impacted by the product but are not members of the company that produces the product.

Facilitator A person specially trained to assist project teams in carrying out their projects.

Feedback Communication of data on quality performance to sources that can take appropriate action.

Feedback loop A systematic series of steps for maintaining conformance to quality goals by feeding performance data back to corrective actuators.

Fire fighting The activity of getting rid of sporadic quality troubles and restoring the status quo.

Fitness for use A short definition of quality, intended to include product features as well as freedom from deficiencies.

Flow diagram A graphic means for depicting the steps in a process.

Foolproofing (also *errorproofing*) Building safeguards into the technology of a process to reduce inadvertent human error.

Glossary A list of terms and their definitions.

Goal An aimed-at target—an achievement toward which effort is expended.

Goods Physical things: pencils, color television sets.

Guild An organization of craftsmen whose purposes include protecting the quality produced by the members.

Immune system A characteristic of organizations that, like biological immune systems, tends to reject the introduction of new concepts.

Improvement The organized creation of beneficial change; the attainment of unprecedented levels of performance. A synonym is "breakthrough."

Inadvertent errors Human errors that have their origin in unintentional inattention.

Internal customers Those who are impacted by the product, and are also members of the company that produces the product.

Joint planning A concept under which quality planning is done by a team made up of customers and suppliers.

Juran Trilogy® The three managerial processes used in managing for quality: quality planning, quality control, and quality improvement.

Key interface The principal channel of interaction between customer and supplier.

Lessons learned A catchall phrase describing what has been learned from experience.

Life behind the quality dikes A phrase used to describe how life in industrial societies requires high quality to maintain continuity of services and to protect against disasters.

Little Q A term used to designate a narrow scope of quality, limited to clients, factory goods, and factory processes. For contrast, see *Big Q*.

Macroprocess An operational system involving numerous tasks, usually conducted in multiple functional departments.

Matrix organization A form of team structure superimposed on a functional hierarchy.

Merchants Those who buy for resale.

Microprocess An operational system involving few tasks, usually carried out within a single functional department.

Monopoly The exclusive right to make certain decisions or to take certain actions.

Operation A task of limited scope.

Operations (1) The general activity of carrying out planned processes; (2) organizations that carry out planned processes.

Optimum A planned result that meets the needs of customer and supplier alike and minimizes their combined costs.

Pareto principle The phenomenon that, in any population that contributes to a common effect, a relative few of the contributors account for the bulk of the effect.

Participation The process of securing inputs from those who will be impacted by an intended action.

Perceived needs Customers' needs based on their perceptions.

Pilot test A test of process capability based on a scaling up, intermediate between the planning phase and full-scale operations.

Policy A guide to managerial action.

President's quality audit A form of audit conducted by a team of upper managers under the chairmanship of the president.

Process A systematic series of actions directed to the achievement of a goal.

Process anatomy See *Anatomy of processes.*

Process capability The inherent ability of a process to perform under operating conditions.

Process control The systematic evaluation of performance of a process, and taking corrective action in the event of nonconformance.

Process design The activity of defining the specific means to be used by the operating forces for meeting the product goals.

Process development A generic term that includes the activities of product design review, choice of process, process design, provision of facilities, provision of software (methods, procedures, cautions), among others.

Process performance The actual result attained from conducting processing operations.

Processing The activity of conducting operations—running the process and producing the product.

Procession A process form in which the product progresses sequentially through multiple departments, each performing some operation that contributes to the final result.

Processor See *Processor team.*

Processor team Any organizational unit (of one or more persons) that carries out a prescribed process.

Product The output of any process.

Product deficiency A product failure that results in product dissatisfaction.

Product design The activity of defining the product features required to meet customer needs.

Product development The activity of determining the product features that respond to customer needs.

Product dissatisfaction The effect on customers of product failures or deficiencies.

Product feature A property that is possessed by a product and that is intended to meet certain customers' needs.

Product goal A quantified expression of the aimed-at values (product tolerances, reliability, and so on) required to respond to customer needs.

Product satisfaction   The result achieved when product features respond to customer needs.

Project   A problem scheduled for solution—a specific mission to be carried out.

Project mission   The intended end result of a project.

Project team   A group of persons assigned to carry out a quality-improvement project.

Project team charter   The list of activities to be carried out by each project team.

Professional   A person specially qualified by education, training, and experience to carry out essential quality-related functions. The most numerous categories are quality engineers and reliability engineers.

Proliferation   The growth, in numbers, of customer needs, product features, process features, and so forth, resulting from the growth of technological activity in volume and complexity.

Public   The members of society in general—an external customer.

QC circle   A volunteer group of work-force members who have undergone training for the purpose of solving work-related problems.

Quality   The word has two major meanings: (1) those product features that respond to customer needs, and (2) freedom from deficiencies. A broad term to cover both meanings is "fitness for use."

Quality assurance   An independent evaluation of quality-related performance, conducted primarily for the information of those not directly involved in conduct of operations but who have a need to know.

Quality audit   An independent review of quality performance.

Quality control   A managerial process that consists of the following steps: (1) evaluate actual quality performance, (2) compare actual performance to quality goals, and (3) take action on the difference.

Quality costs   See *Cost of quality.*

Quality council   A committee of upper managers having the responsibility to establish, coordinate, and oversee managing for quality.

Quality engineering   An engineering speciality focused largely on quality planning and analysis for goods and services.

Quality goal   An aimed-at quality target.

Quality improvement   The organized creation of beneficial change; improvement of performance to an unprecedented level.

Quality instrument panel A report package that summarizes for upper managers the performance with respect to quality.

Quality management The totality of ways for achieving quality. Quality management includes all three processes of the quality trilogy; quality planning, quality control, quality improvement.

Quality planning The activity of (1) determining customer needs and (2) developing the products and processes required to meet those needs.

Quality-planning road map A universal series of input–output steps that collectively constitute quality planning.

Real needs Those fundamental needs that motivate customer action, for example, a real need of a car purchaser is transportation.

Recognition Public acknowledgment of successes that are related to quality improvement.

Reliability The probability that a product will carry out its intended function under specified conditions and for a specified length of time.

Reliability engineering An engineering specialty focused largely on minimizing field failures through reliability modeling, quantification, data banks, and so on.

Remedial journey Those activities of the quality-improvement process that start with the known cause(s) and end with an effective remedy in place.

Responsibility matrix A table that lists the needed decisions and actions, and identifies who does what.

Retrospective analysis Analysis based on feedback of information from prior operations.

Rewards Those salary increases, bonuses, promotions, and so forth that are more or less keyed to job performance.

Salability analysis Evaluation of product salability usually based on a study of customer behavior, perceptions, and opinions, and on competitive product differences.

Santayana review The process of deriving lessons learned from retrospective analysis—conclusions drawn from data on repetitive cycles of prior activity.

Self-control (for an individual worker) A state in which the worker possesses: (1) the means of knowing what is the quality goal, (2) the means of knowing what is the actual quality performance, and (3) the means of changing performance in the event of nonconformance.

Self-inspection (for an individual worker) A state in which the worker makes the decision of whether the work produced conforms to the quality goal.

Sensor A specialized detecting device designed to recognize the presence and intensity of certain phenomena, and to convert this sensed knowledge into "information."

Service Work performed for someone else. Service also includes work performed for someone else *within* companies, for example: payroll preparation, recruitment of new employees, plant maintenance. Such services are often called support services.

Set up The action of assembling the information, materials, equipment, and so on needed to commence operations and of organizing them into a state of readiness to produce.

Simulation A form of planning that makes use of mathematical models or small-scale models; also, a means of providing operating personnel with experience prior to conduct of operations.

Software The term has multiple meanings: (1) instruction programs for computers and (2) information generally: reports, plans, instructions, advice, commands, and so on.

SPC See *Statistical process control.*

Spiral of Progress in Quality A graph that shows the typical progression of activities for putting a product on the market.

Sponsor A manager who is assigned to maintain broad surveillance over specific quality-improvement projects, and to help the project teams in the event of an impasse.

Sporadic quality problems Problems that have their origin in sudden, unplanned causes.

Spreadsheet An orderly arrangement of planning information consisting (usually) of (1) horizontal rows to set out the elements undergoing planning and (2) vertical columns to set out the resulting product/process/control responses.

SQC See *Statistical quality control.*

SQM See *Strategic quality management.*

Stated needs Needs as seen from customers' viewpoint, and in their language.

Statistical process control A term used during the 1980s to describe the concept of using the tools of statistics to assist in controlling the quality of operating processes.

Statistical quality control A term used during the 1950s and 1960s to describe the concept of using the tools of statistics to assist in controlling quality of operating processes.

Statistical significance A term used to distinguish real changes from false alarms. A change is statistically significant if the odds are heavily against it having been caused by random variations.

Strategic quality management (SQM) A systematic approach for setting and meeting quality goals throughout the company.

Suboptimization Pursuit of local goals to the detriment of the overall good.

Supplier Anyone who provides inputs to a process.

Symptom The outward evidence of a quality deficiency.

Taylor system A system of management based on separating planning from execution.

Technique error A species of human error that is traceable to lack of knowledge of some essential "knack."

Translation The process of converting the statement of customers' needs from customers' language into suppliers' language.

Trilogy See *Juran Trilogy*.

Triple role The roles of customer, processor, and supplier as carried out by every processor team.

TRIPROL™ See *Triple role*.

TRIPROL™ diagram An input–output diagram that depicts the triple role of customer, processor, and supplier.

Troubleshooting See *Fire fighting*.

Ultimate user The final destination of the product.

Unit of measure A defined amount of some quality feature that permits evaluation of that feature in numbers.

Upper managers (also *upper management*) The term always includes the corporate officers. In large companies "upper managers" includes the division general managers and their staffs. In very large organizations some individual facilities may also be very large, for example, an office; a factory. In any such case the local manager and his staff are upper managers to those employed at the facility.

Useful many Under the Pareto principle, a large majority of the population that nevertheless accounts for only a small part of the total effect.

User A customer who carries out positive actions with respect to the product, for example, further processing or ultimate use.

Vital few Under the Pareto principle, a small minority of the population that nevertheless accounts for most of the total effect.

Work force All employees except the managerial hierarchy and the "professional" specialists. (The dividing line is not precise, and there are borderline cases.)

Work station An activity center for carrying out the prescribed operations of running the processes and producing the product features.

INDEX

Accounting
    case example of, 35–36
    impact on the dimensions of
        quality, 34
Accumulation
    behavioral inclinations and, 102
    description of, 98–99
    mind-sets and, 101
    success of, 105, 106
Aesthetics
    defining, 29–30
    functional areas in companies and,
        33
Amalgamated Clothing and Textile
    Workers (ACTW), 134
American Express Co., 138
Appraisal menu, 111, 113–14
Appraisal practice choices,
    performance, 120–28
Attribute-control charts, 67–68, 70–72
Availability, 21

Bakken, J. K., 10
Baldrige Award, 3
    winners of, 6, 11, 14, 90
Bar charts, 63, 64, 79–80
Bays, Karl D., 95
L. L. Bean, 143
Behavioral-anchored rating scale
    (BARS), 114
Behavioral inclinations, role of, 102–3
Behaviors, quality enhancement and
    required role, 108–9
Bell curves, use of, 41–43
Bethlehem Steel, 6
Beutow, Richard, 5
Bhote, Keki R., 155
Bluestone, M., 90, 94
Brainstorming, 55, 62
Bretz, Robert, 133, 146
Brunswick, Mercury Marine division
    of, 108

Bubble charts, 53
Buell, B., 6
Business systems
    assessing current, 66–74
    defining, 36–37
    function or conversion process, 39
    inputs/suppliers, 37, 38–39
    outputs/customers, 37, 39–40
    quality and, 41–43

Cahan, V., 6
Capability, measuring, 66–67
Carlzon, Jan, 90–91, 135–36
Cause-and-effect diagrams, 75–78
Center line (CL), 68, 70
Chaparrel, 6
China, competition from, 3
Colgate-Palmolive Co., 144
Compaq Computer Corp., 7
Compensation menu, 111, 114–15
Compensation practice choices
    description of, 128–31
    Ensoniq Corp. case example, 160–62
Competitive strategies
    cost-cutting, 103
    cost leadership, 8
    innovative, 104–5
    matching human resource
        management philosophies with,
        105–6, 107–8
    quality-enhancement, 103–4
    role of quality in, 6–8
    specialization, 7
    technological leadership, 7–8
Conformance
    defining, 21–22, 28
    functional areas in companies and,
        33
Consumer relations and costs, 25–26
Control charts
    attribute, 67–68, 70–72
    P, 73

R, 73
Shewhart, 67
U, 68, 73
use of, 26, 72–74
X-bar, 73
Corning Glass Works, 108
Cost-cutting competitive strategy, 103
Cost leadership, influence of quality
    on, 8
Cost of poor quality (COPQ)
    accounting system, 22
Costs
    appraisal, 22
    consumer relations and, 25–26
    estimating, 60–61, 62–64
    external failure, 22
    internal failure, 22
    preventive, 22
    quality and improved, 4–5
Critical path method (CPM) charts,
    53, 78–79
Crockett, Bruce, 154, 155, 165
Crosby, P. B., 9
Customerization, Swiss Bank Corp.
    and, 168–81
Customers
    defining, 141–43
    differences between internal and
        external, 150–51
    /outputs, 37, 39–40
    relationships with, 148–50
    voice of, 43, 44–46
Customer service, impact on the
    dimensions of quality, 34

Deming, W. Edwards, 5, 9, 23–26, 51,
    62, 155
Deming Award, 3
Desatnick, Robert L., 169–70
Design, 21
    impact on the dimensions of
        quality, 34
Deutsch, C. H., 144
Developmental performance
    appraisal (DAP), 114
Diagrams
    cause-and-effect, 75–78
    fishbone, 75, 76
Dreyfuss, J., 130
Duncan, A. J., 68, 159
Durability
    defining, 28–29

functional areas in companies and,
    33

Eggleston, William, 176
80–20 rule, 62
Employment at will, 100
Employment security, 115, 129–30
Engineering, impact on the
    dimensions of quality, 34
Ensoniq Corp., 119–20, 124–27, 128,
    130, 145–46
    case example of, 154–67
Ernst & Young, 155
Experimental cycle, 81–83

Facilitation
    behavioral inclinations and, 102
    description of, 100–101
    mind-sets and, 102
    success of, 105, 106
Farish, P.,138
Features
    defining, 27–28
    functional areas in companies and,
        33
Federal Express, 131
Feigenbaum, A. V., 4
Field use, 21
Finance, impact on the dimensions of
    quality, 34
Fishbone diagrams, 75, 76
Fisher, George M., 4, 104
Fitness for use concept, 21–22
Fitz-enz, J., 177
Florida Light and Electric, 23
Flowchart(s)
    detail-level, 58–59
    summary-level, 56–57
    symbols, 54
    use of, 53, 55, 56–59, 74–75
Foote, Cone & Belding, 144
Ford Motor Co., 10, 11, 23, 90, 116,
    128, 137, 179
Fowler, E. W., 95
Friesen, P. H., 51

Galvin, Robert, 131–32
Garvin, David A., 20, 27, 155
General Electric (GE), 151
General Motors Corp. (GM), 7–8, 11,
    14, 89, 134
Germany, competition from, 3, 4

Goodman, Jerry, 93
Good Samaritan Hospital, 132
Grettenberger, John, 14
Gryna, F. M., Jr., 21
Gyllenhammer, Pehr G., 10

Hacquebord, W., 51
Halcrow, A., 172
Harley-Davidson, 5–6, 145, 152, 155
Hewlett-Packard, 90, 110
Holusha, J., 4, 6, 14
Honda of America, 137–38
Hong Kong, competition from, 3
Houghton, James, 108
Human resource (HR) function(s)
    creation of vice president of
        quality, 95–96
    Ensoniq Corp. case example, 157–66
    line managers and, 93–95
    managers and, 92–96
    Swiss Bank Corp. case example,
        168–81
    systematic approach to, 97–98
    typology of, 109–16
    unsystematic versus systematic
        approach to, 96–97
Human resource management
        philosophies
    accumulation, 98–99, 101, 102, 105,
        106
    behavioral inclinations and, 102–3
    competitive strategies and
        selecting, 103–5
    facilitation, 100–101, 102, 105, 106
    matching competitive strategies
        with, 105–6, 107–8
    mind-sets and, 101–2
    purpose of, 98
    selecting, 101–3
    utilization, 99–100, 102, 105, 106
Human resource practice choices
    compensation, 128–31
    labor-management, 134–36
    performance-appraisal, 120–28
    planning, 116–18
    staffing, 118–20
    training, 131–33
Human resource practice menus
    appraisal, 111, 113–14
    compensation, 111, 114–15
    labor-management, 111, 116
    planning, 110, 111, 112

    staffing, 111, 112–13
    training and development, 111,
        115–16
Hyatt, Marcia, 118

IBM, 11, 176
Incentive stock options (ISOs), 115
Information
    accuracy andavailability of, 30–32
    functional areas in companies and,
        33
    Swiss Bank Corp. case example,
        171–74
Innovative competitive strategy, 104–5
Inputs/suppliers, 37, 38–39
Ishikawa, K., 68
Italy, competition from, 4

Jackson, S. C., 138, 170
Japan
    competition from, 3, 4
    cost leadership and, 8
    new-product innovation and, 7
    restrictive trade practices of, 6
Junkins, Jerry, 3
Juran, Joseph M., 4, 5, 8, 9, 21–22, 26,
        51, 62, 133, 155
Juran Institute, 21

Kaypro, 7
Kearns, David T., 4, 108
Keichel, W., III, 178
Konrad, W., 6
Korea
    competition from, 4
    cost leadership and, 8

Labor-management
    menu, 111, 116
    practice choices, 134–36
Labovitz, G., 176
Lansing, Douglas P., 143
Lawler, Edward, 135
Line managers, human resource
        functions and, 93–95
Lower control limit (LCL), 68, 70

McDonald's, 112, 118
Main, J., 3, 11, 66, 90, 145
Maintenance performance appraisal
        (MAP), 114
Management by objectives (MBO), 114

Managers
  changing roles for middle, 90–92
  concerns of, 5–6
  creation of vice president of
    quality, 95–96
  executive support and, 9–11
  human resource functions and,
    92–96
  middle, 8–11, 89–90
  no executive support and, 11–12
  no quality-improvement programs
    and, 12–14
  role of line, 93–95
  sphere of influence and, 15–17
  top versus middle, 89–90
Mark, Reuben, 144
Marketing, impact on the dimensions
  of quality, 34
Marous, John, 90
Merck, 94
Miles, G. L., 136
Miller, D., 51
Mind-sets, role of, 101–2
Minnegasco Inc., 118
Mitchell, Michael, 170, 171
Mohrman, Sue, 135
Motorola Inc., 4, 5, 11, 91, 104, 132,
  133, 137
Mowday, R. T., 161
Murray, T. J., 91, 132, 133

Nadler, D. A., 51
Nashua Corp., 23
National Car Rental, 120–24, 128
Naumann, William C., 95
Nissan, 30
Nordstrom, 129
Nucor, 6

Oil, Chemical and Atomic Workers
  (OCAW), 134
Operations
  book-distribution center example,
    35
  impact on the dimensions of
    quality, 32, 34
Osborn, 7
Outlier, 71
Out-of-control point, 71
Outputs/customers, 37, 39–40

Pareto analysis, 62–64
Pareto principle, 62

P control charts, 73
PDCA (plan, do, check, act), 81–83
Perceived quality
  defining, 30
  functional areas in companies and,
    33
Performance
  -appraisal practice choices, 120–28
  defining, 27
  Ensoniq Corp. case example, 158–60
  functional areas in companies and,
    33
Peters, T. J., 9, 155, 179
Petersen, Donald E., 128
Phillips, S., 143
Pie charts, 78, 79
Pinder, C. C., 161
Pitney Bowes, 133, 146
Planning
  menu, 110, 111, 112
  practice choices, 116–18
Porter, Lyman W., 9
Process,function or conversion, 39
Procter & Gamble, 112
Productivity, relationship to quality, 25
Product variation, 41–43
Program evaluation and review
    technique (PERT) charts, 53,
    78–79

Quality
  defining, 2, 20–48
  importance of, 2–4
  need for commitment, 5–6
  reasons for pursuing, 2, 13–14
Quality enhancement
  as a competitive strategy, 103–4
  human resource practice choices
    for, 116–38
  required role behaviors and, 108–9
Quality-improvement plans, steps for,
  14–15
Quality-improvement project
  general process and strategy, 50–51
  major steps for, 49–50
Quality-improvement project,
    example of
  assessing current process, 66–74
  background of, 52–53
  diagnosing problems, 74–80
  identifying the system, 53–55
  measuring capability and stability,
    66–67

publicizing and expanding
improvement, 84–86
quantifying and maintaining
results, 83–84
selecting and developing the team,
65–66
selecting the project, 55, 60–64
testing theories in the workplace,
81–83
Quality-improvement tools
attribute-control charts, 67–68, 70–72
bar charts, 63, 64, 79–80
brainstorming, 55, 62
bubble charts, 53
cause-and-effect diagrams, 75–78
critical path method charts, 53,
78–79
fishbone diagrams, 75, 76
flowcharts, 53–55, 56–59, 74–75
pareto analysis, 62–64
P charts, 73
pie charts, 78, 79
program evaluation and review
technique charts, 53, 78–79
R charts, 73
scatter plotting, 79
Shewhart control charts, 67
U charts, 68, 73
X-bar charts, 73
Quality Institute, 68

Rasmussen, Mary Anne, 138
R control charts, 73
Reader's Digest Association, 35
Reid, Peter C., 6, 145, 152, 155
Relationships
with customers, 148–50
differences between internal and
external, 150–51
with suppliers, 143–48
Reliability
defining, 28
functional areas in companies and,
33
Remedial performance appraisal
(RAP), 114
Reputation, 30
Research, impact on the dimensions
of quality, 34
Richardson Group, 93
Richman, L. S., 133, 146
Robinson, Jim, 138
Romanelli, E., 51

Russell, G., 129

Safety, 21
Sales
case example of, 36
impact on the dimensions of
quality, 34
Sampling, 73
Scandinavian Airline System (SAS),
90–91, 135–36
Scatter plotting, 79
Schaffer, R., 51
Scherkenbach, William W., 9, 43
Schneider, B., 118
Scholtes, P. R., 51, 65
Schroeder, M., 6
Schuler, R. S., 51, 93, 94, 109, 110, 138,
170
Scientific method, 81
Serlen, B., 23, 128
Serviceability
defining, 29
functional areas in companies and,
33
Shamlin, Scott, 91
Sheeran, William J., 151
Shewhart, Walter, 26, 67
Shewhart control charts, 67
Shewhart cycle, 81
Simmons, J., 89
Singapore, competition from, 4
Smith, Roger, 89
South American countries,
competition from, 3
Soviet Union, competition from, 3
Specialization, influence of quality
on, 7
Sphere of influence (SOI)
defining, 16
examples of, 16–17
importance of, 15
Spiess, Michael E., 6
Stability,measuring, 66–67
Staffing menu, 111, 112–13
Staffing practice choices
description of, 118–20
Ensoniq Corp. case example, 162–65
Stark, Ray C., 144
Steers, Richard M., 9
Stempl, Robert, 89
Stock appreciation rights (SARs), 115
Suppliers
defining, 141–43

differences between internal and
    external, 150–51
/inputs, 37, 38–39
relationships with, 143–48
Sweden, competition from, 3
Swiss Bank Corp. (SBC), 93–94
    case example of, 168–81
Systematic approach to human
    resource functions, 97–98

Taiwan, competition from, 4
Tansik, D. A., 118
Target product and variation, 41–43
Team selection and development,
    65–66
Technological leadership, influence of
    quality on, 7–8
Thailand, competition from, 4
Theories,testing, 81–83
Therrien, L., 4, 104
Thomas, Roy, 154, 155, 159
3M, 82
Toyota, 109, 134
Trade protection, impact of, 5–6
Training and development menu, 111,
    115–16
Training practice choices
    description of, 131–33
    Ensoniq Corp. case example, 162
Tushman, M. L., 51

U control charts, 68, 73
Unions. See under Labor-management
United Auto Workers (UAW), 134
United Steelworkers (USW), 136
Upper control limit (UCL), 68, 70
UPS, 112
USX Corp., 6, 136

Utilization
    behavioral inclinations and, 102
    description of, 99–100
    mind-sets and, 102
    success of, 105, 106

Variance
    common-cause/systematic, 24–25
    measuring, 66–67
    special-cause, 25
Vendors. See Suppliers
Vice president of quality, creation of,
    95–96
Virany, B., 51
Vogel, Todd, 151
Voice
    of the customer, 43, 44–46
    of the process, 43, 44–46
Volkswagen, 30

Wagel, William H., 91, 129, 136
Walker, J. W., 51, 172
Wallace Co., 6
Waterman, R. H., 9, 155
Westinghouse, 90
Whitman Corp., 95
Wiggenhorn, W., 108
Williams, Lynn, 136
Woodruff, D., 6
WordPerfect Corp., 31

X-bar control charts, 73
Xerox Corp., 4, 108, 144

Young & Rubicam, 144

Zellner, W., 6
Zero defects, 22